CN00650955

THE GREA

A Biography of
Earl of Tyrone, 1550–1616

Seán Ó'Faoláin

WITHDRAWN

Dufour Editions

MERCIER PRESS

1997 edition published jointly by

MERCIER PRESS
PO Box 5
5 French Church Street
Cork
and
16 Hume Street, Dublin 2
ISBN0 85342 769 0

DUFOUR EDITIONS
PO Box 7
Chester Springs
PA 19425–0007
ISBN 0 8023 1321 3

© Seán O'Faoláin, 1942
First published by Longmans, Green and Co. Ltd in 1942

A CIP record for this book is available from the British Library.

10 9 8 7 6 5

WEST
DUNBARTONSHIRE
LIBRARIES

PRICE	SUPPLIER
9.99	HJ
LOCATION	CLASS
DP	941.505

INVOICE DATE
28.5.97
ACCESSION NUMBER
C020106143

This book is sold subject to the condition that it shall not, by way of trade or otherwise, be lent, resold, hired out or otherwise circulated without the publisher's prior consent in any form of binding or cover other than that in which it is published and without a similar condition being imposed on the subsequent purchaser.

Printed in Ireland by Colour Books Ltd.

PREFACE

Although this book makes no pretentions to be anything but a popular account of O'Neill's life and times it could not have been written without a good deal of help from various quarters. I am especially grateful to Mr. J. K. Graham, Queen's University, Belfast, for permitting me to use his thesis on Hugh O'Neill. It is, as far as I know, the only full-length scholarly narrative of the man's career. I am indebted to Daniel Binchy, University College, Dublin; to T. W. Moody, Trinity College, Dublin; and particularly to Professor James Hogan, University College, Cork, for their great kindness in reading the proofs, though, since I have not been able to make use of all their suggestions, the responsibility for the weaknesses in the text, and they must be legion, is wholly mine. I am obliged for helpful references and suggestions to Aodh de Blacam, James Carty, Edmund Curtis, James de Largy, G. A. Hayes-McCoy, Constantia Maxwell, Gerard Murphy, M. J. MacManus, Major H. F. McClintock, the authority on Irish costume, and others. For assistance in tracing the putative portrait of O'Neill I am grateful to Mrs. de Gernon, the National Gallery of Ireland, the National Portrait Gallery, London, and especially to the Victoria and Albert Museum, London, by whose kind permission it is here reproduced. (British Crown Copyright reserved.)

Above all I am grateful to the Librarian and Assistants of the National Library of Ireland, the Central Students' Library, the Dunleary Public Library, the National Museum of Ireland, Mr. T. S. F. Paterson of the County Museum, Armagh, and, last but not least, my more than patient publishers.

I would like to conclude with a warning and a confession to my Irish readers. Hugh O'Neill has a traditional fame in Ireland which has long challenged a biography. I undertook his biography in that spirit, attracted by the story of the man's ancestry, of his education in England, of his sudden rise to power, of his considerable wiliness in diplomacy, by certain romantic incidents in his private life, by his alleged cunning preparations for war against England, by his seven years defiance of a series of able English generals, and, above all, by the tradition that he represents the last stand of the old Gaelic world against the modern world of the Renaissance. If I confess almost total defeat it is not to plead for a lenient opinion, but to make it the basis of a threefold warning. No intimate details of this great man's character have come down to us, not even an absolutely authenticated portrait, or an intimate letter to a friend: we have nothing to go on except his behaviour. Since his mind was reticent and conspiratorial the reader must constantly be on his guard in interpreting his behaviour. The traditional picture of the patriot O'Neill, locked into the Gaelic world, eager to assault England, is not supported by the facts and must be acknowledged a complete fantasy. He was by no means representative of the old Gaelic world and had, at most, only an ambiguous sympathy with what he found himself so ironically obliged to defend with obstinacy. In fact he never desired to attack England, and avoided the clash for over twenty-five years of his life, more than a quarter of a century. His life proves once again that, to be intelligible, history must be taken on a lower key than patriotism. Indeed it is a sardonic comment on patriotic feeling that, finding him unsuitable to its purposes, it has obliterated his truth with one marching-song, *O'Donnell Abú*, which glorifies all that wild spirit of undisciplined and thoughtless valour which, throughout his life, he set himself to tame. If anyone wished to make a study of the manner in which historical myths are created he might well take O'Neill as an example, and beginning with his defeat and death trace the gradual emergence of a picture at which the original would have gazed from under his red eyelashes with a chuckle of cynical amusement and amazement. Indeed, in those last years in Rome the myth was already beginning to emerge, and a talented dramatist might write an informative, entertaining, ironical play on the theme of the living man helplessly watching his translation into a star in the face of all the facts that had reduced him to poverty, exile, and defeat.

S. O'F.

CONTENTS

THE CHARACTERS

BAGENAL . .	Sir Nicholas Bagenal, Queen's Marshal to 1590. Colonel Sir Samuel Bagenal, Governor of Newry, c. 1600. Sir Henry Bagenal, Queen's Marshal, 1590–1598. Killed at the Battle of the Yellow Ford, 1598. Brother of Mabel, wife of the Earl of Tyrone.
BARON OF DUNGANNON	*Vide* Feardorcha.
BELLINGHAM . .	Sir Edward Bellingham. Lord Deputy of Ireland, 1548–1549.
BINGHAM . .	Sir Richard Bingham, Lord President of Connaught, 1569 onward: a ruthless man. George Bingham his brother, Sheriff of Connaught.
BLAKE . . .	James Blake, the alleged poisoner of Red Hugh O'Donnell.
BROUGH . . .	Lord Brough, Lord Deputy of Ireland, 1597.
BURGHLEY . .	William Cecil, Lord Burghley; Lord Treasurer of England (1572–1598).
BUTLER . . .	*See* Ormonde; Mountgarret; Cahir.
BURKE . . .	William Burke, alias The Blind Abbot, chief of the Low Burkes. This family: two main lines—the Clanricard Burkes of Clare Galway and the Mac William Burkes of Mayo.
CAHIR . . .	Thomas Butler, second Lord Cahir. Lady Eleanor Butler, his wife.
CALVACH . .	Calvach O'Donnell, grandfather of Niall Garv, rival of Red Hugh.
CAREW . . .	Sir George Carew. Lord President of Munster, 1599.
CAROLO . . .	Son of Philip II of Spain.
CHICHESTER . .	Sir Arthur Chichester; Governor of Carrickfergus; Lord Deputy of Ireland, 1604–1616.
CLANRICARD . .	Earls of Clanricard. Ulick Mac William Burke, 1st Earl; Richard, 2nd Earl; Ulick, 3rd Earl; Richard, 4th Earl. Originally De Burgo.
CONN BACACH . .	Conn Bacach O'Neill, 1st Earl of Tyrone, 1542.
DESMOND . . .	Earls of Desmond; first creation 1330. Originally the Fitzgeralds of Munster. The Fitzgeralds of Leinster became Earls of Kildare. Gerald, 16th Earl of Desmond, 1558–1583, 'rebelled' in 1579–1583. James, the 'Sugán' Earl of Desmond, nephew of above, ally of the Earl of Tyrone.

DOWCRA . . .	Sir Henry Dowcra, British Commander at Derry in 1600.
DRURY . . .	Sir William Drury: President of Munster, 1576.
ESSEX . . .	Walter Devereux, 1st Earl of Essex. Robert Devereux, 2nd Earl of Essex. Lord Lieutenant of Ireland, 1599–1600.
FENTON . . .	Sir Geoffrey Fenton. Secretary of State in Ireland, 1581–1608.
FEARDORCHA . .	Matthew, alias Feardorcha (the Dark Man), O'Neill Baron of Dungannon, alleged bastard of Conn Bacach O'Neill, 1st Earl of Tyrone, rival of Sean O'Neill, killed 1558.
FITTON . . .	Sir Edward Fitton. President of Connaught, 1569.
FITZMAURICE . .	James Fitzmaurice Fitzgerald, cousin of 14th Earl of Desmond (q.v.) 'rebelled' in 1578.
FITZGERALD . .	*Vide* Desmond; Kildare; Fitzmaurice.
FITZWILLIAM . .	Sir William Fitzwilliam, Lord Deputy of Ireland 1571–1575, 1588–1594.
GREY . . .	Lord Grey de Wilton, Lord Deputy of Ireland 1580–1582.
HOVEDEN . .	Harry Hoveden (Hovendon), foster-brother to Earl of Tyrone.
HUGH DUV . .	Hugh Duv (Dark) O'Donnell, father of Red Hugh O'Donnell; ruled 1566–1592.
HUGH THE DEAN .	Hugh O'Donnell, illegitimate 'O'Donnell,' really the son of Dean O'Gallagher: killed by Ineen Duv, 1588.
INEEN DUV . .	Fionola O'Donnell, mother of Red Hugh O'Donnell.
JENISON . . .	Thomas Jenison: Auditor General.
JONES . . .	Thomas Jones, Protestant Bishop of Meath, 1584–1605; Archbishop of Dublin, 1605–1619. Lord Chancellor of Ireland, 1605–1619.
LEICESTER . .	Robert Dudley, Earl of Leicester. Presumed 'Guardian' of Hugh O'Neill, later Earl of Tyrone.
LOFTUS . . .	Adam Loftus, Protestant Archbishop of Armagh, 1563–1567. Chancellor of Ireland, 1581–1605. Archbishop of Dublin, 1567–1605: Provost of Trinity College.
LOMBARD . .	Peter Lombard, Catholic Archbishop of Armagh, 1601–1625.
MACCARTHY . .	Florence, or Fineen (Fionán) MacCarthy, made Governor of Munster by Tyrone, 1600.

MACDONNELL . . (The MacDonnells were freebooter immigrants from the Scottish Isles.) Sorley Bwee MacDonnell, leader of the Scots of Antrim: submitted 1586.
Sir Randall MacDonnell; later Viscount Dunluce; 1st Earl of Antrim, 1620.

MACMAHON . . Hugh Roe MacMahon. Chieftain of Monaghan; killed by Fitzwilliam.

MAGENNIS . . Catherine Magennis, fourth wife of the Earl of Tyrone.

MAGRATH . . Meiler Magrath, Protestant Bishop of Clogher, *c.* 1570–1571; Archbishop of Cashel, 1571–1622.

MOUNTJOY . . Charles Blount, later Earl of Devonshire and 8th Baron Mountjoy. Lord Deputy of Ireland 1600–1603, when he became Lord Lieutenant.

MALBY . . . Colonel Malby, President of Connaught, 1576.

MOUNTGARRET . . Edmund Butler, 2nd Viscount Mountgarret.
Richard Butler, 3rd Viscount Mountgarret.
Viscountess Mountgarret, née Margaret O'Neill, daughter of Earl of Tyrone.

NIALL GARV . . Niall Garv (*Asper*, or Rough) O'Donnell, second cousin of Red Hugh O'Donnell and married to his sister. Red Hugh's rival supported by the English and later abandoned by them.

NORREYS . . Sir John Norreys, President of Munster, 1584. Governor in the Queen's forces, 1593–1597.
Sir Thomas Norreys, President of Munster: Lord Justice of Ireland on death of Lord Brough.

O'BYRNE . . . Fiach MacHugh O'Byrne: 'The great firebrand of the mountains between Wexford and Dublin.'

O'DONNELL . . Red Hugh O'Donnell, Tyrone's ally.
Rory O'Donnell, 1st Earl of Tyrconnell, created 1603.
Joan O'Donnell, second wife of the Earl of Tyrone, sister of Red Hugh.

O'MORE . . . Rory O'More, and son Owny: of the O'Mores or O'Moores of Leix (Queen's County). 'Spoilers of the Pale.'

O'NEILL . . . The unqualified surname always connotes the Chief. When translated into English the article is prefixed e.g. 'The O'Neill.'

1. Conn Bacach O'Neill, created 1st Earl of Tyrone, 1542.
2. Sean O'Neill (Sean an Diomais—Sean the Proud) 1528–1567.

O'NEILL—*con.* . . .	3. Turlough Luineach (i.e. fostered by O'Luinigh) O'Neill, ruled 1567–c. 1587.
	4. Hugh O'Neill, 1550–1616. The Great O'Neill: 2nd Earl of Tyrone.
O'NOLAN . . .	Thaddeus (Thady) O'Nolan, succeeded Thomas Whyte, q.v. as Chief Apothecary: failed to poison Fiach MacHugh O'Byrne.
ORMONDE . .	Thomas Butler, 10th Earl of Ormonde, died 1614.
O'ROURKE . .	Sir Brian O'Rourke of W. Breffni, or Leitrim—'That sottish and cowardly traitor O'Rourke'—Bingham.
PERROT . . .	Sir John Perrot, Lord President of Munster, 1569 onward. Lord Deputy of Ireland, 1584–1588. Reputed natural son of Henry VIII. Conciliatory: magnifico: direct.
RUSSELL . . .	Sir William Russell, Lord Deputy of Ireland, 1594–1597.
SMYTHE . . .	Thomas Smythe, Chief Apothecary in Dublin Castle: 'Bottle Smith.'
SORLEY BWEE . .	*Vide* MacDonnells.
ST. LEGER . .	Sir Anthony St. Leger. Lord Deputy of Ireland 1540–1548, 1550, 1553–1556.
SUSSEX . . .	Thomas Radcliffe, 3rd Earl of Sussex: earlier Lord Fitzwalter. Lord Deputy of Ireland 1556–1558, and 1559–1565. Lord Lieutenant, 1560.
	Rival of Earl of Leicester, q.v.
SIDNEY	Sir Henry Sidney. Lord Deputy of Ireland, 1559: 1566–1571; 1575–1578.
STUKELEY . .	Sir Thomas Stukeley: soldier, pirate, and adventurer, associated on the Continent, 1570–1578, with Catholic proposals for an invasion of Ireland, financed by Pope Gregory XIII. Claimed to be natural son of Henry VIII.
TURLOUGH LUINEACH	Turlough Luineach O'Neill. *Vide* O'Neill.
TYRRELL . .	Captain Richard Tyrrell; Leinster guerilla leader.
WALLOP . . .	Sir Henry Wallop, Lord Justice.
WINGFIELD . .	Jacques Wingfield, Master of the Ordnance in Dublin. Served in Ireland 1534–1587, when he died, in debt to the Crown. Typical corrupt English official. Sir Richard Wingfield: served under Mountjoy.

PART ONE

CHILDHOOD, BOYHOOD, AND YOUTH: 1550–1568

I

UNDER THE DATE 1505 the Gaelic chronicle known as *The Annals of the Four Masters* records the passing away of one of the last intact pieces of the old Gaelic world, the death of an Irishman whose long life was a summary of one of the venerable civilizations of Western Europe. Even when translated into modern English the entry retains a good deal of the antique dignity of thought and language which the event evoked. It says:—

> 1505. Aedh Ruadh O'Donnell, son of Niall Garbh, son of Turlough of the Wine, Lord of Tyrconnell, Inishowen, Cinel Moen, and Lower Connaught, died: a man who had obtained hostages from the people of Fermanagh, Oriel, Clannaboy, and the Route, and from the O'Kanes and also from the English and Irish of Connaught, with the exception of MacWilliam Clanricard, who, however, did not go unpunished for his disobedience, for O'Donnell frequently entered his territory and left not a quarter of land from the River Suck upwards and from Slieve Aedha westward that he did not make tributary to him. This O'Donnell was the full moon of the hospitality and nobility of the north, the most jovial and valiant, the most prudent in war and peace, and of the best jurisdiction, law and rule of all the Gaels of Ireland. There was no defence made in Tyrconnell during his time except to close the door against the wind only; the best protector of the church and the learned; a man who had given great alms in honour of the Lord of the Elements; a man by whom a castle was first raised and erected at Donegal that it might serve as a sustaining bulwark for his descendents; and a monastery of Friars de Observantia in Tyrconnell, namely the Monastery of Donegal; a man who had made many predatory excursions around through Ireland, and a man who may be justly styled the Augustus of the north-west of Europe. He died after having gained the victory over the devil and the world and after Extreme Unction and good penance, at his own fortress in Donegal, July 20th, in the seventy-eighth year of his age

and forty-fourth of his reign, and was interred at the monastery of Donegal.

That O'Donnell came from the remotest, north-western corner of Ireland, the immediate ancestor of the O'Donnells who were to prove the greatest allies of the O'Neill of this story.

This Aedh Ruadh, or Red Hugh, King of Tyrconnell, was succeeded by his son Aedh Oge, or Young Hugh. A very different kind of chronicle records a very different event in which this young man took part a few years later. The chronicler, this time, is Holinshed ; the date is February 13th, 1511 ; and the place is London. That night one of the most brilliant pageants of the year was creating a great hubbub in and around Whitehall. The Christmas festivities were over, and the court had left Richmond for Westminster, but Henry VIII was still celebrating the birth of his first son by Katherine of Aragon. There has been a jousting in the forenoon, and after it Henry and Katherine had heard evensong, and supped at a great banquet with all the ambassadors of Europe. Now in Whitehall, hanged richly, scaffolded and cordoned for sightseers, the pageants began, the music, and the dancing. This time the pageant was an arbour of gold, on wheels, with a great cloth or arras drawn before the entrance. Henry had stolen away to dress for his part while the minstrels played and the ladies danced, and was now waiting behind the curtains. In the arbour the crowd saw six ladies all apparelled in white and green satin, all set and embroidered with the letters H and K in gold, knit together with lace of gold and damask and all their garments were replenished with glittering spangles gilded over. On their heads were bonnets opened at the four quarters. When the arras fell the King and five gentlemen appeared in purple satin, with cuts of H and K, and every edge garnished with friezed gold and every garment full of posies made of letters of fine gold, in bullion as thick as they could be, and every one of the six had his name in like letters of massive gold—Cure Loyal, Bon Voloire, Bon Espor, Valiant Desire, Bon Foy, Amour Loial. They glittered as they moved. And at every gesture the people saw that their hose, their caps, their coats, were so full of posies, with more H's and K's of fine golden bullion, that the very background could scarcely appear and yet in every void that peeped there were more spangles of gold. Out of the whole dazzling arbour and garden lord and lady came down on the floor, in couples, and many minstrels in disguise danced before them, and the lords and ladies danced, and says the chronicler, 'It was a pleasure to behold.'

It was a long night as it had been a long day of triumphant joy. Earls and Viscounts in mummers' costumes wove their way through the hours. Golden canopies swayed. The masque, the feast, the procession, the dancing, the music, jibed each other's heels. The crowd jostled. Once the rougher public broke through the cordons and tore the tasselled hangings and one prentice later sold some of the bullion letters of H and K for several pounds. Through it all the young Henry passes from point to point, roseate with wine and joy and pride.

Somewhere in the ante-rooms, while these festivities step down the programme, young O'Donnell is awaiting his cue to enter, how ill at ease or how overborne by curiosity we do not know. He had been on a pilgrimage to Rome and was now on the last lap of his return journey to his remote Atlantic home. His presence at Whitehall was natural enough because he was the ally and intimate friend of one of the greatest dynasts of the century—Garret More, the Great Earl of Kildare, who had linked his name with that of Henry of Lancaster when he married the King's cousin, Elizabeth St. John. At his due moment he is ushered forward, and kneels before Henry. The hubbub falls; the crowds watch the brief ceremony of knighting; O'Donnell rises, Sir Hugh O'Donnell. At once the chattering swells again, and the games go on as before.

The historical facts on which these two chronicles open windows are simple, though one hesitates to state them too simply lest we should add to these two pictures what they do not contain, namely, the historical perspective of the twentieth century. For if we are to understand the story of Ireland and England in the sixteenth century by living it over again we, too, must allow ourselves to be, as they were, a little troubled and confused; we must be satisfied to learn by an experience (even though it only be through words) as near as possible to theirs. On one or two things, however, men were even then sufficiently clear. This was the sixteenth century, the peak of human achievement. England had come to the end of her internal troubles and, in Henry VII, Henry VIII and Elizabeth, was to be blessed with three strong monarchs in one century. Her soldiers and sailors were eager for adventure and conquest. She had no colonies and her mercantile period was in its infancy. There, beyond the Irish Sea, was an island at which she had often nibbled but which she had never succeeded in exploiting fully. The elegy on O'Donnell is a glimpse of the unabsorbed Ireland. The picture of his son ceasing to be an Irish king and becoming a feudal knight is a peephole at the process of absorption. To be more intelligent than that would be to leave the century altogether and to know things and see things with a clarity that the times did not possess.

Before closing those heavy volumes of the contemporary historians we may glance at one other event which shows the process of absorption much farther advanced. The date is thirty-one years after that knighting at Whitehall, when another Irishman, lame of one foot, one Conn Bacach O'Neill (linked in marriage to those O'Donnells; his sister to O'Donnell's son) limps on the deep-strewn rushes of the Palace at Greenwich, before Henry, heralded by trumpeters, sided by two Earls, the Garter carried before him, accompanied by his own bishop, to become the first Earl of Tyrone. We are told that the solemn ceremony was performed fittingly and honourably down to the twenty angels that Conn paid for his gown, the ten pounds that he paid to the Office at Arms, and even the tip of forty shillings to the captain of the buglers, all 'according to the old and ancient custom.' O'Donnell's knighthood and O'Neill's earldom were indeed customs 'old and ancient' but the two events are an epitome of the surrender of custom far more old and ancient, the declension of a Gaelic kingdom to the rank of a feudal state, the entry of yet another of the last remaining pieces of a world older than Christianity into the modern Tudor system.

We are not, however, to imagine that these events indicate some quite simple process. If it were so Ireland would almost be one of those happy lands without a history, and this biography would never need to be written. The process was of a labyrinthine perplexity. That perplexity arose chiefly from the fact that in England's decision to make Ireland her first real colony two civilizations became interlocked that were in spirit utterly divergent. That may seem evident even from those two glimpses, in Holinshed and the Gaelic *Annals*, of London and Ulster. The sixteenth-century wars of conquest there mingled what was by nature immiscible. It is the same forced juncture of modernity and antiquity that comes with every imperial conquest, whether it is the conquest of Mexico by the Spaniards, or the colonization of India by the Hanoverians, or the plantation of Ireland by the Tudors. For out of it emerges a kind of Siamese duality of mind just as indissoluble, and just as incoherent, producing at first, on the side of the conquistadors, extremes of idealism, loyalty, persistence, stubborness, folly, by which all first puzzlements or stirrings of conscience are smothered up or brushed aside; and then, on both sides, when the confusion rises, mountains of treachery, an otherwise unimaginable brutality, indescribable savageries, recantations, selfishness, contempt, every known weapon of human ingenuity and bestiality to obliterate the enemy and justify his obliteration. In such a clash there is no simple story because there is no clear mind. In the final stage of all nothing remains but the oversimplified story of the victor and the oversimplified memories of the defeated, both of them unfaithful to the always confused and occasionally troubled split-mindedness of the time.

The truth is that Englishmen were fantastically ignorant about those countries which they assailed so blithely in the flush of their passion for adventurous conquest, and that the assailed were just as ignorant as to the nature of the forces and the order of life that assailed them.

For English contemporaries the entry into sixteenth-century Ireland was an entry into a world as strange as the Indies were to Columbus, nine-tenths of it an uncharted Thibet, and the O'Neills and O'Donnells and all its chief princes as remote and as unimaginable as the Great Khan. So that had some English traveller reported that there lived deep in Ireland tribes who wore their heads, like the anthropophagi, beneath their shoulders, London would have believed him; and in fact, well after the Tudors, men were still picking up books from the counters of the booksellers under St. Paul's that made report of things just as fantastic. One has but to look at the old map-books. Thus Speed's map of 1610 could repeat from Giraldus Cambrensis such tales as that there exist in Ireland islands 'some full of angels, some full of devils, some for male only, some for female, some where none may live, some where none can die.' Just as it also repeated the legend that the map-maker wrote on the map of Ortelius (1574), that there was no Lough Erne until the people who once farmed the solid earth there committed 'filthy abominable acts with beasts' and the waters rose and smothered them. In that same treacherous map of Ortelius which smoothened away vast headlands of rock to doom the pilots of the Armada, the Aran Islands are helpfully marked in Latin as places where no corpses can putrefy; and students of the fate of the Armada conning the Map of the Westerne Oceane (1609) found it as seriously enlivened at Sligo by the legend that here lie 'the high hills of Ben Bulben where yearly limbereth a falcon esteemed the hardiest in Ireland,' as at Derenishe that here 'three Spanish shipps were caste awaye.' The usual sea-monsters are doubtless a convention, but other things are conventional in a different way: thus the farther islands are suggested much as modern maps suggest the unexplored Arctic with incomplete guess-work outlines; and the general position of lakes and rivers is indicated with an imaginative abandon. In Norden's map of 1609, when our story is well-nigh over, small lochs like Carra spread to the size of the widest waters of the Shannon: scores of others, including one entire Shannon lake, Allen, have vanished completely; or a lake like Lough Conn can appear two counties away from where it should be. A modern, searching the maze of rivers for a familiar clue, is lost among streams that have neither beginning nor end, but devour their own tails like the impossible beasts in the intricate medieval designs of the Book of Kells, and the whole river-system looks less untracked than the upper waters of the Amazon a hundred years ago. In Ortelius all Tirconnell is as blank as the Sahara. In the best of these maps, Speed's of 1610, forests and mountains lie haphazard and there is not one road. In others the picture is like a film which has melted away, hither and thither, into distortion. There is no really effective map until the *Hiberniae Delineatio* by Sir William Petty in 1685, almost at the threshold of the eighteenth century, and if one goes back behind those I have mentioned—behind Speed, and Camden's *Britannia* of 1607, and Peter van den Keere's of 1599, to the first map of the British Isles ever engraved, at Rome in 1546—not, of course, the first map drawn—only fifteen places in all Ireland are marked, and all we see in Ulster is Lough Foyle (*Lacus Foilus*), Armagh (*Armacaną Metrop*), and one great black entry into the bowels of the earth, like the entry into Hell, marked *Purgatorium Sancti Patricii*. The rest is a waste land.

That wonderment existed, apparently without discomfort, side by side with the staid facts of constant contact by trade, on the periphery of a wholly commonplace commercial communication between London and coastal towns like Dublin and Wexford and Drogheda and Dundalk, and the stories came back undiminished of their wonder by rubbing with the beef, salmon, suet, butter, lard, hawks and horses, linen, wool, and leather exported from the Irish ports in exchange for the coal and cloth of England, or the guns and ammunition smuggled back for the Gaelic captains fighting the same England in the hinterland. All the varied trade from the Continent into Ireland, wine from Canary and the Levant, spices for Irish *uisgebaugh* from Italy, Spanish wine, salts and dyes from Toulouse and Picardy (one could build it up without trouble into an impressively solid record as well as a prettily sonorous litany from such studious books as Alice Stopford Green's *Making of Ireland* or Ada Longfield's *Anglo-Irish Trade in the Sixteenth Century*) did nothing to diminish the basic feeling that Ireland was behind it all a lost land. And this is natural, because all this communication was on the fringe of the hinterland, and these ports and towns—barring one or two like Donegal—were Norman rather than Gaelic, Anglo-Irish rather than Irish, and the core of the life of the country was that of people who never developed any kind of town-life, being satisfied, rather, to develop rural life to the point where, normally, it should have spilled over into urbanity—and most obstinately would not. The island, accordingly, was to its neighbour ringed with entries, familiar lighthouses, behind which lay a great deal that was quite unknown.

Indeed that may be seen also by reference to the maps, in so far as none of them shows any real focus or centre. The city of Dublin appears as a castle no more impressive than any other castle along the coast, such as Knockfergus, Carlingford, Dundalk, Wexford, Youghal, Kinsale; and every inland centre of any size promises us as fair as the next to develop into a city as Kilkenny did or to decline like Cashel into a ruin. Clearly each centre is the centre only of its own *locus*. No hierarchy or predominance has been established. History is still a complete gamble. To the stranger the past of this island is darkness and its future can only be written in blood. There are not even these firm local centres in Ulster, unless we count the Cathedral of Armagh in the east or the Monastery of Donegal in the farthest west. The fort of Portmore on the Blackwater River, so jealously watched by both colonist and native, its capture repeatedly claimed as a victory, proves to be a small wooden blockhouse on a little mound about forty feet in diameter. So that it is not surprising that Sir Henry Sidney's march from Ulster through Munster and Connaught should have been seriously compared to the march of Alexander three hundred years before Christ, across Persia, into the Swamps of the Oxus; and indeed his own descriptions seem to invite the comparison—'Never saw I a more waste and desolate land . . . such horrible and lamentable spectacles are there to behold . . . yea, the view of the bones and skulls of the dead subjects who, partly by murder, partly by famine, had died in the fields, as in troth hardly any Christian with dry eyes could behold!' It might be the record of the entry of some Elizabethan adventurer into a new Panama. And that, as far as this story is concerned, is what it was.

That physical incoherence is merely a hint of the obscurity that outdid it on the mental plane. For the English colonist the country and its ways were such a black-out of all sympathy and understanding that they solved the matter easily by calling all the simpler inhabitants, except their own settlers, by every conceivable epithet from 'savages' to 'beasts.' These words in the despatches of the sixteenth-century generals became boring by repetition. As for the more important men, they were merely puzzled. Thus, though we do not know what they thought, that night at Whitehall in 1511, when O'Donnell knelt before Henry VIII to be made a knight, for all that Holinshed says is that he was a powerful Irish prince, we do know what they thought twenty years farther on in the century, when the famous Seán O'Neill (1528–1567)—the uncle of our O'Neill, known as Seán the Proud, and the first man to be called Great O'Neill—visited the spangled court of Elizabeth in 1562, and with an admirable bluster swept the Queen off her balance. They looked at him, says the historian Camden, 'with as much wonderment as if he had come from China or America.' It was as when Indian princesses were brought to Spain by Columbus, and the Spanish court, allowing imagination to take the place of knowledge, saw behind them visions of empires made of gold.

They naturally knew many of the facts; though, naturally they concentrated on all that, in being strange to them, they took for barbarity, and in expecting the barbarous concentrated in turn on what was primitive or archaic. Just as historians and propagandists of the counter-reformation, like the Sanders whom we shall presently meet at close quarters, concentrated on all the barbarities of Elizabethan England, true and untrue, fact and rumour, and did not hesitate to believe the worst. To revert to this Seán O'Neill of 1562, they knew for example that here was a typical Irish captain, lord, noble, prince—for they hardly knew what to call him, not knowing a word of his language and next to nothing about the antique society out of which he came; they knew that he was enormously rich—he must have owned more than a hundred thousand cows; that he had murdered his brother, or caused him to be murdered; killed off his rival nephew, or caused him to be killed; believed that he kept his mistress, the Countess of Argyle, in chains in a cellar until, of evenings, when the wine was in his brain, he chose to have her up for his pleasure; as they guessed that she had betrayed her husband to become O'Neill's woman; and knew that while she was in O'Neill's arms, her husband Calvach O'Donnell was being shown to the people outside in chains like a baboon. They believed that he had had swarms of bastards. They had heard of his gigantic potations, of the vast cellars at Dundrum where two hundred tuns of wine were commonly stored at a time, and of his strange habit of burying himself to the neck in sand to cool his mad blood. They knew that he was dangerous and would have to be placated.

On the other side they may have known—all the Queen's counsellors certainly would know—of his bards and his rhymers, his annalists, priests, and friars, of his kernes, mercenaries and urraghs, his endless and always victorious feuds, and his great influence and unassailable courage, as they were to discover later that he secretly corresponded with Charles IX and the Cardinal of Lorraine. They may have been puzzled when on his death he was found to possess a score of velvet and golden suits and wondered how to reconcile the grandeur and the squalor.

But with it all before them, when they looked up at him and his escort of gallowglasses, armed with battle-axes, bareheaded, their curls long, their shirts bright saffron, their sleeves flowing, and their tunics brief beneath their furry cloaks, they still looked at him 'as if he came from China or America.' Perhaps it was because they were uninterested in anything that was not narrowly essential to their power-politics, were satisfied that he was powerful at home and was here making obeisance at the feet of Gloriana. Even as Elizabeth 'believed his tale,' in Camden's words, surely not because she took his tale of loyalty for truth so much as that she was indifferent to everything but the formality and could not possibly hope to pierce farther. But her courtiers revealed that they really noted only the superficies when, half in derision, half in admiration of their savage's hauteur, they styled him 'O'Neill the Great, cousin to St. Patrick, friend to the Queen of England, and enemy to all the world besides'—which is the kind of uneasy joke one makes when one vaguely feels the presence of another and completely unintelligible civilization. We find the more frank and fearful counterpart of that derision and lack of understanding in the amazement of their general, Carew, that in his own country the title of The O'Neill is 'a name more in price than to be entitled Caesar.'

The whole run of Tudor propaganda is of the same order, the scorn and contempt of every adventurer, colonist, and general, for which so many of them paid dearly, as Bingham did with his reputation, or Brough and Essex with their lives; it is that of men who could not so much as conceive that behind the outer ring of port-towns, behind those wild Irish woods, and those dark Irish bogs with their gleaming pools of water, there was another mode of life as valid, as honourable, as cultured, as complex as their own. They saw nothing there but 'savages,' 'wild hares,' 'beasts,' 'vermin,' 'churles,' 'rascals,' 'felons,' 'slaves,' either to be 'rooted out' and 'civilized' or 'exterminated.' And sometimes both were suggested simultaneously, as when Elizabeth told her Lord Deputy in Ireland that she particularly wished 'the people to be trained from the inordinate tyranny of the Irish captains and to taste of the sweets of civil order' in the year after the elder Essex brought back to Ireland her warm praise for his action in slaughtering the sick and wounded Scots on Rathlin Island as men stamp out running vermin; and Lord President Malby reported that he had now, in two years, hanged four hundred people in Munster alone in the interests of peace, and was presently about to tame Connaught. The conquistadors saw, in short, so little that they saw in effect only the fundamental weakness of the Gaelic world from the military point of view—indeed its fatal weakness—and their power-politics crashed into it with a contemptuously brutal disregard for everything else.

That weakness, which aroused so much scorn in the Tudors, has been described by scores of writers, but by none more intelligently than Dr. David Mathew in his *The Celtic Peoples and Renaissance Europe*. Ireland suffered, as he puts it, from the fact that she had never had any 'share in those common memories which still united the other nations of the West, memories of Roman order and Roman law, of a hierarchy of officials, and the sovereignty of the State. Even feudalism had suffered a sea-change as it crossed the Irish Sea. It was this barrier which led the English to regard as 'savages' the magnates who ruled west of English law, an inevitable consequence of the profoundly alien character of Celtic civilization. The society dominated by Seán O'Neill was a legitimate development of that of the Cúchulainn cycle. Few customs could be more remote from sixteenth-century Europe than those which still survived in the elaborate ritual of the chief's "*dún*," the right to the "shoulder piece," the "hero's portion," the precedence of the well-descended kinsmen, the presence of the bought women and the wolf-hounds. Such a life had been an anachronism in the medieval system, and there was no place for it in Renaissance Europe. The mutual incomprehension of the Irish chieftains and the officials of the New Monarchy suggests that the Irish wars would have been inevitable even if Catholicism had remained the State religion of England. Doctrinal differences only served to embitter the struggle and to emphasize its cause—the fundamental divergence between the *Celtic conception of a ruler and the new conception of the State*.'

It remains to observe how the colonist-invaders induced these Gaelic rulers to come into the new system. On the surface the answer is Power. But the thing is not on the surface. Power, indeed, was the mainspring, but the machinery was of the mind. Just because these Gaelic captains were petty dynasts, cogs only of their own local engines, they were mentally subject to the greater moral force of *the nation* that assailed them, one by one. That attack had, of course, been going on for centuries—now pressing in, now being rolled back, now being absorbed, now establishing hard cores or cells in the middle of the native life, sometimes even clearing and planting whole counties, and always claiming titular government of the entire island from their bold little centre at Dublin. It was Henry VIII who invented the final, ingenious solution, and this, taking an actual case, is how his plan worked out.

Dónal O'Connor Sligo, a petty captain, is sorely pressed. The colonists find it difficult to defeat him in the field, and offer a compromise. If he will surrender his entire estates to England, he will receive them back at once, as the gift of the Crown—together with his legal titles and every possible security. He will pay a small levy, but, in return, he will always be entitled to claim assistance against any neighbours who threaten his power. O'Connor Sligo, whose whole military outlook was governed by the technique of the raid, retreat, and counter-raid, and the tactic of temporal local alliances and feuds, would not have looked very deeply into this offer, nor very far beyond it. He probably said to himself that it was a good bargain if these meddling English could be placated for the time being with a formal obeisance that cost nothing. He agreed.

There were many inducements. It all came down to what modern society calls 'muscling in on the racket.' The English adventurers had simply observed that Gaelic society was broken up into many parts, that every man was out for himself, that the stronger commanded the weaker, and that there was nobody strong enough to be what the modern racketeers have called The Big Shot. They said to whatever O'Connor Sligo they happened to be handling at the moment: 'You are a small man. You are paying levies to your local dynast, O'Donnell, merely because you are not strong enough to make him pay levies to you. We are stronger than O'Donnell. We mean to take over all this countryside, and rule it. Sign on with us and we will give you protection. True, we want a levy too, but you will get a slice of the spoils, and be for ever safe, powerful, wealthy, and, so, honoured.' Henry VIII called this system 'Surrender and Regrant.' Denuded of its legal phraseology it was more crude than simple. O'Connor Sligo, in agreeing, simply threw off O'Donnell and took on Queen Elizabeth. Nothing else arose, least of all patriotism, since (or so he argued) at best he might profit by the scheme—get lands and feudal tenure in which he had formerly had only an interest as chieftain; take over land seized from the Church; get hereditary possession of lands that by Gaelic law belonged to the people. At worst the scheme altered nothing.

But it did alter a great deal, as he and hundreds like him found to their cost. The chief who thus compromised weakened his local authority since he weakened the traditional system of which he was a part. He provoked suspicion among his neighbours and anger among his 'tenants' and the caste which depended on the old system frowned on him to a man. The poets (and only those who are familiar with the temper of Irish literature will realize the awful significance of this), might even satirize him. He would indeed keep on saying that it all really meant nothing, and for the time being speak the truth; but, presently, the inch of his compromise would lengthen to its mile, and he would find himself being brought, bit by bit, within the ambit of English law. He would be asked to acknowledge the foreign legal system of possession, inheritance, landlordism, against all of which his followers would furiously protest. Officials would come to shire his land and sheriffs follow. The boot would begin to pinch, his pride revolt, his peace become disturbed, his people rise against him, and when the law to which he had agreed was finally quoted against him, his conformity expected and his obedience demanded, he had no option but to fight as he might better have fought at the start—or compromise again. If he compromised once more for the sake of a quiet life he would find himself retreating little by little until he ended by finding himself hamstrung on a peak midway between the old Gaelic code and the new English code. He became a white blackbird. He was demoralized. He could rely neither on his old friends, whom he had virtually rejected, nor upon his new allies, who would always suspect him. Now he was raided by his own people, his cattle stolen, his houses burned; now he was assailed by his new English associates, who asked him, with the insolent and brutal peremptoriness of the boss-racketeer, why he was not earning his living by raiding his own friends on their behalf. The fate and position of the suborned Gaelic chieftain was thus as pitiful as that of every man who sells his loyalty to the highest bidder of the underworld and finds that he has won neither mental, moral, nor material security.

Invariably he lost everything in the long run. For he could never keep to his promises, the old ties pulled, his people held him to the old way, and the old way was in his own blood; he began to hate the new master as he had often, doubtless, hated the old; endlessly he resisted and compromised, and resisted and compromised, until he grew weary of compromise as his masters grew weary of his vacillation, and the next time he resisted the thing was final—that is if *they* won, though not if he did. For they would never stop. They never could stop. They were too deeply involved. They had to pay their middlemen, the Carews, Raleighs, Grenvilles, Bagenals, Binghams, Gilberts, and hundreds more, endlessly pouring into this exploitable *lebensraum* of sixteenth-century England; and these middlemen, who were perpetually increasing in number, could only be palliated by the obliteration of more and more Gaelic little-lords. At which point the stool-pigeon was thrown to the hungry wolves, and his Title, his Letters Patent, his Articles, vanished into the storm which swallowed him, and sent his line reaving, like all dispossessed men, on the edges of the land he had lost. On the general morality of all this, supposing that anybody was interested in such an abstraction, Froude remarks two hundred and fifty years later, in the exact spirit and vocabulary of its times, that 'the exclusive right of a savage population over lands which they will not cultivate is always disputable.' It is the morality of all colonists, the semi-invulnerable doctrine of the Superior Race.

It does not matter and we need not doubt that Conn O'Neill likewise, in submitting formally to the new monarchy, did so for many of these reasons, and that like all the other Gaelic captains who from time to time made formal obeisance to Henry VII, or to Henry VIII, or to Queen Elizabeth, he did it in the same dangerous spirit of a decision nullified by secret reservations and a loyalty precluded by unuttered cynicism. It does not matter, because as time went on and the consequences became apparent it was left to his sons to suffer a dissatisfaction that broke all bounds, and the result was with the O'Neills as it had been with O'Connor Sligo, what the English blandly called revolt, treachery, rebellion, and the country swam in blood in the effort to avoid the effects of what O'Neill had so unwittingly accepted and to recover what he had so cynically pretended to resign.

Only a very few Irishmen tried to think out the meaning of all this upheaval. Only one or two ever really understood what was at stake. Of these the greatest was a grandson of that Conn O'Neill who became Earl of Tyrone in 1542. He was Hugh O'Neill, second Earl of Tyrone, known to the foreigner because of his power and success by every name from Arch Traitor to The Monster of Ulster, from Arch Rebel to The Running Beast. It is because he did understand what was at stake that he was of such size in his own day and of such interest to ours. He is one of the very few figures in the Ireland, indeed in the Europe of the sixteenth century, who stands up like a rock above the tossing seas of men struggling to defend and resist and achieve they hardly knew what.

That has always to be held in mind, especially about this Ireland, that the issues were not yet articulated, and indeed many of them are only beginning to reveal themselves clearly to our time. The centralized patriotism of England was already clear enough. It is strikingly clear in the whole spirit of Holinshed, who published his work in 1578. One turns for instance from the magnificent speech of Shakespeare's Henry V at Agincourt —the Saint Crispin's Day speech:

> Wish not a man from England . . .
> God's peace, I would not lose so great an honour
> As one man more, methinks, would share from me . . .

to its direct source in the practical prose record, and one realizes at once that this people is consolidated as a political nation, and tremendously, and selfconsciously proud of itself. The spirit of Ireland was not articulated in the same way, certainly not to the same extent, because it was too disparate and individual and politically unformed. Individual poets, the custodians of the general racial pride, did occasionally speak out nobly, like the poet of the O'Carrolls who so resented that surrender of Conn O'Neill in 1542—it was a year in which many such surrenders occurred, following the meeting of the Dublin parliament in 1541:

> *Fúbún fuibh, a shluagh Gaoidheal,*
> *Ní mhair aoineach agaibh :*
> *Goill ag cómhrainn bhur gcríche,*
> *Re sluagh síthe bhúr samhail . . .*
>
> *Fúbún on ye, O race of the Gael,*
> *Not one of ye has any life in him :*
> *While the Foreigner is sharing out your country*
> *Ye are like a fairy host . . .*

But such men were speaking, in effect, to an audience of shadows, not to a solid national phalanx. There *was* a Gaelic people. There was not a Gaelic nation. O'Neill was the first modern man who gave that people a form, by giving it a speech that it could understand and which made it realize itself intelligently. Before him, war meant to the Irish cowherd, ploughman, peasant, mother and father in rude sod-cabin, child weeping for hunger and often dying of it, only a sudden rush of horsemen, hoarse shouts, the flash of knives, screams, a rush through the woods, cold night on the cold ground, and the uninforming stars through the branches: a break in a hard enough peace, no way of tending the crops or of sowing new ones; a peeping down from some safe eyrie at the soldiers trampling and burning the corn to starve the land into famine; and thereafter no food, so that they crept weakly from pool to pool in search of cress, and from cress they declined to grass, and died of racking pains of hunger and disease, their mouths green with grass and bile—dying so like beasts for no better reason than Misfortune, or that they had tried to preserve their bits of property. Sound reasons indeed, but poor ones beside the vast and exciting issues, national and international, that they could not have known. Such misery is tedious to record, horrifyingly fortuitous and aimless; meaningful only in the name of Conquest. But with O'Neill the Wars began to move towards an end. The people saw a plan and a purpose, even though it was far less clear than later patriotic over-simplification would have it, and even though—as we shall see—unwillingly enough on his part, until at last the forces that he realized and therefore freed took possession of him and made him the symbol as well as the vehicle of their necessity and their pride. The clash, in sum, was between two civilizations that disliked one another at sight.

But do men really fight for 'civilizations' or for any principle so abstract? Do they not, rather, fight for hearth and home, for the familiar nook in life which custom has warmed, the content of wife and lover and child, all the ritual that the generations have sanctioned, the seat by the fire, the comfort of the table, the decencies of friendship, the habits that time has found good? Are not these things and ways the symbols like speech and writing that express for every common man the principles underlying all civilization—simple things, like a song at a country inn, dress, country customs, idle sport and humour, feast-days and holidays, or arrogant things like great monuments in great cities? The Irish fought, in short, for their own way of life, and the Tudors' contempt for sixteenth-century Ireland was not, in practice, for its code of laws, of which they knew little, and apart from a general dislike cared nothing at all; or for its religious beliefs, which had been in any case the beliefs of their own fathers; or even for its military tactics, which they soon learned to respect.

The Tudors despised the (to them) outlandish and disgusting ways of life that they met everywhere in Ireland outside the narrow ring of port-towns.

Let us, then, go with them into one of these country homes where the old ritual was still at its height.

2

It is the equator of the century, 1550. Ireland. The heart of Ulster. Roughly sixty miles from the coasts, north, west, or east. Dungannon Castle.

This castle is on top of a brief, steep hill, at a juncture of ten roads; obviously an important centre. The country around is curiously unemphatic although its nature is defined clearly enough by an endless series of little scrubby hills, knolls in fact, between which lie moist meadows or the heavy bogland from which they have been reclaimed. There are many little lochs, and in the evening what one remembers is the pure gleam of water and the dark outline of these little hills against the sky from which the water seems to have stolen the greater part of its brightness. From the look-out one sees the sun rise beyond the mist of the Great Lake seven miles away, over the great woods that creep to the water's edge, and then the long, cold rays slowly light up the view, a dew-wet champaign that slowly rolls under its broken covering of trees down to this inland sea. Full daylight shows miles upon miles of waving land, broken by streams and the meandering line of the Great River, as they called the Blackwater, shadowed by the clouds piling up from the lake, shadowed too by immense roving herds of cattle, this country's gold. The sun sets behind the replicated horizons of craggy hills that mount from far south to far north into the ridges of high mountains, where, north of Slieve Gallion, are the oak-forests and glens of the impenetrable fastness of Glankankyne. This is all O'Neill territory, the land of Tyrone, held inviolate from time immemorial.

Southward the champaign fades off into the level land below Lough Neagh, land constantly wrestled for by downward and upward thrust, the battle-ground of all ambition creeping in from the coast, the envy of all colonists. Here the ancient cathedral village of Armagh is another great meeting place of many roads, the only real counterpart to Dungannon between the mountains and the sea. Down there on a great inlet is the abbey of Newry, and then comes Dundalk on the coast itself, where all adventurers land and prepare for the entry into the hinterland; the town from which they advance, to which they retreat, where they rest and huddle, according to the fortunes of the war of conquest. The Newry marks in 1550 the practical boundary of settler penetration, that is—about five miles inland. One Nicholas Bagenal had been granted there, by London, the Lordship of Mourne, the good abbey lands of Newry, and his inestimable chances. He was a Newcastle tailor's son whose political career had not been stainless; he had become involved with the notorious adventurer Stukely, and Ireland was his opportunity to recover his reputation and build his fortune, very much as the Spanish Main was for the bankrupt Drake. The Newry was now full of his sons, and his line was to be the spearhead of attack for two generations against Dungannon and the O'Neills.

To spread the eye wider, there was another set of claimants, the Hebridean Scots, led by James MacDonnell, calling himself Lord of the Isles, over from Strathclyde and Galloway, and settled among the Antrim glens north-east beyond the Great Lake. There were thousands of these professional fighters, known as Redshanks, pouring across the narrow sea when the Irish captains lit their beacons on the cliffs to show that a fight was on. They were too-splendid fighters. Men often hesitated to invite them in because they had a way of refusing to go home again. They were virtual pirates. They founded the modern line of the Earls of Antrim. West to the Atlantic was in the main the country of the O'Donnells.

The settlers on the coast, i.e. men living in places such as Carrickfergus or Newry, accustomed to towns and a central government, looked on all this wild land beyond their narrow pale of influence with a natural awe and some distaste. To them it was but one unexplored fastness after another, and, of evenings, if they went beyond the lights of their little villages, the fading west must have effected their imaginations with an uneasy gloom. Out there they would not come to another cluster of even moderately friendly lights until they came to Armagh, thirty miles away, a whole day's journey, and after that the enmity of Clanbrassil and Clancam, Killultagh and Kilwarden, Killitragh, and Glankankyne, some of them forests as large as the New Forest, all of them impassable except by those born and bred to their uncharted geography. No towns; no roads, only muddy, beaten paths; forests; few buildings; the desert.

But to the Gaelic lord, at this date Conn O'Neill, to the English Earl of Tyrone, to the Irish The O'Neill, it is all as homely and familiar as boyhood. He knows that southward on the Great River is Sean, his son, in the castle of Benburb. The little cluster of churches and friaries at Armagh with the huts sheltering under their wings is wholly friendly to him. Over at Strabane, a good house for the salmon season, is kinsman Turlough. Away up on the lovely, luxuriant Bannside, where he can go for more salmon-fishing, or see the elvers flashing in the moonlight, is Castle Roe. There are other similar houses here and there.

But it is not merely of buildings that he would think as he sets out on some long ride through his demesnes but of his *urraghs*, or lieges,[1] bound to him by bonds of service and fealty, or by those links of fosterage and gossipred which form a stronger alliance than blood—O'Hagans and O'Hanlons, Quinns and MacMahons, O'Cahan and Devlin, Magennis and O'Donnelly, close and distant O'Donnells and O'Neills—the inextricable network of Gaelic society from which every captain like himself gets his lawful dues of oats and oatmeal, butter, and hogs, and mutton, and rents. He would see every one of these at least twice a year, at May and Hallowtide, when he weaves his way with his retinue of swordsmen and horsemen, lawyers, chroniclers, and poets around the spring-to-autumn woodland camps. At these camps O'Neill would dismount. The food would be laid out on great stone slabs or on the beaten fern. He would sit to it under the clouds of heaven. His host's *reacaire*, or orator, might relay a poem of welcome. The harper would strum a simple accompaniment on his little eight-stringed harp. A friar would recite the Grace. It would all be a simple ceremony, as unromantic as habit. If it were dull weather they would eat indoors, almost certainly a wooden building. After the meal O'Neill would settle down to business, to the discussion of crops, and cattle, and rents, and raids, for the whole source of his power was his capacity to protect his liegemen against other men, and that nexus bound them to him, and him to them in a bond of mutual advantage.

They were not ignorant of, and might in passing mention the towns whose affairs filled most of the history of Anglo-

[1] See Notes on page 282.

Ireland, since they might trade through them for some of their necessities, such as salt, or Spanish iron, wines, or spices, or even the famous shaggy Irish mantle in which towns like Waterford did such a steady trade both with Ireland and the Continent. O'Neill might, for grandeur, be wearing some fine garment—as of crimson velvet, with aiglettes of gold, even a double cloak of crimson satin guarded with black velvet, and a bonnet with a feather (as in a well-known contemporary description of the dress of the great Maghnus O'Domhnaill; though it is added that he was more richly dressed than any other Irishman), and this would have come to him from one of these port towns; or, for the occasion his hostess might wear a town-bought dress, with the yards and yards of linen piled on the head like an eastern turban and the immensely long flowing sleeves. But, in the main, these men would have little to do with the towns, since, obviously, they were not traders or merchants or manufacturers; and in fact the whole mercantile economy of the towns typified the forces that aimed at the destruction of their way of life. Anybody who knows the life of the Gaelic-speaking parts of Ireland in our own day will guess how centred they were in their own rural world and the slight extent of their interest in the distant towns. And that would be more true of Ulster than of any other part of Ireland: because it was more remote it was more archaic.

We must not in modern nostalgia idealize that Gaelic world too much. It is doubtful if any modern would find it particularly comfortable in practice, unless he happened to be well at the top of the structure. Its dominant features were the hereditary nexus qualified by an elective succession. It was not therefore a clan system in the simple sense of family groups. It was rather a system of dynasts whose ambition to rule was encouraged by a traditional affection for a succession by blood; and they extended their power and property partly by sheer buccaneering, partly by this loyalty to old families. One may easily imagine the result: constant unrest and internecine strife. 'It is a usual thing in the case of great princes,' wrote the great Gaelic genealogist Dubhaltach MacFirbhisigh in the seventeenth century—he was the great exponent of the pre-Christian Brehon Laws, and knew chiefs who governed by them in his own day—'when their children and their families multiply, that their clients and followers are squeezed out, wither away and are wasted.' That was not written of some ancient and outmoded practice but of the time of Cromwell.

Two other powerful traditional elements in this world of the O'Neills were intermarriage and patronage, and through them manifold alliances and dependencies which were, in every human sense, firmly cemented, but in every political and military sense brittle and unreliable. The merest glance at the story of Hugh O'Neill shews that it was because of these that he had to crawl every inch to power, circumspectly and circuitously, and because of them fell like a shot bird, weighted in both rise and fall by the fabric that entangled him. In these elements too this 'pre-medieval society was a hard world. Marriage and patronage were in the main a business deal, and indeed one would not expect gratuitous emotion to be anything else but a luxury in such a stern life-mould.

There, men of ambition got possession of land in order that they might give it out on what we would now call the hire-purchase system, generally however to their own kin, thereby creating dependents and becoming proportionately nobilitated and powerful. A man like our O'Neill did not therefore fight for land, year after year, merely to enjoy its products, but rather to create scores of clients whose legion lifted him to the highest rank of noble. Indeed, O'Neill climbed so high that he took for clients men who were nobles themselves.

Below king, noble, client, swordsman, horseman, gallowglass, and kerne, all freemen, there came the helots—men without a vote, mere tenants, inferior craftsmen, the common labourer, strangers in a district, and those who had deliberately made themselves outlaws. That large and varied class never, naturally, appears in the annals of politics; in war, only as camp followers, churls, cow-keepers, vivandiers, people not even expected to come so near the honourable profession of fighting as to be allowed to groom a horse, and horse-boys were 'the very skumme and outcaste of the country.' These poor people appear in literature as fools, bodachs, cailleachs, churls, and that rarely, and always in an atmosphere of folksy buffoonery. It is of these that English travellers are thinking when they describe the triple or quadruple ploughmen trudging after the rank of horses, the ploughs attached by ropes to the bare rumps, or even to the tails, and the men 'hanging by the ends of that unwonted labour'; or when some traveller speaks of the sight of women working with children on their backs, 'laying their dugges over their shoulders to give suck to the babies without taking them in their arms'; or it is of these that another traveller says that they go half-naked in summer, wearing only shoes and the notorious Irish mantle, 'and sleep under the canopy of heaven or in a poor house of clay, or in a cabin made of the boughs of trees,' although he adds that 'such are the dwellings of the very Lords among them'—as no doubt they often were in times of war, or in the hot summers, or on the hunt. It is most likely of these, from the drudge to the mere tenant, that the English repeatedly said (to quote one typical statement of the kind) that 'the common Irish people have desired to leave their own lords and live under the English if so they might,' and even claimed for them that they were in favour of the Plantations that drove their chiefs to the bush; 'the common people who live by their labours and yet are hardly suffered by these unruly idle swordsmen to live in safety or to enjoy of that which they get by their own labours so much as to sustain their lives, expect to be relieved by the due execution of the laws—which they hope . . . by the success . . . which hath appeared . . . where the English are planted.' But of course one does not, sensibly, take all such claims as facts, since colonists the world over always say such things, and the contemporary churl elsewhere in Europe was probably no better off.

That general system existed nowhere, at this date, in its purity. Feudalism had come into Ireland with the Norman invasion, and although the Normans had become largely hibernicized there had, naturally, been a strong seepage of Feudalism into the old Gaelic system. It gave the chief more power, and so far he would have welcomed it. But in this Ulster the Gaelic system was to last longer and exercise its power more fully than anywhere else. One can almost see that, to revert to the contemporary maps, in the elemental vacancy of the whole of the north as compared with the rest of the country. Moreover, along with the seepage of feudalism there was the leakage to the towns, to England, even to the Continent. In these the new Anglo-Ireland was growing up. Here there was room for craftsmen of every kind, and this is pertinent to the wars of O'Neill because it was these migrants, Gaelic and Catholic, through whom information, guns, and ammunition were constantly smuggled in to the hinterland. Once again, however, there was far less leakage in Ulster than anywhere else, and far more of what there was to the Continent than from the one or two towns on the east to England.

To emphasize, finally, the independence and antiquity of the North, and here one might also add the West, the effects of the mercantile policy of the new England were felt here hardly at all. The whole of that policy was based on the fact that Ireland produced valuable raw materials, such as wool and linen, yarn and hides, and imported only luxuries, and that her exports had for centuries gone in Irish ships to France and Spain and farther; so that when she bought from England she did so on good terms, and bought largely re-exports from the Continent which she could and did buy much more cheaply elsewhere by direct trade. By the sixteenth century there were religious and political objections as well as selfish commercial ones to this continental free-trade. Gradually the English commercial class set out to capture the whole Irish export trade and it is a matter of common knowledge that the ultimate result was the blocking of Irish industry—since the raw material now went direct to England, in English ships, and English industrialization grew proportionately. But Ulster, being practically bare of town life, was hardly concerned, so that we may picture our O'Neill and his client as men for whom the outer world existed only as a remote and practically irrelevant detail. Their interests were personal and local. And if we want to know those specific services over which they would check and bargain as they sat in the fern we may take this typical list of the conditions under which one sub-captain, Owen O'Sullivan More, held his estate from his chief-captain, the MacCarthy More:

1. To aid him with his whole strength on summons and to be marshal of his army.
2. Every arable ploughland to pay five gallowglass or kerne, or six shillings and eight pence, or a Beef for each, at the choice of MacCarthy More.
3. That MacCarthy shall have a half-crown for every ship that comes to fish or merchandize in O'Sullivan's harbours.
4. To have merchandizes brought at the same rate as O'Sullivan has his.
5. To entertain MacCarthy More and his train two days and nights at Dunboy, and at all the times he has occasion to travel that way, to entertain MacCarthy More and his Body Servants, and to quarter the rest on the Country.

6. He is to send horse-meat to Pallice for MacCarthy's saddle-horses, and pay the groom two shillings and eight pence out of every arable ploughland.
7. He must feed the hounds, grey-hounds, and spaniels of MacCarthy whenever they come, and sixteen pence per annum to the Huntsman out of every arable ploughland.

That was their business. It would take them a long time. The little intimate touches cannot, alas, be recaptured—the snatches of private talk, the humour, the significant pauses, the glances, the unwritten ritual, the private suppressions, the whole unrecorded code of nice behaviour. And it is these things that it would be most precious and informative to record, as when, to-day, some traveller into the less-trafficked parts of the world notes them with pleasure; as when, say, in the desert, the Arab slave hands the coffee to the guest before the master, but expects him to refuse precedence, or the sheik tears the choicest morsel from the steaming carcase for his friend. Curiously, too many Irish historians, the most patriotic the least sensitive in this, are happiest when they are proving that these Gaelic folk lived, in effect, quite as formally as the foreigner and had all his sophisticated ways; whereas their lives are most interesting where they did not and had not; but rather—let us say—lived like some modern Emir who will end a meal with hands greasy to the wrist, rise openly from the group to go to his wife, love best his sharpest rather than his richest daggers, take the fleas as part of the luxuriance of nature, speak with the freedom of the libidinous desert, seem to the foreigner a savage, be in effect a king. It is the interest of this Ulster that here the world of Ireland was at its oldest and youngest, so that to try to deck it with modern circumstance is as tasteless as it would be untrue.

So the day would pass for O'Neill and his client, and their clerks and lawgivers would be weary before the setting sun sent them to a last meal and sleep—which would come to them as they lay down under the open sky, or in a bothy, shoulder to shoulder, like the king-shepherds of Palestine.

There is a long poem by the blind poet Theigue Dall O'Huiginn, one of the latest of the race of classical poets, recording such a night on such a tour, spent in the stronghold of Mael Mordha son of Maol Muire MacSweeney of Sligo, a *gallóghlac*, or gallowglass chief. He praises the 'domed castle with ivory-hilted swords,' and then tells how there sat beside the chief 'the choice of every craft in the world,' including three famous poets; namely, Brian MacOwen O'Donnellan attached to MacWilliam of Clanricard, the 'Iarla Búrcach,' and the poet Brian MacAngus MacNamee attached to Turlough Luineach O'Neill, and the poet Conor O'Huiginn attached to MacWilliam Burke. After they had 'eaten to the soothing strains of harps,' and were replete with the 'sweetness of honey and the elation of ale,' drunk from cups of gold and goblets of horn, they lay down for the night, the blind man in the middle, and the poets and the host to his right and left. In the darkness he began to tell them a long story to wheedle sleep and fulfil the custom of his craft and the economy of his life. When his voice fell away into silence the other recumbent figures gave their judgment on the tale and listed their rewards. MacSweeney ('O blossom of Tara') gave a dappled horse. Brian MacAngus gave one of the choice hounds of the world. Brian O'Donnellan gave the flower of the royal books of Ireland, the history of all famous 'Cattle Raids, Wooings, and Destructions.' Conn gave a harp, 'such a precious jewel as even a king would not bestow.' Alas, says the blind man, for as he writes his four companions are all dead and those times passing away,

Alas! for my beloved lovers,
My bedfellows of one bed, my secret-sharers:
Four streams from a fruitful forest,
Trees that were rich in gift to me . . .

That picture of life as lived in the golden world of Ulster is of the greatest psychological interest if we put it beside the records of contemporary travellers. Read the description of a Gaelic household in the 'Itinerary' of Fynes Moryson, who was Lord Mountjoy's secretary in the last stage of the war against Hugh O'Neill. He takes what we should call, in the popular use of the word, the realistic angle. For Moryson sees only the great malodorous candle made of reeds and butter, the fire in the centre of the room smoking indecisively up to the central vent of the roof, the clay walls or their anatomies, the boughs of trees, the heaps of straw for beds. He retches at the food—milk strained through unclean straw, and stew made with all the entrails in the pot, swimming about with great greasy lumps of butter. The clothes were to him merely one garment over naked bodies, the famous Irish mantle, a great shaggy thing like a bearskin. Indeed he is remarkably like any tourist who thinks that everything foreign is beastly and enjoys nothing. In another mood Father Goode (1566) a man educated at Oxford and settled at Limerick, describes soberly the dress of the 'wild Irish kerne'—the saffron linen shirts whose wide sleeves swayed by their knees, the short woollen jackets, the tightfitting breeches, and the inevitable shag-rug Waterford mantle, with its hood of fur and triangular shape, fringed colourfully; he describes the womenfolk with their heads wreathed in fine linen, and their neck and arms loaded with bracelets. Yet a fourth, the Sir John Harington who translated Ariosto's *Orlando Furioso*, describes a visit, in 1599, to our Hugh O'Neill, a meal and a conversation—'his fern tables and fern forms spread under the canopy of heaven. his children in velvet jerkins and gold lace after the fashion of an English nobleman's sons; the two tutors; the bodyguard of beardless boys, stripped to the waist, devoted as slaves to their master: "Who in the frost wade as familiarly through rivers as water-spaniels ; with what charm such a master makes them love him I know not, but if he bid come they come; if go, they do go; if he say do this, they do it."' And he tells how he read them, and they eagerly heard, with a quizzical twinkle passing between visitor and Arch Rebel, that 45th canto of Ariosto—which begins:

By how much higher we see poor mortal go
On Fortune's wheel, whither runs a restless round,
We so much sooner see his head below
His heels ; and he is prostrate on the ground.
The Lydian, Syracusian, Samian show
This truth, and more whose names I shall not sound ;
All into deepest dolour in one day
Hurled headlong from the height of sovereign sway.

By how much more deprest on the other side,
By how much more the wretch is downward hurled,
He so much sooner mounts, where he shall ride,
If the revolving wheel again be twirled.
Some on the murderous block have well-nigh died
That on the following day have ruled the world.
Ventidius, Servius, Marius, this have shown
In ancient days ; King Lewis in our own. . .

One could read many other accounts, as different as these in mood and in degree of sympathy, and take their measure from nothing but the choice of words, as when Harington speaks pleasantly of 'the *fern* tables and *fern* forms,' while Moryson says, 'What do I speak of Tables? Since indeed they have no tables but set their meat upon a bundle of *grass* and use the same *grass* for napkins to wipe their hands?' And which is true, in the end—the idyllic mood of Tadhg Dall O'Huiginn, the satirical amusement of Derricke, the 'savage and heathenish' picture one gathers from men like Moryson, the sobriety of Goode, the interested detachment of Harington?

Is it not all an illustration of how convention plays on reason and the imagination? Thus, Holinshed's brilliant account of the festivities of Richmond, Westminster and Greenwich that winter of 1511 is clearly 'true' in that there *was* all this gold, and colour, and gaiety. Yet nobody, nowadays, would be so ingenious as to take it as a complete picture of the events it records, let alone of the life of the time. Prince Arthur, the baby greeted so joyously by Henry, died a few weeks later: We know the long and not too tasteful story of Katherine, and have taken full measure of Henry's *amours loials*. A tragic series of private lives and a dreadful squalor and brutality of common life lie behind the gilded page of the chronicler, and the elementary habits of sixteenth and seventeenth century England are too well known, even to those who only read in the most cursory fashion through the Elizabethan novelists and pamphleteers. After all, Bardolph and Nym were among those who heard that splendid speech on St. Crispin's Day.

O'Huiginn's poem on the stronghold of MacSweeney is infinitely more unliteral, as unliteral and conventional in some ways as Chinese court verse. It may be that the MacSweeney of that poem had a stone peel, but it is much more likely that his 'domed castle of ivory-hilted swords' and his 'purple fort,' so 'polished and bright of hue' never existed as such outside the poet's imagination, or that it was ever anything but a clay and timber affair of one room; probably lime-washed, probably inside a rath set with a ring of thorn-trees, with the cattle driven into the corral for the night, breathing and chewing against the wooden wall. His poetry is called 'classical' precisely because it *is* conventional, and it went on being written—there were considerable shifts of style and content but hardly any of outlook—

into the eighteenth century, long after every castle was a ruin, and every Gaelic 'high-king' dead, and all that antique society had faded into the mist.

Another even more conventional poem by the same man might be compared with this one, the thirty-seven verses on Maguire's castle at Enniskillen with its description of the fleet which was like a grove; 'the slender-lipped, satin-clad maidens, weaving wondrous golden fringes'; soldiers with their weapons hanging over their heads, 'artificers binding vessels, smiths preparing weapons, wrights from many lands at work, dyeing of textures, polishing of blades, fitting of javelins'; and then, to break all sense of reality, on the battlements—he mentions incidentally the *wooded* rampart—'a mighty band of elfin (i.e. fairy) youth on whom no eye dared to look because of their splendour.' And it should at least be mentioned that this poet was a blind man.

How, then, do these conventions strike us? Surely, even from our puny vantage-point of three-hundred-and-fifty years later, we have seen the passing away of too many conventions to be likely to condemn any completely, or to be overwhelmed by complete admiration for any, and we have recorded the rise and decay of too many states and cultures to be inclined to base a judgment on even the most dazzling descriptions of material splendour or the least pleasing pictures of physical discomfort? Whatever the gross faults of our time we have, at least, learned the pre-eminence of the human element in life over every other element. For if it is merely a question of material splendour, what is the most bullion-laden pageantry of Henry VIII or Elizabeth compared to the fabulous wealth of the Incas, which was in that same century being rifled by the Spaniards and lusted after by the English? What, in those terms, is the tomb of any English king beside the great halls of the Inca dead in the Temple of the Sun, low under the snowy glimmer of the Andes de Carabaya, literally plastered with gold, where the sallow-faced kings sat embalmed in rows, their dusky faces lit by the dim radiance of their niches, drooping in a calm more like dream than death? If it was a question of displays of joy and grief what can compare with the immolation of four thousand Peruvian concubines and servitors on the pyre of the last Inca monarch before the Spanish conquest immolated the whole of that barbarously brilliant empire from Cuzco to Cotopaxi? If it is a question of 'savagery' does one need to go farther than the equally ruthless and revolting religious persecutions of Europe from the thirteenth century to the seventeenth, enjoined and approved by the most saintly men of every known faith? If one thinks, pertinently, of these concomitants of splendour, what remains of the contempt of any traveller for these Gaelic chiefs and churls whose ignorance was to eat like shepherds, and sleep under the sky, and be ruled by rulers descended from the time of St. Patrick? There remains, at least, small room for the sort of patronage the English gave them.

But something does remain. That old blind poet lying in the dark and telling his saga to his fellow-poets was part not merely of an old convention but of a convention that was already growing weary. It was growing too old to adapt itself to Change; like himself it had grown too blind to observe the realities behind the formula. For it is, as we shall see and may already have guessed, not a question of superficial culture. (The Persians had been far more cultured and suffered from the same weakness: which was inflexibility.) That world of his and of O'Neill's, and of all the Gaelic nobility reached back too far, and was far too conscious of its own age and dignity, two things about which the intruding adventurers knew nothing and cared not a fig. They cared nothing that O'Neill claimed a descent to the fourth century, that his greatest ancestor, the conquering Niall of the Nine Hostages, had enriched Tara with the spoils of Rome, heard the crackle of burning cities when the great outposts of Roman power in the west, Chester, and Caerleon, and Caerwent, and Uricanium fell to the sound of his name; did not know or care that he had given the poet Claudian a theme when Britain heard his hosts 'making the sea foam with hostile oars.' But the poet knew it all, and loved it too much, and all those 'savage and heathenish' Gaels, if they did not expressly know it, had the arrogant feel of it in their bones. They were too embedded in their world, historic and prehistoric, and hyper-glorified in the imagination, to know that another had long since come—sometimes too embedded in it to realize that any other existed.

Thus, that same poet O'Huiginn wrote another pathetically significant eulogy on Sorley Bwee MacDonald, the Scotch pirate, in which, he compares Sorley to Julius Caesar—the famed High King (*Ard Ri*) of Rome. With an odd confusion of history he tells how Caesar was in Spain when the barbarians threatened Rome, and was there visited by Rome in a vision in which she took on the likeness of a tearful woman. (This Vision Poetry is one of the most elaborately perfected conventions of all Gaelic poetry, repeated over and over again for three centuries with endlessly ingenious variations.) Rome begs Caesar to return and save her, which Caesar does, as Sorley Bwee is now presumably about to do for Ireland. Thus, concludes the poet, were saved 'the lime-washed castles of Rome'—the only kind of noble building he could imagine. Those 'lime-washed castles,' Caesar as Árd Rí, Spain as the natural enemy of 'Rome,' (i.e. England), the implicit opinion of all invaders as 'barbarians' like Attila's Huns, makes such a counterblast to Tudor opinion about Ireland that one is left in no doubt that two irreconcilable worlds met in these Anglo-Gaelic wars and that there could be no end to them but some tremendous catastrophe.

When we widen the sweep of our eye backward the explanation becomes self-apparent. In this Gaelic world life had always been turbulent, and heroic, but it had also been too secure. And wherever life becomes too secure, or too easy, it decays for lack of change. Granted that these men would raid as heroically as Arabs, when the need arose, they might otherwise evade all the insecurity and instability and need for adaptability inherent in a more complex, competitive, compressed, and developed kind of civilization. The *leit-motif* of Gaelic society since time immemorial was the lowing of the vast herds of cattle, so persistent and dominant a note in the lives of the generations, raised almost to the stature of a Myth by the national epic of the Táin Bó Cuailgne (The Driving of the Bull of Cooley) that the Bull should by right have become the Bull God, adored as the emblem of fertility, a guarantee of a life that need never languish. About these beasts had centred the raid, the counter-raid, the ambition of Kings and Queens, the great battles, the scandalous loves, the tremendous exploits of the sagas. It was these lowing mobs of cows that had created the Rolands, and Beowulfs, and Brunhilds of the Celtic epic—Cuchulainn, and Ferdia, and Maeve. That comparatively easy pastoral life had been sealed in the minds of the people as the one true and lovely life, to be elaborated and adorned by every invention of the imagination, in law, poetry, saga, religion—for they peopled it with their gods and it was honoured by the druids, and the poets chanted it, and many of the observances that depended from that sort of life had to be tolerated even by Christianity until, in horror, the Norman priests began to reform Church and Society alike. But it was an attractive existence, and like an Oriental sun it drowsed even the most disciplined invaders, and every settler from the Danes and Normans on tended gradually to fall subject to it. And though it decayed over the centuries, and lost many of its best features one by one as outside pressure fissured it, and frayed away finally before the new mercantile spirit creeping in from England and the Continent, it still held its attraction, powerfully nostalgic, atavistically resurgent, long after the rest of Europe had begun to move forward to new ideas, new inventions, new codes, greater and finer elaborations in every branch of life—manners, education, architecture, social organization, politics, dress, food, philosophy, methods of war, letters. Nowhere did it so obstinately persist as in this remote Ulster. There especially evident, everywhere else less obviously, it had conditioned a racial psychosis, and its psychological effects—what men liked, what their instincts desired, their way of looking at everything—were the chief obstacles to the reforming, modernized minds of men like our Hugh O'Neill: its racial arrogance, its indiscipline, its rashness, its lack of thought, its impatience, its incogitancy, its hatred of change, its shallow opportunism, its lack of foresight; all were antipathetic to him, and out of them all he could make use only of the brilliant dash and deathless courage of its fighting-men.

In the end, it is a question of intelligence, of taking thought and of not taking thought. For there is in our respect for all such ancient ways of life much more than a mere veneration for something that in lasting so long seems, by its very endurance, to have established an *a priori* right to our respect. What we venerate, surely in those customs is their intimations, as yet only half-realized, of a sensible philosophy of life which those who practise them have no other way of expressing. Sometimes this expression takes on the form of a religion as with the Arabs, who thereby can preserve life-modes that would otherwise vanish from the face of the earth; as have, to all intents and purposes, the Eskimos who travelled from the Urals to the Arctic and left not even a wrack behind. Sometimes this racial aptitude expresses itself more practically, as with the Romans who found in Law and Organization a mould to preserve their natural proclivities. But in all cases the racial bent must ultimately come, in some way or another, to the surface of the mind; though, long afterwards, it will sink back again as sentiment—like a metaphysic that, as Pater says, only becomes effective when it is felt. If speculation does not in this way inform custom society decays. Custom will ossify as a series of automatic tabus and fetishes, an imbroglio of superstitions that become more and more debased, and end as a subject for the student of decayed races or arrested developments, the anthropologist of the might-have-beens. The history of the world is full of these examples of embryonic philosophies that came to nothing or ended as heresies, whole tribes and races that have died out, cultures that have performed the amazing miracle of garrotting themselves in cul-de-sacs. There is a terrifying disease of the body which may be vulgarly described as forgetting how to breathe: some hiatus occurs in the brain; a link is snapped in the communication-system between mind and body; and unless somebody is at hand to perform artificial respiration the victim finally asphyxiates himself. The old Gaelic world had suffered for centuries from this inactivity of the brain, which threatened repeatedly to deprive it of the breath of life. It was the task of our Hugh O'Neill to be the physician and surgeon of this suffocating Ireland.

For if some such great figure did not come to its assistance that ancient world *had* to face a catastrophe, and that we should come to see this through the arrogant minds of the poets is natural, both because *caste*, as stubborn and haughty as inca or cacique, is the symbol of the old native tradition, and because *caste*—poets, lawyers, professional soldiers, local captains—fought to maintain what maintained it. Hatred of the foreigner, hatred of their own people who yielded to the foreigner, the exasperation of their captains who felt obliged to yield, the contempt in which these captain's rivals held them because they had yielded, the inevitable intriguing on all sides, sporadic outbursts of resistance on all sides, the bitterest family division—this is the litany of daily life ever since the Tudor pressure became intense, with the poets, at the peak of *caste*, all the time hissing their incitements,

> *The seed of Brian of Banba,*
> *under Murrough they are*
> *bound to the Saxon king:*
> *they have turned—O woe*
> *the doing!—their backs on*
> *the heritage of their sires.*

Fubún on the grey foreign
gun!—Fubún on the golden
chain!—Fubún on the court
that talks not English!—
Fubún on the denial
of Mary's Son!

Disunity among the people, a unified purpose in the invader, that is the summary of it all. The pathetic coda, or tail-piece, comes at the beginning of the seventeenth century, when the poets start to contend among themselves in that colossal piece of pedantry known as 'The Contention of the Bards,' in which the poet of the Earl of Thomond and the poet of the O'Donnells lead a mighty combat in words about the mythical theory of a mythical fifth century poet about the mythical origin of Ireland —this at a time when the conquistadors were in secure possession of the real Ireland from end to end. The comment of an observer is apt—'The great poets are like dogs, blown up with scent, snarling in the empty straw . . .'

3

We have begun this story with the year 1550, and chosen to picture the ruling O'Neill, Conn first Earl of Tyrone, on a pleasant tour of his demesne; as no doubt it was pleasant. But we also know that his thoughts were often unhappy and that his life for many years had been far from pleasant. Ever since that day in 1542 when he took his patent of nobility from London the shadows had begun to creep over his house; for whatever about the political wisdom of his surrender he had done a most unwise thing in naming his son Matthew as his successor; known from that day as Baron of Dungannon. Indeed what he really bestowed on Matthew was the role of a doomed Banquo to the Macbeth of his son Sean. (The fortunate Fleance of that story was the Hugh of this biography.)

Here is the sequence of events. Conn said that Matthew was his eldest son, although a bastard, by one Alison O'Kelly, the wife of a blacksmith of Dundalk town. Sean, who had hitherto been thought the eldest son, denied this as soon as he was old enough to realize the consequences to himself. He asserted passionately that the thing was a trick to defraud him of his rights, that Matthew was not his father's child but the veritable child of the blacksmith Kelly; and that Matthew had always been known as the blacksmith's child until Alison found herself a widow, and he proved, at least to the satisfaction of the English courts that Matthew was a Kelly. As he put it to Elizabeth herself: Matthew's mother 'for vain glory and for a name to herself declared him to be O'Neill's son, alleging and boasting of her unhappiness, how that O'Neill lay once with her. And O'Neill being a man that never refused no child that any woman named to be his, as he had divers beside the said Matthew, accepted and took him to be his son. His nature was such he never refused no man of nothing that they asked of him.' From which it follows that Matthew's sons were likewise blacksmith blood, and that the second of them, our Hugh, is not Hugh O'Neill at all but Hugh O'Kelly. Yet it is hard to see why Conn should have disinherited Sean for Matthew if he did not wish to acknowledge a fact—that Alison was his first passion. The truth will probably never be known. It is merely the first of many mysteries that darken the long and tangled story of the house of O'Neill.

Whatever the truth, the results were terrible. Bitter war between the two claimants to the title: the misery of the old and too-compliant father who wavered to the end between his two children, thereby exacerbating both; bitter war between Sean and his father; war even between Matthew and his father. The story becomes a typically tragi-fantastic family squabble when, in the year of our Hugh's birth (1550) Matthew found the old man wavering towards Sean and ran to the English with the cry of treachery. Conn was summoned to Dublin and, Earl or no Earl, imprisoned. Whereupon Sean, enraged at this double treachery of his brother and the English flew to arms. He metaphorically tore up the covenant implicit in his father's title. The colonists inevitably took the side of Matthew—though not because he was the stronger but because he was the weaker, since it was their policy at all times to keep the natives in a balance on which they ultimately swung themselves to power. Sean procured the murder of Matthew. His people despatched Matthew's first son Brian four years later. The remaining sons kept up the vendetta to the end of Sean's career and long after. Thus, Matthew's second son, our Hugh, was said to have hanged one of Sean's sons with his own hands ; he harried the rest without pity and finally jailed most of them. The vendetta outlived the century.

The child Hugh, therefore, grew up at Dungannon in an atmosphere of raid and counter-raid, bloodshed and danger, bitter argument, divided loyalties. As soon as he could absorb anything he drank in through his very pores the lesson of his murdered father, his murdering, rebellious, haughty uncle Sean (known to all as Sean the Proud, and among a host of arrogant Gaelic captains the most arrogant of them all); he absorbed the highly pertinent lesson of his murdered brother, of the whispers about his father's origins and his own, and behind it all the two essential lessons—there must have been men in plenty to make him see it: the value of power, and the great power of England.

Youths matured quickly in those days and boyhood was brief. Essex was with Leicester in Holland when he was eighteen, and with Drake in Portugal when he was twenty-two. Henry VIII was married when he was eighteen and was leading a war of conquest in Europe when he was twenty-three. Grotius was the pupil and companion of Scaliger at the age of eleven, at fourteen went with the ambassadors of the States General to Henry IV, and was called to the bar at sixteen. Francis Bacon was admitted to the Society of Ancients at Gray's Inn when he was barely sixteen and accompanied Sir Amyas Paulet, the Queen's ambassador to France. Sean O'Neill was in arms for his rights in Ulster almost as soon as he left his teens. So, although the child Hugh was only nine[2] when Sean seized full power on the death of Conn O'Neill, the first Earl of Tyrone, (1559) we must remember that he belonged to a precocious age and was older than his years. The natural rivalry of families, always savagely intense in Ireland, must have thrown before him day after day the taunting picture of his young cousins, those often-to-be-mentioned 'sons of Sean,' Hugh and Henry, Conn and Toirdelbach, Brian, Art and Sean Oge. His clan was indeed raiding bloodily back on Sean, but the bitter fact remained that on Conn's death people acknowledged Sean as The O'Neill, and at the old crowning-stone of Tullyhogue gave him the white staff of sovereignty, symbolically—though in his case somewhat unaptly—white and straight.

It would be a dwindled Dungannon where the boy sat and heard over and over the whole hateful story of his grandfather's frailty, his father's death, and the futile dying curses on all who should ever again 'build houses, sow corn, or learn English'—the summary of the terms of the English patent. The only sweet news would be of some setback for Sean, and every word of his success would sting. The fact that Sean, in the characteristic anarch way, was attacking the O'Donnells on the west would make their names sound friendly to Dungannon. When the O'Donnells raided Sean and he barely escaped by diving into a river, Dungannon laughed. When the colonists, headed by Sir Henry Sidney, threatened him from below in Dundalk no patriotic feelings would prevent Dungannon from being delighted. And when Sidney, instead of attacking him made friends with him, even came up to Benburb and stood godfather to his child the news was vinegar. If the Turk had offered help, then, against Sean they would have embraced it. Their only feelings about the Tudor colonists were those of the dying Conn, that the man who trusted them was a fool. Men in that mood, foiled by stronger characters rather than defeated by braver hands, are ready for anything, so that it must have been in a coldly calculating spirit that they suddenly heard (1559)[3] from this same Henry Sidney that he was willing to take the lad Hugh back with him to England. They agreed and let him go.

There is something extraordinarily pathetic and dramatic about this sudden lifting up of a little 'rascal horseboy' from those lost woods west of the Great Lake, out of the laps of his fosterers, the O'Hagans and the O'Quinns, to be fostered now (as Sir John Dowdall observed) 'by the heat of Her Majesty's favour unto nobility and counsellors with other great men and captains.' What memories he was leaving, how he had lived with those foster-parents we can only guess from the general picture of the times. We may dismiss any poetic idea of a boyhood in castles, with gold dishes and silver goblets and fine clothes and soft beds. Being fostered out, he hardly lived in Dungannon 'castle' itself at all. Probably the nearest modern analogy to the child's exile would be some poor little tatie-picker from Donegal going off via the clanging city of Glasgow to the big farms of Ayrshire.

Far later, when he was himself a great man and captain, we get a hint—perhaps too faint and subtle to be reliable—from the finer way in which he reared his own children—wonder that is if, as so often happens, father did not try to give to son what he himself had lacked. Then he sought out a young tutor, one of the most delicate and sincere poets of the new times, Aodh MacAingil—the young man whom Sir John Harington bade read Ariosto to his pupils—later to become Guardian of the College of St. Anthony at Louvain, Archbishop of Armagh, and at last to be buried in the Church of St. Isidore in Rome to the resounding eulogy of Vernulaius, the President of Louvain—'Nemo adiit qui non laudaverit, nemo novit qui non amaverit, nemo spectavit quin virtutis amorem ex eus vultu atque totius corporis compositione hauserit. . . .'[4] Whatever force there may be in such a hint lies only in the fact that we know of no such man about his own father's house, know of no teacher at all, know so little that we cannot help feeling that it must have been an anxious and uneasy sort of home, unhappy, lacking in all urbanity, from which no image whatever remains beyond the name of that murdered brother; and we hear of the other two brothers only as angry restless raiders. There is one other hint, also from those later famous years, when the Deputy wished him to send his boy Henry to Trinity College, just founded in Dublin, and O'Neill's letters in reply make clear that he wanted *his* boy to be educated where there was a regard for the Old Religion, so unlike (was he remembering it?) his own boyhood now about to begin, in Sidney's great castle at Ludlow in Shropshire, and at Penshurst in Kent, and with Leicester at Holkham in Norfolk, and in these powerful men's houses in the city of London.

But even there, where he spent the most formative years of his life, the shadows are about the boy O'Neill. Indeed only one solitary sentence remains to describe his life during all those years, that of the contemporary soldier, Thomas Gainsford, who records that 'he trooped the streets of London with sufficient equipage and orderly respect.' To Sidney who took him in his train he was just 'a little boy, very poor of goods and full feebly friended.' To himself, recalling it nearly thirty years later, he was 'a child of tender years,' which when put beside Sir John Dowdall's phrase, 'a rascal horseboy,' evokes compassion for this small traveller leaving the tossing boat at Beaumaris that September of 1559 and starting on the Welsh roads down to Ludlow. For Sidney was Lord President of Wales since the year before, and resided there in his great keep on a tributary of the Severn. At Ludlow Castle Aodh O'Neill would have met another child whose fame was almost to be as great as his own, Philip Sidney, then aged five.

The next main break in the journey would be in London, and then down into the Kentish uplands to Sidney's great house, of which Ben Jonson had such an unbounded affection and admiration, and whose solid, homely virtues he described in the measured lines beginning

Thou art not Penshurst built to envious show . . .

The little Hugh, wandering the gardens, would have been shown the sapling, now but five years old, planted for Philip, 'where all the muses met,' relished the fine game-preserves, the deerpark, the pampered cattle, the pastures by the river, and with eye roving from the ancient pile beyond to the gardens at hand, seen in astonished admiration all the blandishments of this so civilized English world of which no word had ever come to him from his poets back in the Irish hills. There were the fish-ponds, the flower-gardens, the orchards where still

the cherry and the plum
Fig, grape and quince, each in his time doth come;
The blushing apricot and woolly peach
Hang on thy walls that every child may reach . . .

and in the years he spent there seen it as a place which habit had already established as a centre of a local ritual and tradition, a home bound closely to the humble life about it by loyalties born of experience as well as tested by it. For Hugh, like Ben Jonson, would have seen how each peasant would bring in his gifts on feast-days—capon, or country cake, nuts, and apples, and fine cheeses,

or else send
By their ripe daughters, whom they would commend
This way to husbands, and whose baskets bear
An emblem of themselves in plum or pear,

and though homesick, no doubt, and loyally critical, possibly even loyally scornful, found in the end that it was too honest a house and Henry Sidney too honest a man to keep up the antagonism year after year. Up at Norfolk or in Leicester's town-house, whichever he visited, things would have differed only by the greater degree of magnificence. And he was, it seems, in some ways closer to Leicester than to Sidney, for he spoke afterwards of Leicester as 'my honourable patron who from my youth had a special care of my bringing up and well-doing,' and said on Leicester's death that he had now lost the only friend who could patronise his 'good actions.'

So in that Penshurst society he lived for seven years a life utterly at a pole from the meals under the sky, the vast uncontrolled Ulster champaign, the roving herds, and the gallowglasses with their long glibs of hair, talking over the smoky fire of ambushes and sudden raids. His guide now was the Sidney who had been bedfellow to Edward VI, felt the young king die in his arms at Greenwich, was linked by marriage to the famous or unfortunate houses of Dudley and Northumberland, Berkeley, Beauchamp, Talbot, Leicester, and Grey; and all the interests and memories and gossip about him—even the religion, for he was now a little 'Protestant' boy—a world removed from such names as Niall of the Nine Hostages or old blind Theigue O'Huiginn's poems in difficult Deibhidhe about Sorley Bwee and the visions of Julius Caesar, and the fairy host on top of Maguire's castle, and MacSweeney's stronghold wet with the spume of the Atlantic.

It does not require a great deal of imagination to realize that the influence of those eight years in England must have been profound. He had left Ireland as a boy of nine, in August 1559, and he did not return to it until June 1567, aged seventeen, and we have already noted the precocity of the age, and how soon in life childhood ended and responsibility was handed over to an early maturity. As he returned to England in October 1567 and spent a last Christmas there, returning finally to Ulster in the new year of 1568, he actually spent nearly eight-and-a-half years in that powerful atmosphere. It is probably fair to say that two main elements composed it—two complementary elements supporting and enriching each other: an eager seriousness and a hardy opportunism, both exemplified at their very best in the life of that young contemporary of his, Sir Philip Sidney. Like him, he was brought up in the new religion, with its infusion of a Puritanism that was always solemn and earnest, and sometimes hard and narrow, but fundamentally conscientious, laborious, humble, elevated, and—as in the case of Bunyan, later—capable of producing a tremendous idealism near to the obsession of the fanatic. There is a curious letter extant, written by his patron Sir Henry Sidney to 'my little Philip,' then at Shrewsbury, which is a veritable Code of the ideal conduct expected of English gentlefolk turning from Papistry to the new faith. What it suggests is a picture of an Archangel with a Flaming Sword. It advises most weightily and seriously, prayer, study, modesty, courtesy to all men, moderation and discipline. . . . 'Seldom drink wine, yet sometimes do, lest being enforced to drink upon the sudden you should find yourself inflamed.' Bodily exercise, cleanliness of body, attention. . . . 'Be you rather a hearer and bearer away of other men's talk than a beginner and procurer of speech. . . . If you hear a wise sentence or apt phrase commit it to your memory.' It advised thought and consideration, remembering 'how nature hath ramparted up the tongue, as it were, with teeth, lips, yea, and hair without the lips, and all betokening reins and bridles for the loose use of that member.' Truthfulness above all, a recollection of his noble blood, and the call to a virtuous life and good actions. Did Lady Mary Sidney ever drop some of this character-building wisdom and piety into the ears of her Irish page?

Side by side with this earnest seriousness went a burning zeal for achievement which, as by the play of practical experience on noble theory, always assuaged the priggishness of the code and in deflecting its rigidity often belied it. For an image of that one may turn from young Philip Sidney to young Francis Bacon, and compare the adult lives of both. Sidney did not hesitate to fight bloodily, though he never besmirched his escutcheon, never became a *labes generis*. Bacon, though reared in a much more puritanical home, utterly devoted to learning ('I have taken all knowledge for my province'), thirsty for its possession, his whole life aimed at the noblest purposes of intellectual enlightenment, leaves us with the image of a man in whom opportunism so corroded all integrity that, despite the fact that his work ranks him among 'the few chosen examples of human achievement,' he remains in the memory as one of the least attractive characters of the period. The compression of Power, then one of the most lustful ambitions in the hearts of men, the ruthlessness of Adventure, the threats of Intrigue at every turn of the labyrinthine channels of court-life—an almost indispensable preliminary to all achievement—the urge of a financial Necessity that pressed heavily on the scruples of the most high-born, all these were a concomitant of that romantic thirst for conquest—of England's enemies, of the forces of nature, of the bounds of knowledge—which was just beginning to bud in the years during which O'Neill grew up, sensitive to it all, in those powerful, courtly houses in the country and in London city: a world where men could at once labour in humility and reverence for their vocation, and that vocation be in many ways if not in every way noble, and yet achieve their ends by methods which can only be called unscrupulous—that adaptation of ideals to ends which, in effect, is Opportunism.

It was too soon for O'Neill to see the ships of Raleigh on the Thames quaysides: he and Ireland lived to know the man's utterly ruthless nature. He could have stood at the waterside to see Frobisher set out on one of his annual expeditions to Africa and the Levant, or young Drake set off with the buccaneers for the Spanish Main, or slave-bartering Hawkins (his arms, a demi-moor, proper, bound with a cord). He came to know the elder Essex fairly intimately, and his nature, too (as Ireland found) was far from fastidious. Popular opinion as to the morality of his other patron, the Earl of Leicester, survives in Scott's sinister novel *Kenilworth*. He saw the new comfort, lavishness, delicacy, refinement, and to-day we would be inclined to emphasize hygiene, of the modern world beginning to replace the old feudal-medieval adoration of strength and commonalty; he also saw the obverse of this gallantry in men who 'wore a manor on their backs,' and who, in the thriftlessness of the gambler and the recklessness of the adventurer then set off to recoup their losses with their swords. He met scores of them in Ireland on his return, fought beside them, and helped them eagerly to recoup themselves on the flesh of his own country. And beside it he also saw the poverty of the London ghettos, and the filth of their vagrants on the road, liable to be hanged by the first magistrate.

What he read or saw in the way of letters and the arts we do not know, beyond the fact that Harington introduced him to Ariosto, and that Leicester was in the way of providing masques and pageants full of all the colour and allegory of the travelled world for Elizabeth at Kenilworth, and he was as likely—indeed more certain—to have visited the court for some of its brilliant entertainments as his grandfather Conn whom we saw there seventeen years before. But he probably saw very little, actually, of these things. And is it worth recalling that famous *cénacle* of Leicester House which Sidney's sister attended, since it was not until after (if only shortly after) his return to the wilds that it flourished as a literary coterie? Indeed he missed the great burst in literature and the arts by over ten years, for all the great men of the first school—Hooker and Sidney and Spenser and Marlowe—were of his generation, and came to their powers when he was coming to his, elsewhere and in another field. We do not know and, judging by the temper of that none too-wealthy and rather serious household, it is unlikely, that even Ascham's *Toxophilus* or Tottel's *Miscellany* lay on a Penshurst table—it was, in any case, more of an old-time feudal house, with the communal castle-hall strewn in rushes as its centre, than a modern Elizabethan house with 'drawing-room' and 'parlour' for family privacy. And if O'Neill saw a Miracle Play in a country town it was probably his entire and, *if* he saw it, doubtless, bewildered experience of the Drama.

No ! The seriousness of life, the zeal to achieve, the earnestness of the struggle, the force and technique of competition, the excitement of the growing spirit of adventure—*these* were what he must have imbibed most of all. These built up his character, for good or ill. There were plenty of examples to fire his uncritical admiration, as there were for any youth of his age. He had over eight years in which to observe and con and be filled with emulation. Those years left their mark. Their suave memories so overlaid those earlier homespun memories that if some gentle English visitor came in the after years on Hugh, feasting in the fern, he would laugh wryly and excuse his simple habits, comparing himself to wolves who eat well at a time and fast long after it. Their deeper informative mark on his mind as he grew old enough to be judicial about it all must disentangle itself gradually from his story, which is thereby proportionately more subtle and intelligent than that of the courageous bluntness of Sean, his uncle, or the thoughtless dash of his magnificent ally, Red Hugh O'Donnell.

This, then, was the world in which the boy grew away from his memories of Ireland—Shropshire's 'coloured counties,' the Kentish chalk-hills, the narrow streets of London, one of the most modest and serious homes in England, glimpses of the court, murmurings of that new learning, both colourful and sober, which was the blending of the Renaissance and the Reformation, the company—even though it was at the great distance of their differing ages—of men of parts and responsibility, hints of the great issues being fought over in the Continent. This, too, was what he was to leave behind on his return to Ireland, where he was never to know that Learning and the Arts were bursting behind him into the greatest flowering they were to know in England, and that Humanism was reaching there its peak of grace and enlightenment; since, alas, for it seems that such things must always have their sinister corollary, he was to experience only the savage reverse of the medal, and forget whatever he had seen of England's humanistic grace and kindness in her imperial brutality and greed.

But that was years away, and in the meantime which are we to imagine, that the lad was storing in a wily heart the secret intention to turn all this that he was enjoying to good use against it, or that he simply relished it like any natural boy? The whole of his after life when circumstances had made him aware of a conflict inside him, shows him painfully caught in a dual loyalty —one of the very first, perhaps the first modern Irishman so divided by the impact of a complex and sophisticated civilization on the quiet certainties of a simpler way of life.

Not that Ireland was ever altogether to be forgotten. The insistence of Sean O'Neill saw to that, and through the thick foliage of this many-serpented Eden his name hissed ever so often. It sounded through the Penshurst gossip about Condé and Guise and the proposed marriage between Mary Stuart and Navarre, for Sean had a close Scots connection and at one time was considered by his people a fit match for Mary Stuart. His name cropped up in connection with Sir Henry's secret missions to France and Scotland in '62. It fanned the whispers about the rival house of Sussex, for Sean was incredibly supposed to be asking for the hand of Lady Frances Radcliffe, sister of Sussex; it spoiled the happy flutter when Sir Henry's name went on the eighth stall of Windsor Chapel and it mingled with news of the French fighting. And however little else the boy was in discretion permitted to hear about Ireland he had to be told at least (1562, he was then aged twelve), when Sean with a magnificent effrontery borrowed several thousands of crowns from Elizabeth in order to visit her in person, duly arrived in London with his native bodyguard of six-foot gallowglasses, and his own private poet, impressed Her Majesty, and went back to Ireland as the acknowledged Lord of Tyrone. Though there really could be no question either of keeping that from Hugh or of telling him about it since the visit was the talk of the town, with people saying here how well his English dress became Great O'Neill and there how he 'feasted a good number at once,' or, again, how the Bishop of Aquila was charged with having brought Sean and twelve or fourteen of his household to hear secret Mass in his chapel. The whole visit can only have been regarded by the Sidneys as a disturbance of the quiet of their young ward, and they must have sighed with relief when Sean was gone. Besides, underground were the unspoken things, such as Sean's sharp mistrust of the favour being shown to young Hugh (it is mentioned expressly in the State Papers) and his fears that at some time this child might be given power in Tyrone. The exiled boy would not hear of that directly but he would sense the tension of the general atmosphere. And then the news had to be broken to him that his brother Brian had meantime been murdered in Ireland by Sean's kinsmen, and that he was now Baron of Dungannon. Nor need we doubt that Leicester passed on to him, by way of consolation, that Cecil had noted his existence and remarked: 'And so the title for the Earldom is undecided?' At that point the most innocent of boys must have realized why he had been brought to England and what was expected of him.

The fact is, his destiny was closing in on the young Baron of Dungannon, and childhood and boyhood were coming to an end that was premature even for the times. Sean, on his return to Ireland, 'began to play the knave as lustily as ever he did'—we are now thinking westwards into the wilderness with a Londoner's mind—and two years later the colonists could stand his ravages no longer. Sidney himself was sent over to lead an expedition inland. Behind him he left his ward, the heir presumptive to the Earldom, aged fifteen, aware at last that only his father's murderer stood between him and the title, and that his English friends were dangling it before his eyes.

4

Sidney was in the field in January 1565, and so stoutly pressing into the Ulster woods that time and again his 'avaunt-couriers felt the couch warm where the rebel lay last night.' His reports back to England declared that 'Lucifer was never puffed up with more pride or ambition than O'Neill. He continually keepeth six hundred armed men about him and is able to bring into the field one thousand horsemen and four thousand foot.' (Those figures, in passing, were very large for the period: one remembers that Cortez marched across all Mexico and conquered it with three hundred men and a handful of horse, relying, as the English did with this nearer Mexico, on native supernumeraries and internal dissension.) 'He is the only strong man in Ireland,' went on Sidney. 'His country was never so rich or inhabited, and he armeth and weaponeth all the peasants of his country, the first that ever did so of an Irishman.' An unhealthy example, obviously, for master Hugh. Especially when Sean mocked their English titles saying, 'I care not to be an earl unless I be better and higher than an earl, for I am in blood and power better than the best of them. . . . My ancestors were kings of Ulster, and Ulster is mine and shall be mine!'

Meantime the youth had other examples to compare with his uncle. There were the fortunes of other restless Irish 'earls' to watch and ponder. There was, for example, the Desmond house of the Fitzgeralds, Normans who had been so long in Ireland that they had become virtually gaelicized. Their traditional enemy was the house of Ormonde and it was notorious in London that Elizabeth favoured Ormonde and disliked Desmond, who had, in any case, grace neither of mind nor body to attract her or commend himself. He, also, was in London in 1562 with Sean, and like Sean made formal obeisances, promising to pay his feudal dues, and suppress the Gaelic poets and brehons and come back to English ways. He had failed his promise—his Gaelic followers would not allow him to keep it. He was in London again in the year that Sidney left for Ireland, and he was *not* allowed to go back. Young O'Neill may well have seen and certainly would have heard of this wretched man who, during the next eight years, suffered the penury and humiliation of so-called honourable confinement in London, hanging about the low taverns and lodgings of the city, ill-clad, half-fed, constantly sick, as poor as any broken down knight of Eastcheap, before final disaster ended his career in a mountain cabin in the wilds of Kerry. But we must return to that terrible story of Desmond and merely throw a glance at it here because that, too, was dangled before the youth as one of the salutary lessons of his London life.

Sidney, meanwhile, never did come to grips with Sean, and Sean might well have made good his boast to hold Ulster, if, in his super-egotistical arrogance, he did not care more for private glory than any sort of national 'front' against the conquistadors. It was local rivalries that ended him—his efforts to crush his neighbours on the west, the O'Donnells, and those Scots of Ulster who were led by the saviour of Ireland, Sorley Bwee (according to O'Huiginn's flattering poem). The O'Donnells finally hurled Sean back from the Swilly in 1567, and in his extremity the foolish man took refuge with the Scots, who promptly murdered him. Hugh, Baron of Dungannon, was in Ireland that year, and on the June of Shane's death joined his patron, Sir Henry, at his camp in the north. With that visit his adult life began, at the age of eighteen.

If the young man thought, in his eager ambition, as he sniffed Power through the turf-smoke, that nothing now remained to be done but to proclaim him Earl he still had a great deal to learn about the ways of the world. His grandfather, Conn, it appeared, had had a grand-nephew named Turlough. This Turlough now made his unwelcome appearance in Sidney's camp as claimant to the Lordship of Tyrone, and presented himself, truthfully, as the accepted captain of his people. Since he was a man of influence, and since he was prepared to come to terms with the colonists, the colonists agreed to acknowledge him. To the sanguine Baron of Dungannon these political compromises must have seemed not only puzzling but dampening; and as a matter of history this Turlough was to go on chilling his high hopes for many years to come.

Then the long, tangled intrigues began in earnest. The hot young heart felt the first pangs of deferred hopes. Slowly the skin of the heart hardened, and the eyes began to peer their first suspicions. If others were calculating he must calculate too. Then he would be reassured, and his hopes rise again, and his trust revive. It clears the air a little when the colonists agree, the next month, that Turlough's acknowledged territory should be confined to the north part of Tyrone and that their baron should hold the south. By September he has the further satisfaction of hearing them declare that Turlough shall have no control whatever over him. By October the cockerel is learning to crow for himself: he has procured from the courts the exemplification of that first patent of October 1542 which made earls of his grandfather and all his successors. He is obviously impatient to find out exactly what legal claims he has on the major title.

A week later he had to set off for Dublin with his patron. Sidney's work in Ireland was finished, and in proof of it he brought with him half a dozen Gaelic and Old Norman captains who would make their obeisances in person to Elizabeth and take a chance on coming back safe to Ireland: they were O'Connor Sligo, Ely O'Carroll, Fitzmorris of Lixnaw, Breffini O'Reilly,

Ross MacGeoghegan, Sir John of Desmond. Having duly stuck Sean's head on a spike over the gates of the castle of Dublin, where all these Gaels could see it grinning at the sky whenever they passed in or out, Sidney left for England.

That second journey of Hugh O'Neill differs from the first in that it touches a sardonic as well as a pathetic note. It is not he, however, who is now the subject either of pity or irony. For he is now a prosperous, well-set, low-sized, red-haired young gallant, English-trained, intimate with the ways of courtly houses, within grasp of an Earldom. But—about him this time, on the boat and on the muddy London roads, are his own folk, looking at him with an uncomfortable mixture of reliance and mistrust, admiration and dislike, none of them quite certain whether he himself is a guest or a prisoner. There happens to be a precise description of the arrival of this motley train at Hampton Court, where Elizabeth was then in residence: it emphasizes the sardonic pathos of the thing.[5] Sidney, followed by about two hundred of his gentlemen freebooters, came walking along the wide, bare-branched avenues and through the arches, with the fallen leaves drifted in the corners, to the Queen's rooms. In the middle of his retinue were these uneasy Irish, and somewhere in the crowd the confident Baron. Elizabeth was looking out of a window and saw them, and in surprise asked who these men were. She was told that it was Sir Henry Sidney back from the Irish wars with some hostages, and she remarked, with an idle indifference, 'It is well. He has two of the best offices in the kingdom'—one man, at least, who would not need further reward. Sidney was shown into her presence, then, proud of his satisfactory tale, only to be galled bitterly by the murmurs of some courtiers who echoed their Queen's mood with such remarks as, 'This scuffle in Ulster was not worthy to be called a war. Sean O'Neill was nothing but a beggar and an outlaw.'

Outside, meanwhile, in the November cold, stood Hugh and the Gaelic captains, staring and stared at, their eyes on magnificence and their thoughts on their own parlous future, wondering whether their worst premonitions—now keyed to peak in this general atmosphere of contempt—were or were not to be realized. They were: another salutary warning for the Baron. He saw O'Connor Sligo and Sir John of Desmond taken away, rowed down the river to the Tower and the fog over the marshes. O'Neill probably had only a vague idea where this fateful 'Tower' was. To these wretches, as to so many of their kin then and after, some of whom were never heard of once the Tower received them, it was a dark nowhere. Such lives became bounded by a hole called a cell, by hunger and cold, by the loneliness of endless days during which they would hear only scraps of talk from a jailor, or shouts from the quays outside in a language they did not understand, or in the quiet night the whispering mud of the foreign river. He knew that all they would have to keep them alive would be the illusion of hope and agonizing memories of forays on the Irish hills; memories that would soothe them in their sleep and torment them as their eyes slowly opened to another day. May one be permitted a mild guess that O'Neill, seeing them go, stiffened his jaw, and noted the price of the gamble, and measured the horror of a fate than which it would surely be better to grin like his uncle Sean, back in Dublin, from a spike in the free air? May one venture to believe that when his own time came he remembered the looks on his friends' faces?

That was the last Christmas that O'Neill spent in England. He and Sidney were in a mood of satisfied exaltation. At the end of the Irish campaign Sidney had been low and irritable. His rival Sussex was then in the ascendant with his plan for the marriage of Elizabeth to the Archduke Charles, while he had to remain stuck in the wet Irish bogs far from the roulette of courtly favour. Now Sussex was on the down grade, his plans awry, and in token of Elizabeth's continuing satisfaction with her Irish Deputy, she had confirmed him in his office as Lord President of Wales. He would not need to go back to Ireland for many months, probably not until after the next summer. O'Neill, on the other hand, was about to begin his career. He was to go to Ireland in the new year, take over his barony, and enjoy a maintenance of 1000 marks a year from the Treasury.

He was there in the spring of 1568 in the old house at Dungannon, now *his* Dungannon, with the winds of March sweet over 'Tyrone of the Bushes' and the gulls from the lake following the churls' ploughs, and the old childhood smell of the peat in every breeze. The country was in a pause after the collapse of Sean. Some were dismayed by the surrenders of Turlough and the lesser captains, some waiting to see what way things would go, but most were indifferent as usual to any larger politics than their own familiar ritual of local life. Even the arrival of this forgotten son of Matthew, backed by English money, reared in

English ways, presumed at best indifferent in religion and at worst a heretic, was no matter to arouse more than a passing interest. When the first gossip died away, the recollections of his father's curious story and his brother's violent death, and when he had shown himself to the curiosity of the people, he would be at peace to confer with his brothers, Cormac and Art, and with his fosterers the O'Quinns and O'Hagans—these at least would have welcomed him with a warm affection—count his friends and enemies, and for the rest, like everybody else, wait and hold his counsel. As yet he was but an English Baron, something infinitely less important than a Gaelic chief. He must like Sean, be more than the one and wholly the other before any crest of power could float him to his tide.

PART TWO

PREPARATIONS: 1568–1595

I

SIDNEY WAS DUE back in Ireland in the autumn. During the spring and summer O'Neill spent the days analysing his prospects. It was a tricky business, where family relationships and local rivalries led him at every hand's turn into a maze. Every step had to be supremely tentative.

His chief rival and the pivot of the situation was his cousin Turlough Luineach O'Neill, the man who had been the instrument of his brother's death. The disturbing thing about Turlough was not his power, which was measurable, but his chances which were unpredictable, largely due to the recognition which the English had decided to give him. That was from the rear, worrying, intangible. In time both Turlough and the Baron discovered that this dubiety was the whole point of the English game. They sowed unease deliberately in the minds of rivals and profited thereby. The elegance of this technique was that it cost them so very little. What Turlough actually got was less than the beads that early explorers are said to have given to American natives in exchange for gold. He was given a recognition which his power made inevitable; permission to rule a territory that he absolutely possessed; later offered the title of Earl of Clanconnell, than which his own name carried far more weight. There was even in these concessions to Turlough a considerable hesitation and a convenient ambiguity. They did not finally get down on vellum until some nine years later (1578). Then articles indented between him and the Lord Deputy of Elizabeth declared in the best legal Latin that it was 'agreed and conceded to Turlough Luineach that during his life, and by the grace of Her Majesty, he should have and inhabit all the territory from Lough Foyle to the Great River.' Some years later still the Attorney-General Coke was asked to examine these articles. He wrote in the margin—'Nothing passed in law by these articles and letters patent to Sir Turlough Luineach.' And how could it, observes Coke, since on the death of the arch-rebel Sean everything was given to Her Majesty (i.e. confiscated) by articles and letters patent? Even when Sir Turlough Luineach became Earl of Clanconnell, adds Coke, not only was nothing thereby granted, but a proviso was added that he should claim no other lands on the strength of his new dignity other than those mentioned in the said articles, and once again his hand writes in the margin, 'by these letters patent nothing passed by law to Sir Turlough Luineach only the dignity.' In the brutal American phrase, whose cruelty is justified by the need for something astringent to cut through the slime of this Renaissance diplomacy, they had played the old man for a sucker. To the end of his days the pathos of it is that Turlough never quite admitted even to himself that nothing passed to him in law 'only the dignity.' To the end of his days he was under the delusion that he could if he chose become an accepted, respected, valuable peer of the realm, whereas he was to the Burghleys and the Walsynghams nothing but a pawn. Shortly before he died he offered with a touching simplicity to give up his castle at Strabane, and to control all Ulster, if they would give him three thousand men to lead. As if the colony could possibly consider handing over three thousand men to a potential enemy at a time when the Deputy was overruled by his own Council in wishing to ask for two thousand to control all Ireland!

These discoveries, maddening to Turlough, delightful to the

Baron, were, however, far in the future. For the moment these spurious offers of English assistance to Turlough prevented O'Neill from raiding his rival in the immemorial fashion of his ancestors. For what he immediately wanted was cattle, thousands of cattle, and land, thousands of acres of it. In acknowledging Turlough's rights the colony prevented O'Neill from seizing them for himself. As soon as the young man realized this he began his real education in the exasperating political methods of his masters.

That Turlough was thus partially acknowledged as 'Lord of Tyrone' meant something else of the greatest importance to Hugh O'Neill. It meant that the sons of Sean, the dead rebel, were his second batch of enemies. He saw that in passing them over the English colony had turned them into outlaws and landless men, every one of them a potential Fortinbras ready, on the skirts of Ireland here and there, to shark up a list of lawless resolutes to win the land thus by their father lost. These wild men would naturally oppose any English nominee most bitterly, and to oppose them in turn, the sons of his father's murderer, was wholly palatable to Hugh. Moreover, he saw that if he should ever rise to power these bandits would swing over at once to Turlough—as they did. He must have marked them down early as absolute foes.

If we were to go beyond that we should have to follow him into a labyrinth as treacherous as the caverns of Minos. The family trees of a people so long established cross like wild brambles that have not been pruned for generations. We may leave him to his subtle and tedious task and be content to accept each new name of enemy or friend as it crops up in the path of his ambition; this one to be cut down, that to be trained to his purpose. Only one other set of names is essential—that of the O'Donnells of the neighbouring country of Tyrconnell. And there the key-name is a woman's, Ineen Duv, The Dark Girl, Fionola MacDonnell—one of the Scotch pirates of the Isles who had married into the O'Donnell country and became the mother of Red Hugh O'Donnell, one of the finest fighters of the century and the life-long ally of O'Neill; who later married Red Hugh's sister, Siobhan, or Judith. Ineen Duv was the driving force, the typical fighting matriarch, imbued by a relentless hatred of the English, the great inspiration behind her son in all his fights. One other name he linked briefly with his own when he married the daughter of Brian MacFelim O'Neill. Of that marriage nothing now is known except that it was within the forbidden degree of relationship and was therefore subsequently dissolved.

If we should go farther into that welter of 'clans,' what would surprise us about it all is not his diplomatic weavings but that the colonists, however much they hated and feared this maze of alliances and family entanglements, were able to find their way through the maze as well as he—and that from three hundred miles away. To see the gouty Cecil at Hampton or Whitehall or Richmond, noting with his quill-pen on the backs of pieces of paper the track through the maze, and advising Secretaries, Deputies, Presidents, and Generals how to find their way through it, and remembering it all so well in the midst of the most worrying national and continental business, is to form a considerable respect for the statecraft of Tudor England.

Immediately he recognized his enemies O'Neill began to raid as many as he dared. It was what was expected of him. Every newly-fledged chieftain did it. For whatever he was, Baron, or Earl, or Captain, he would count for nothing except in virtue of the blood caking on his sword and the healthy respect of the 'clans' for his fighting men. He did not stop even when Sidney arrived back in Ireland that September: he was still in the field in October taking great preys of cattle from unfriendly O'Neills —just as if he had never been a respectable little English gallant swaggering in the streets of London.

Then, in the following January, Sidney called a parliament in Dublin and Hugh went down to it, a fine, upstanding, red-headed young man of nineteen, and sat and listened among all the bishops, archbishops and temporal lords of the realm—i.e. those of the established Church and State. It was, of course, largely a paper parliament. Connaught and half Munster were not represented; nor, apart from himself, more than the merest edge of Ulster. Behind him he left Turlough spoiling and raiding to his heart's content in the old manner of his predecessors; a course which was, as Turlough failed to see, exactly the behaviour most suited to the advancement of the English nominee.

At that Parliament O'Neill saw, for the first time, the importance in Irish politics of the religious question. He found that there was a powerful resentment among the towns and the old (Norman-English) houses against any effort to force the Reformation on the country, and as a matter of historical fact the ultimate result of this was that by the end of the century there were less penal laws against religion on the statute-book of the Dublin parliament than on that of London. But there was nothing to suggest to his mind that there was any anti-English feelings in the port towns. On the contrary those present were ready to proclaim anybody a traitor who resisted the government, and otherwise to fall in with Sidney's policy of anglicizing the country, in law and custom—provided only that their religion was left alone, their titles to their property not interfered with, and their feudal influence left undiminished. But these three things were just the three things that England would not abstain from reforming, so that in this little Dublin caucus O'Neill saw in *petto* the whole problem of Ireland's future, and the future of every man like himself charged with a part of it.

Religion was for the moment passed over. But he heard the Act which aimed at preventing 'lords and great men of this realm' from 'exercising absolute and regal authority within large circuits,' and even before the parliament rose the interference with titles—in other words the grabbing of land by fresh adventurers—had set the whole south in violent commotion. He came back from Dublin to Dungannon with news of these southern disturbances. And, probably, *eager* news since he had an eye keen enough to see that the more disturbed the country the quicker was his advancement likely to be—or of any man whose use to the colonists would increase in proportion as there was danger to themselves. That is clear from the fact that he had no scruples about taking a part, with a troop of horse in the Queen's pay, in those southern wars against his fellow Irishmen—'in which and all occasions he behaved himself valiantly' says the English reporter Moryson. It was, for the moment, little to him that these risings were the result of Sidney's threat to the power of every man like himself. The amount of power that he, so far, had to lose by the Acts of Sidney's Parliament was not sufficient to make him consider their ultimate effect on himself.

These disturbances became known to history as the Desmond Rebellion. For many reasons they must have had a real influence on the career of O'Neill. He could see in them a picture of what happened to any man who failed to balance himself adroitly between the two worlds—the Renaissance and the Medieval; he could here measure the full gamut of English and Irish power: these wars involved Spanish military aid—the one thing which he considered, through all his subsequent career, to be the crucial element in any resistance to the spread of the Reformation spirit in Europe; and it was his first experience of a really bloody war. For all these reasons it is well worth while to follow the young man with his hired horsemen as he canters eagerly to the south.

2

The Earls of Desmond had come to Ireland as Fitzgeralds, with the first great wave of twelfth-century Norman adventurers. Over the centuries they had broken up into the House of Desmond and the House of Kildare, both feudal titles; but by this date both had become almost completely absorbed into the Irish system. Thus, in 1537 Justice Luttrell observes that in Kildare land which used to be, like the country immediately about Dublin, 'more parte Englyshe,' there was not now a husbandman who could speak English, or make any use of the language at all, 'and there gentyllmen be after the same sort.' And when, following the foolish rebellion of young Silken Thomas Fitzgerald, he and his five uncles were executed and all the Geraldines of Leinster exiled and banished (1537), the *Annals of the Four Masters* speaking in the name of the Gaelic world said—'these were great losses and the cause of lamentation throughout Eire.' The Gaelic poet Muireadach Albanach later chanted their line as he would the line of the oldest Celtic heroes. The only other Norman settlers who outdid them in this respect were those Normans who had pierced to the west, such as the De Burgos who became Burkes, or the de Angulos who became Costellos, and went completely native. The Desmonds, however, were a far more civil line than any of these and to find a proper analogy one must go to some English house like the Sidneys or De Veres. Some of the most charming Gaelic love-poems, for example, of the sixteenth-seventeenth century are due to the influence of the French lyric introduced into Ireland by the fourth Earl of Desmond, Gerald the Rhymer, and the unusually rich contents of the library of the Earl of Kildare, of 1526, are well-known.

Their traditional rivals were the Butlers, Earls of Ormonde, who had established a pocket of Norman-English around Kilkenny, and with these they were endlessly squabbling about land, chiefly their *marches* in Tipperary, very much as O'Neill was to do later with his cousin Turlough. These rivalries were constantly before the English Court where Ormonde had the advantage of having been playmate in childhood to Elizabeth, all of whose favour his charm, personality, and intelligence had by this date, won from his rival. In fact, as we saw, Desmond had been in honourable confinement in London for the past three years under the care of Sir Warham St. Leger. This July of O'Neill's return to Ireland his fortunes had fallen so low that he was under open arrest for alleged disloyalty, and purchased his life only by the surrender of everything he possessed: 'all his lands, tenements, houses, castles, signories, all he stood possessed of, to receive back what Her Majesty was pleased to allow him.'

The territory was enormous. The inevitable adventurers smelled the loot. Up out of Devonshire and Somersetshire there poured a bevy of brave and ruthless men, ready to hack out a fortune with their swords—Gilbert, Herbert, Grenville, Courtenay, Carew, St. Leger, Raleigh, all eager to hold this rich land of the south for the Queen. They promised her to bring the wildest and most idle natives to obedience and civility, and if the savages, the usual word, offended by idleness then the savages would die. They would, with native labour, build castles, forts, harbours, and roads, fish the seas, till the soil, and pay just revenues to the Queen. It was the ideology of the typical sixteenth century soldier and wandering privateer, blooded on the coasts of Barbary and in the wars of France, as indifferent to the lives of any number of natives as ignorant of their ways, but at the same time sufficiently informed by the legalism of the Renaissance imperialistic mentality to look for courtly sanction and a guarantee of title before embarking on their adventures. The court, through Cecil, with a characteristic mixture of humanity, unscrupulousness, and caution, advised against precipitate confiscations but suggested that a modest beginning might be made in the region of Desmond's escheated estates around County Cork.

The falcons flew. Then Sir Peter Carew made a sad, and even for the times, an almost incredible blunder. With a colossal contempt for established or traditional titles he ignorantly laid claim to lands that had, over the centuries, come into the possession of two brothers of the favoured Ormonde. He raided and ejected the followers of Sir Edmond Butler. At once the whole countryside was in crackling flames. The Butlers tore down on him, burned, plundered, slaughtered, raped virgin and mother alike. For two days the orgy of brutal retribution went on; the fire spread like a burning heath. The Butler raid became a mere trigger-incident when the standard of not merely a just but, what was far more dangerous, a Holy War was raised by Desmond's cousin James Fitzmaurice, one of the most interesting and in some ways attractive characters of the whole century, an idealist, a humanist, an unboasting man of valour, all his letters and proclamations headed IN OMNI TRIBULATIONE ET ANGUSTIA, SPES NOSTRA JESUS ET MARÍA. It was his aim to combine the whole restless South into a national confederation.

This danger redoubled when he appealed to Philip II for assistance: his story knitted there with that of the raffishly baroque adventurer Sir Thomas Stukeley, and one feels the threat of the Armada budding in the background. For the next few years messengers continually passed to and fro between Ireland and Spain until by 1571 the English Deputy was reporting that the country was overrun with 'Spanish spies and vermin.' This was the last thing desired by Elizabeth, threatened with Catholic unrest at home and the Spanish challenge abroad. Mary was in prison again, but Alva's brutalities in the Low Countries against the Protestants had at once been encouraging Catholic unrest and infuriating Protestant opinion at home. The northern earls were in revolt. The Pope had at last issued his Bull of Excommunication and Deposition against her. Not until Cecil exposed and executed Norfolk and Northumberland (1572) was that danger allayed.

Fitzmaurice pursued his course with a guerilla's dash. He seized a ship belonging to Sir John Hawkins in the harbour of Kinsale and bore down on the St. Legers and the Grenvilles. The masters were by chance away, pressing their suits in London; the wives fled into Cork; the raiders cut the windpipes of the entire household; the 'Earl of Clancarty' according to the usual schedule, came down from his English peak, shook off the trammels of Earldom, became Irish MacCarthy, and overnight what had been a rabble became an army, the sight of whose ragged thousands squatting on the high hills around the city of Cork, and under the walls of the little county towns—for this Munster was much more developed in that respect than our Ulster—must have struck terror into the colonists.

It was a strangely contrasted army, for Fitzmaurice knew how to bear himself nobly, and the letter he sent to the Mayor of Cork reveals a mind both refined and controlled, and like all idealists pitiless:—

'Mr. Mayor,—I commend me unto you; whereas the queen's majesty is not contented to dispose all our worldly goods, our bodies, and our lives as she list, but must also compel us to forego the Catholic faith by God unto His church given, and by the See of Rome hitherto prescribed to all Christian men to be observed, and use another newly invented kind of religion, which for my part, rather than I would obey to my everlasting damnation, I had liefer forsake all the world if it were mine, as I wish all others who profess Christ and His true faith to do: therefore this shall be to require you in the way of charity that ye ought to have towards all them that profess to be Christian men, to abolish out of the city that old heresy newly raised and invented, and all them that be Huguenots, both men and children, and to set up the service after the due form and manner which is used in Rome and throughout all Christendom, and as our forefathers have ever used before. Assuring you that if you follow not this our Catholic and wholesome exhortation, I will not nor may not be your friend, and in like manner I wish and require the chapter and all the clergy of Cork and of the bishoprick thereof to frame themselves to honour God as your ancestors have done, and destroy out of the town all the Huguenots with the first wind.

'From Martyrstone this 12th of July, 1569.

'Spes nostra Jesu Maria.

'Yours if ye be in good faith, James Fitzmaurice of Desmond.'

Sir Peter Carew meanwhile fanned the flames by taking a bloody revenge for Butler's bloody revenge. He seized Butler's house and he slaughtered every man, woman and child, even to the tender age of three. Butler duly retorted, say the State Papers, with 'outrages too horrible to hear.' The South was now fully roused. 'None but fools or knaves,' cried Sir Edward Butler, 'would sit still to be robbed.' The Burkes and Thomond combined. Kildare began to waver. Even the favoured Ormonde himself grew restless. It seemed as if Fitzmaurice might bind them all into a phalanx. And now we see clearly the reverse of that medal which bears the delicate features of Sir Philip Sidney, that perfect personification of all the bright ideals of the Elizabethan world, when his father, O'Neill's patron, with O'Neill at his side, raced through the land, burning villages, blowing up castles, hanging every man he caught alive, flinging down their corpses from the battlements to terrify others. The old, frightful, futile slaughter that follows on all colonization was in full swing.

As O'Neill partook of all this in person, the north felt it from a distance. Cousin Turlough began to champ the ground, spoiling the neighbouring country, now known as Fermanagh and then called Maguire's Country. He was promising fair, as observers reported to Cecil, to become like his predecessor Sean. We see him, all that year of '69, now playing for better terms with the colonists, now sending for Scots mercenaries, now welcoming messengers from James Fitzmaurice, now threatening to waste Newry, and finally so terrifying the settlers that messengers went galloping for help to Dublin. That autumn of '69 Dublin actually had to abandon the south to violence and drive north against him. Fortunately for the government and possibly for himself he married that autumn, and for purely domestic reasons somebody (a 'jester' the State Papers say with unconscious humour) put a bullet through his shoulder whilst he sat at table with his new wife and he was out of the game for the rest of the winter.

The South felt the recoil. Ruthlessness, that centralized drive which always told against the disparate clans, and a clear-cut purpose won for the time being. 'I slew,' said Sir Humphrey Gilbert, writing to Sidney, 'all those from time to time that did belong to, feed, accompany, or maintain any outlaws or traitors; and after my first summoning of any castle or fort, if they would not presently yield it, I would not afterwards take it of their gift, but won it perforce, how many lives so ever it cost, putting man, woman, and child of them to the sword. Neither did I spare any malefactors unexecuted that came to my hands in any respect; using all those that I had protected with all courtesy and friendship that I might, being for my part constantly of this opinion that no conquered nation will ever yield willingly their obedience for love, but rather for fear.' MacCarthy More was soon on his knees under the weight of this treatment. James Fitzmaurice fled for refuge to Kilkenny. The Butlers never joined this confederation but, despite a promise of safe conduct, were nevertheless treacherously arrested and flung into the cells of Dublin Castle.

We may accept Froude's comment on all this. 'The English

nation was shuddering over the atrocities of the Duke of Alva. The children in the nurseries were being inflamed to patriotic rage and madness by tales of Spanish tyranny. Yet Alva's bloody sword never touched the young, the defenceless, or those whose sex even dogs can recognize and respect.' And then Froude goes on to point out the disadvantages of the ruthless method. 'It must be carried out to the last extremity, or it ought not to be tried at all. The dead do not come back; and if the mothers and the babies are slaughtered with the men, the race gives no further trouble; but the work must be done thoroughly; partial and fitful cruelty lays up only a long debt of deserved and ever-deepening hate.' And that is true of the whole century—a wavering between total war and tentative compromise—which ended in frustration and futility, combined with and emphasized by the obstinate persistence of the native spirit, which kept rising from the grave like a myth, when, by all the laws of nature it should have been counted dead, and by all the laws of reason it might well have decided that it had died and risen often enough both for wonder and for honour.

Sure enough, three months after Sidney was writing contentedly to Cecil, in January 1570, that Fitzmaurice was now a bush-beggar with not twenty knaves to his back, and that the very name of an Englishman was now more terrible than the sight of a hundred had been before, the dead arose again. Elizabeth began to count her losses in cash. Compromise succeeded slaughter. Weakness followed strength. Gilbert, having achieved nothing whatever, was recalled from Ireland. Fitzmaurice became lord of Munster within a week. In the north Turlough O'Neill became bold, sent his Scottish wife home with orders to bring back more mercenaries, and by the summer he was so haughty as to claim the complete lordship of all the countries, and all the titles and dignities, that any O'Neill before him had ever had.

Hugh's attitude is clear in this crisis. Young, but no longer poor, and no longer feebly friended, his whole aim is to get that title of Earl and the lands that go with it. Nothing else matters. Nobody else counts. Power is paramount. His only way of getting it was to play fair with the English. He was working hard for their favour all that winter during which Turlough had lain in bed, and Turlough's new contumacity now played into his hands. In April, 1570, the Deputy recommended that he should be proclaimed Earl of Tyrone and given the task of expelling Turlough's Scots. But Turlough saw the danger and in the winter of '70–'71 began to play a softer tune, and his Scots wife now starts to write to Elizabeth that she is holding Turlough back, that she is all for peace and tranquillity, and she begs that her husband should be given some title to his possessions in Ulster. Indeed he puts away his Scots and writes himself to Elizabeth offering to pay tribute, recounting his long services—though it is hard to know what his services had been seeing that he had aided Sean's revolt and been troublesome ever since—and begging to be allowed to rule his country in peace. Elizabeth, however, seems to have had enough native wit (it did not require much) to see through this palaver. She knew that it usually came up with the weeds every spring in Ireland when the fighting men wanted time to sow their crops; and sure enough when the harvest was well in and the days were short and the nights dark Turlough was in the field again. He was not a patient intriguer.

To the fighting men on the other side all these truces, and compromises, and endless shillying-shallying were demoralizing and exasperating. Sidney having long cursed the beastly country to which misfortune had consigned him returned to England. His successor, Fitzwilliam (1571–1575) is soon complaining that he is all but beggared and has to pawn his plate to raise a few men to hold Dundalk. A new President sent to Connaught finds himself shut out of his own garrison town of Athlone, on the Connaught border, because he cannot pay his way to the citizens. Within a year Fitzwilliam is begging release as heartily as any of his predecessors, or, if not that, men and money, and if not that they can 'devise to bury him." Indeed money was always the key. Without it nobody could take any policy to a conclusion. Without it the Deputy had to try to pay himself out of what he could grab, and his levies became freebooters, revolting against all discipline, and still further exasperating the whole island. As one historian puts it, Elizabeth did not pay her Deputies, the Deputies could not pay the officers, the officers could not pay the men, the men could not pay the shop-keepers, the shop-keepers could not pay the farmers, the farmers could not pay the landlords, the landlords could not pay the Crown and so the circle of bankruptcy and demoralization was complete.

3

During the lull in the fighting we may observe the general picture which, as we must always remember, was O'Neill's first real experience of the greater Ireland. Wherever he looked the picture was disturbing, and if he had the wit to draw general conclusions from particular instances, he must have begun to form some unfavourable general opinions about the efficacy of English rule. The instances would, in any case, have sunk into the back of his mind, to be revived on a later occasion to support conclusions forced on him from bitter personal experience of that rule. Since it was at the core of Fitzmaurice's rising, we may take the example of Religion. First of all, let us glance at the corruption and idleness of the clergy; and then at the general level of public morals.

Even here money was the key since, without it, the Reformation clergymen could not take up their duties, and those that did gave too many examples of unashamed corruption to be ignored even by a young soldier chiefly intent, like them, on attending to his own interests. Some of these clergymen became a byword in their own day, and persist in to our's almost as a legend. The famous Myler McGrath was the extreme example. Originally a Catholic he became one of the most clear-headed, if most secular of the new Reformation prelates. Having apostatized he collected in time eighty-one benefices, and having exploited so much in his own church lived to see his children appropriately become Catholics. It is no wonder, therefore, that when Sidney toured the country on his return in 1576 he found in the county of Meath alone two hundred and twenty-four benefices, of which one hundred and five belonged to the Crown, and in not *one* of these was there a resident clergyman. 'There is no divine service in the country,' wrote one Andrew Trollope to Walsyngham as late as 1587, 'and all the churches are clean down, ruinous, and in great decay. The ministers will not be accounted ministers but priests. They will have no wives. If it would stay there it were well; but they have harlots, which they make believe it is no sin to live and lie with them, but if they marry they are damned. With long experience and some extraordinary trial of these fellows, I cannot find whether the most of them love lewd women, cards, dice, or drink best.' Some dioceses were occupied by laymen. The Bishop of Killaloe was a boy at Oxford. The Bishop of Cork sold the livings of his diocese to horsemen and kerne, and when upbraided said in a sermon, preached before the Lord President, that unless he sold his livings he had no means of livelihood. But then the fount and origin of the Reformation was not itself particularly redolent of idealism; on which it is better to quote the accepted Protestant historian again: 'Scandalous dilapidations,' says Froude, 'destruction of woods, waste of the property of the sees by beneficial leases, each incumbent enriching himself and his family at the expense of his successors—this is the substantial history of the Anglican hierarchy, with a few honourable exceptions, for the first twenty years of its existence.' The same seems to be true of Ireland at the later date. Whether it was that there were far fewer wealthy religious establishments in Ireland or that the loot went astray, the Crown had made very little profit out of confiscations, so that although a large number of the churches and monasteries had been confiscated or fallen into decay and their occupants turned loose on the country, very little was done to replace them. O'Neill would have seen only a slightly prettier picture if he turned to the Catholic Church. To quote a modern Catholic historian, the report of Edmund Tanner, later Bishop of Cork, spoke of a 'demoralization so great that a pious Catholic scarcely existed anywhere. The priests were regarded as being very depraved. So insufficient was religious instruction, that few knew the Lord's Prayer, the Creed, or the Ten Commandments, and fewer still understood them. Sermons were rarely delivered. Sacraments were scarcely ever administered, and an ignorant people did not know whether they were the work of God or the invention of men.[6]

But, perhaps, the real test of the efficacy of any Church is the general level of morality. The Counter-Reformation had plenty of work to do here. Take some examples. Sean O'Neill had had small respect for the clergy, but for morality, as far as we can see, none at all. The Gaelic cheftains themselves had not been above seizing church lands. Illegitimacy was common in every family, and seems to have shocked nobody: it did not, for instance, bar either Hugh O'Neill's claim to succession or his father's. There does not seem to be any doubt that many of the chieftains had mistresses as well as wives. O'Neill's third wife, Mabel Bagenal, left him when she discovered that 'he affected two other gentlewomen' besides herself. The second Earl of Clanricard, a Burke, who died in 1582, had five wives, and three of these marriages had been contracted during the life of his first wife, a stormy woman of the O'Briens'. It seems somewhat excessive that Turlough of the Wine O'Donnell should have had ten wives, even if he had them all lawfully. John, Lord Leitrim, had a son by his own sister, Lady Mary Burke, who later married and bore a son to an O'Rourke. Without necessarily believing the general run of English travellers like Rych, Moryson, Trollope, Tremayne, their consistently unfavourable comments about the common run of life cannot, when all is said and done, have been conjured up out of the air.

But morality was not high anywhere at the time. Few people, for example, anywhere in Europe believed in a natural sudden death in the sixteenth century. O'Neill would have known that poison was considered a legitimate weapon by the most chivalrous statesmen. At a banquet in London at Holborn the father of the 10th Earl of Ormonde was poisoned together with his steward and sixteen servants. His uncle Sean O'Neill barely escaped death by a potion. The chief apothecary at Dublin Castle, Mr. Thomas Smythe, was known to the public as Bottle Smythe and recognized popularly as the poisoner-in-chief of the government. His successor in office Thady O'Nolan is best remembered for his failure to poison Fiach MacHugh O'Byrne. Tradition maintains that Red Hugh O'Donnell died by the potion of an agent, one James Blake, sent after him to Spain for that purpose. O'Neill's own son Bernard was strangled in Brussels by an undiscovered assassin. Several attempts, as we shall see, were made on his own life, all specifically encouraged by the Queen's most trusted counsellors. We have seen the murder of his father and of his brother by Sean. There are two instances in his own life that have a sinister air, the cutting off of his rival Hugh Gaveloch O'Neill, and the murder of Phelim McTurlough O'Neill. One could multiply those examples endlessly.

Honour was as besmirched. The entire course of Elizabeth's political relations is an endless tacking against the squalls of her own indecisions, deceptions, and ambiguities bursting about her from every point of the compass. There is hardly a straight run in all her treatment of the Protestants abroad. She broke the heart of the Prince of Orange by behaviour which her own minister Walsyngham described as 'dishonourable and dangerous.' Her relations with Catholic Spain have, in popular opinion, crystallized as a magnificent war of religion and empire crowned by the destruction of the Armada: whereas she played for years so tortuous and indecisive a game with Philip that at one time, when Mendoza seriously suggested that she should revert to Catholicism, she could reply, however disingenuously, that while present change was impossible she would consider it at a more favourable moment. Spanish policy was no less disingenuous, as O'Neill was to discover to his cost. Spain, for instance in 1574, for the sake of better commercial relations with England, ejected hundreds of Catholic refugees such as Nicholas Sanders, the great friend of Fitzmaurice, and when, aghast, they appealed to the Pope to check Philip he gave them no assistance. Indeed, O'Neill's general experience of Philip was that as compared with the interests of his own dominions religion always definitely took second place, and the same is true of the English Queen. Indeed it is probably fair to say that it is the experience of history that Catholicism could be for the one a profoundly felt emotion, a knitted part of common life, a magnificent stimulus to the culture of the nation; and Protestantism a sincerely-felt moral idealism, giving fibre and strength to the national character, and emerging in the sincerity and intelligence of a Milton or a Donne, or even a recusant Bunyan—but, for all that, neither people would ever permit, and never did permit religion to interfere with business. What, after all, were a few score zealots to Philip as against a sound commercial treaty that covered the ships seized by English privateers and even the treasure stolen by Drake in the Indies and on the Spanish Main?

Beside all this the confusion of Ireland, seen at its most chaotic at all periods of unrest like this of the Desmond wars, is not abnormal; except in so far as here alone there was no central recognized government to assuage its worst effects, no central line of thought to evoke any intelligible public morality or promise any workable social order. Considering the history of the country there was only one quarter from which guidance could come, and it is the superlative interest of the part Fitzmaurice played—and can O'Neill have failed wholly to catch something at least of the spirit of Fitzmaurice's ideals?—that he typifies this new influence. For Fitzmaurice tied the wagon of national resistance to the star of religion, and so strengthened both. Despite the general laxity he saw what the poet Spenser saw: 'The great wonder to see the odds which are between the zeal of Popish priests and the Ministers of the Gospel. For they spare not to come out of Spain, from Rome and from Rheims, by long toil and dangerous travelling hither, where they know peril of death awaiteth them and no reward or riches are to be found, only to draw the people into the Church of Rome; whereas some of our idle ministers, having a way for credit and estimation thereby opened unto them, and having the livings of the country offered unto them without pains and without peril, will neither for the same, nor any love of God, nor zeal of religion, nor for all the good they may do by winning souls to God, be drawn forth from their warm nests to look out into God's harvest which is even ready for the sickle, and all the fields yellow long ago.' That contrast became more and more true as time went on and the Counter-Reformation made itself felt. Even the seizure of church property and the dispersal of priests and friars assisted Fitzmaurice, for these homeless men wandered all over the country and for the first time in the long history of Irish national idealism began to spread the well-nigh invulnerable gospel of Faith and Fatherland. These, in *his* wanderings, O'Neill would have heard—at least, heard about: though, for the moment, he did not heed.

He did not guess that the old primitive, antique, patriarchal, shambling life of churchman and layman alike, so undirected, so easily ravelled, so mesmerized by the lure of an ancient memory of days before the Tudors when all men could live 'as they lived in the golden world'—a world, as we know, far from being as pretty as the lustful phrase—was, in its roughness and rudeness, about to be touched by an almost vernal breath of a great imaginative idea: an idea that was, at the beginning, part chivalrous, part pious, symbolized by an idealisation of the power of Spain and the dignity of Rome. It is one of the refreshing things about this otherwise tragic story of Fitzmaurice and the Desmond wars that he was the first man to bring in this note of a finer spiritual invigoration, like a man born before his time, to anoint what would otherwise have been a mere jacquerie. So that as we watch and compare the simultaneous fortunes of Fitzmaurice in the south and the fortune-hunting of O'Neill, north and south, we know that we are watching an Ireland fumbling out of the complete darkness of an uncouth and selfish preoccupation into a half light of understanding—call it a glimmer, if one wills—as to the great issues of which it was her fate to be the final battleground. There the comparison with Turlough

O'Neill is informative. Hugh finally saw the merits of this Idea. Turlough *never* guessed what rivalry of world-forces had come to his remote corner of Europe to play about him and his hordes of frieze-cloaked kernes and long-haired Scottish janissaries from the isles. To the end he was a figure out of the *Tain*, a rude Homeric Scythian, never to be hellenized, a baby Cyclops, fooled and blinded by a childish trust in his rough strength; 'a timorous and savage man' as some contemporary truly described him.

Not that it was necessary, even if it was possible, for men to be quite clear-sighted. Fitzmaurice was usually so. O'Neill ultimately became completely so. Desmond himself—to look forward a little—is the most amazing example of a man who was a tool rather than a manager of these forces. He had been a boy-husband and therefore never at court in his youth; he was a hunchback, palsied, tentative, tortuous, shifty to the last degree, and though he did vaguely feel the stirrings of knowledge, he was informed mainly by fear, and when at the end he rode at the head of his people—they had to lift him into his saddle—to fight in the name of Christ, under the ensign of the Pope, he is a figure driven to his course by stronger men rather by the impulse of an overmastering idea. Whereas Fitzmaurice, now, and Hugh O'Neill later, both travelled men, both thoughtful men, the one an inspired idealist, the other an astute man of the world, were the first and second thoughts of a people otherwise thoughtless as children.

That Ireland, then, of the 1570's which O'Neill saw at close quarters was indeed chaotic, and the chaos became worse all through the Desmond wars until at the end all Munster was a desert, strewn with bones in the tangled grass and those briars which all contemporaries unite in describing—a wilderness that choked every growth, symbolic of the apparent choking of all thought, wisdom, order, hope for the future. But it was not wholly anarchy, since it contained at least a budding idea whose memory was to live. It is a strange picture, that of O'Neill set against Fitzmaurice, cantering in the trail of these ruthless Tudor adventurers, while all the time this informative Idea is growing about him if he could but feel it. Here were the friars coming out of their anonymity, the priests in their tens and twenties marching through the country to proclaim a crusade, great conventions of friars in Donegal and Galway, and the hope of

Spanish and Papal aid growing year by year. But his mind is, for the moment, elsewhere. It is on his own power. The young dynast shuts his ears to everything but that.

4

After the lull, the slaughter started up again when a new figure appeared in the spring of 1571 from England, as Lord President of Munster—Sir John Perrot, the reputed bastard son of Henry VIII. He was soon trotting the mountains after Fitzmaurice, never able to catch him. Instead of fighting the kernes and gallowglasses he fought the enmity of the shaking bogs and splashing pathways where his men could only march two abreast, and the invisible assaults from the dark forests where ambush lurked. Perrot was a severe man but a man of genuine nobility, whose qualities the Irish—although he scourged them unmercifully—fully recognized. On that there is the remark of the Four Masters when he left Munster—it may be also a sign of their contempt for the helot class—'his departure was lamented by the poor, the widows, the feeble, and the unwarlike.' He cared far less than the majority of his colleagues about money but he cared much for pride. He was overbearing and ruthless. The Anglo-Irish disliked him and conspired against him, and he was to end, long after Fitzmaurice's revolt had been crushed, the victim of their official intrigues, escaping the scaffold only by the mercy of a natural death in prison.

Like Sidney he now burned, hanged, and slew where and when he could. When he could not catch the midges 'who stung his nakedness' he became so crazy with offended pride that he offered to fight out the revolt with Fitzmaurice in an old-time feudal combat of twelve knights; and the meeting was actually arranged. It was a characteristically gallant Renaissance gesture, and when Fitzmaurice, fearing treachery, did not turn up for the joust, it ended in an equally characteristic orgy of further hanging and burning. Instead, Fitzmaurice went up to the North, ravaged down the Shannon, threatened Dublin, and so terrified the Lord Deputy that he sent expresses to Elizabeth, as usual for more men and money, only to be told by her that she could not be troubled by his Irish trifles and that he must 'take his chance.' Perrot raced to meet Fitzmaurice in Limerick, cut up his Scots, flung half of them into Lough Derg, was held up by a mutiny among his unpaid men, again surprised and pummelled Fitzmaurice, and having exhausted his cash and done his worst—made peace. It was another of those compromises that reflected credit on neither side since they both were entirely disingenuous about it.

Meanwhile, where was the man chiefly concerned about this devastation of his unfortunate country, Desmond himself? He was still being held in London, either 'pent up in a little room,' at Sir Warham St. Leger's or wandering down-at-heel about the London streets in his misery, lifting his hunchback shoulders to complain that all the Queen allowed him was twenty-six shillings a week, that his lodgings cost twenty, that he could not afford meat, and his clothes were in rags. What a wretched existence the creature must have had, his wife now big with child, every news from Ireland worse than the next, his health never good, his mind melancholic by nature. One may surmise it from the picture one forms of his meeting with Frobisher—Where? In some Holborn tavern?—whispering over his shoulder about the chances of a ship off the Welsh coast that would land him in Munster: and then the sickly smile and the feeble evasions when he is duly informed that Master Frobisher has been betraying him all the time, and that the authorities are fully informed of his plans for escape.

Better luck attends O'Neill, still pulling strings for his Earldom. By June, 1572, he has so flattered his neighbour in the Newry, Sir Nicholas Bagenal, the Marshal of the Queen's army, that we read of his willingness 'to support the young Baron.' On the other hand cousin Turlough is again taking an arrogant tone, actually to the point of upbraiding the Queen's Deputy for daring to call him Turlough Luineach instead of The O'Neill. But, somehow or other, the semi-comic note is never long absent from the story of Turlough, and once again domestic matters come to the aid of the government when his wife falls out with him and vanishes to Scotland with the greater part of his Scots, and her's. So that it must have been a disappointment to the Baron when these fruitful Desmond wars seemed again about to peter out at the opening of 1573.

In that year the Earl of Desmond was at last sent home with his wife to his castle at Askeaton on the Shannon, a remote place, the Shannon like a great lake, from whose meadows the Great Forest (Kylemore) stretched south and west for miles and miles to meet the Galtees and the Ballyhouras, and whose quiet battlements—for this was a real Norman keep—were quietly reflected in the creek of the Deel beneath. There, in rejection of the conditions forcibly imposed on him in London and Dublin, he heard the bells of the monks begin again to toll over a countryside for the moment as peaceful as it looked. For, apart from the darkness of the forest, it was no place for fighting; and far less so to-day when the forest is gone and the nearest stone wall makes a blue horizon and the slightest eminence catches the attention—a hillock man-high, the ruins of some old Desmond peel, or a spire as eventful as a poplar in Flanders. It was a happy release from the mud of London, a welcome contrast of harper and poet and brehon and kerne to the frigid suspicion of that household at Southwark: a contented place if only cousin Fitzmaurice were safely out of the way.

5

But if this new quiet was unwelcome to O'Neill other excitements replaced it. In this year there comes the first breath of suspicion about the loyalty of 'the young Baron.' It comes from that Queen's Marshal already mentioned, Sir Nicholas Bagenal. These Bagenals were the type of men who really won and for centuries held Ireland for the Crown. They were the typical colonist, half-soldier, half-merchant, for whom the political horizon is always bounded narrowly by Government House on the one side, and an implacable distrust of the native on the other; the sort of men who turn into a profession what began as an adventure. (Sir Nicholas had come out of Staffordshire in 1542, of humble origin, his name smirched by his part in a case of manslaughter.) Such men were very different in class and outlook and technique to a Walter Raleigh who might win half a county by sword-work; or to a Richard Boyle, armed with a signet ring, a public-school polish, an overdraft, and a lordly insolence, who would win an Earldom by the sheer cuteness of the carpet-bagger—and make a good job of it after. The Bagenals would be content with a fair estate and be prepared to take plenty of kicks. They were the sort that never make a great deal of money, but make enough and keep it. They were the first of those 'Deputies of deputies of deputies' of whom Lecky speaks when recording the climax of landlordism in the eighteenth century—by then they would have had deputies of their own—and to whom the Gaelic poets always refer as 'upstarts.'

Bagenal's suspicion of O'Neill probably originated in fear. Turlough Luineach, apparently sick of playing the courtier's game had suddenly turned directly on the Baron, raided his country, arrested his brother, and swept off triumphantly with thirty-thousand head of cattle, just as any one of his ancestors might have done in the days of Cuchulainn and the *Táin.* It probably infuriated him when the Queen's Marshal stepped into the picture to point out that this was the sixteenth century. Turlough replied, in the language of the third century before Christ, that the interloping Baron was no O'Neill and must yield absolutely all his lands in Ulster. At that Bagenal counted Turlough's forces, which were large, and reported to Dublin Castle that there was going to be trouble with 'the natives.' Three months later Turlough is still in the field, and it is then that the Marshal drops this first word of suspicion, remarking that he believes that the baron is 'about to join Turlough.'

It is unlikely. The thing was probably part of the general movement in the south which realized that the only possible northern leader was Turlough. At any rate the English spies reported that Ulster had been marked out for him by the Pope as Munster had been for Desmond. As this was a new angle for the ambitious O'Neill it is just possible that in his surprise at finding that there could be any alternative to English force, or that this religious question could have any part in practical politics, he may have begun conversations with his cousin. The real interest of the incident is the suspicious mind of the Marshal. Time and again O'Neill came up against that suspicion and was infuriated by it. What an O'Neill thought of a Bagenal it would take a Gaelic satirist to say!

If he really was toying with career-suicide a further opportune insanity from the English side saved him. The southern adventure had failed. But the elder Essex, Walter Devereux, Lord Hereford, hearing that the Ulster region then called Clandeboy, now in Antrim, had been deserted by the Scots, repeated to Elizabeth all the offers made by the southern adventurers—to build castles and forts, to establish towns, and incorporate them by charter, to spoil, besiege, raze, or destroy the castles of the Irish outlaws, and so on, down to the destruction of all traitors, pirates, and felons and the chaining in galleys of treasonable Scots and Irishry. The government blessed him as he set out with the usual bevy of bonneted young lords—Hunsdon,

Champernowne, Wilsford, Bourchier, Carew smarting from his southern failure. The Irish, forewarned by Catholic English friends, burned every conceivable castle or fort that they possessed, as they always did on such occasions, and vanished into the woods.

Essex landed with his company of gallants at Carrickfergus, in the pleasant August of 1573. Before he sailed he had heard all the usual tales: no Drake or Hawkins heard worse. The day he landed the coast was quiet: the fields smiled at him; the people proved mild and courteous; he looked about him at the peaceful scene, and with a laugh he sent back a courtier to deride the wild tales of earlier travellers. Sir Phelim O'Neill, as Elizabeth had dubbed him, came in hurriedly to do the usual obeisance, and better still brought a gift of ten thousand cows. Essex's spirits rose proportionately. The following morning the ten thousand cows had vanished, and with them all Essex's beeves—Sir Brian having seen and taken all he wished to take. Within two months, when the rains were falling ceaselessly on the shivering men, now so thin in numbers that not a sixth remained serviceable; when disaster had swooped time and again out of the black woods and the quaking bogs, Essex was adding to the legend he had derided; a little more of it and he was begging the Queen to be released, cursing (like the younger Essex after him) this rotten, moist climate, the beastly Irish, his own base, godless, cowardly slaves who had not the resolution to endure travail, and who 'through long peace in the fat, delicate soil of England,' as his friend Wilsford complains, 'have lost the minds of soldiers, while the Irish have learned the use of weapons.'

It is unnecessary to follow the fortunes of this piece of buccaneering closely. Its main interest is that Hugh O'Neill assisted in it, against his own father-in-law, and again won the favour of an influential Englishman as the price of his treacherous support. To see to what dastardly things he lent his name, we may glance at the two main achievements of Essex in the course of his adventure. The first was the revenge that Essex took on Brian O'Neill. He invited him, and two hundred of his men, to a meal; after the meal the Irish retired for the night, and in the dark Essex's men burst on them and in their confusion slaughtered them with the sword, men and women alike. For this, in a letter of the following April 11th, Elizabeth told him that he was a 'great ornament of her nobility,' and she 'wished that she had as many like him to spend their lives and fortunes in the service of their country.' She further encouraged him to break every Northern chief in the same way. Essex was preparing eagerly for further ruthlessness, when—less than six weeks later, and before he could do anything, in a letter of May 22nd, he found himself ordered by the Queen to make peace with the Ulster leaders on the least dishonourable terms that he could obtain. He did so.

The second achievement of Essex annotates the lack of meaning in even this parlance of irresolution. In the calm summer of that year he heard that the Scots—the kin of Sorley Bwee—had sent their women, children, aged, and wounded for safety to the island of Rathlin. The seas being unusually calm, and a wind offering, Essex sent a troop of his men to the island, and they killed there every living soul, making again no distinction between men, women, and babies. The massacre went on, Essex reported calmly, while Sorley Bwee himself 'stood upon the mainland of the Glens,' and as he watched the little black figures of the murderers and the doomed race madly to and fro, he was, writes Essex to Elizabeth, 'likely to have run mad for sorrow, tearing and tormenting himself, and saying that there he lost all that ever he had.' On the quiet air, with only small waves on the shore, the wretched Sorley must have been able to hear the faint, shrill screams as the caves were poked out for the hiding women—those whom Essex speaks of as 'his pretty little ones and their dam.' For this Essex was again complimented by Elizabeth. Yet, it was a pointless piece of devilry. It had no object: it produced no result; and a further 'peace' was made almost immediately. Essex arranged his affairs, went to England, and came back in the hope of recouping his damaged fortunes. It is an irrelevant coda to the adventure that he died within five weeks, in Dublin; people thought by poison. It is also irrelevant that his wife was suspected, because she presently married her lover, Leicester (as all readers of *Kenilworth* will remember). Or it is irrelevant unless as a general commentary on the times, and because one may, at this point, remark that no historian has ever found any assuagement of Essex's behaviour in that general savagery. In any case nothing can detract from its futility.

Hugh O'Neill had no scruples about allying himself with this man, because, as far as he was concerned, the position was that there, to the west, was Turlough, fat with his thirty thousand cattle, and here in the east was a useful link with the Court. The wisdom of his choice is evident in Essex's report back to the Privy Council two months after his arrival that the Baron is the only man in Ulster to be trusted; followed, the next month, by the recommendation that the Baron should be made Earl of Tyrone. If, then, O'Neill would work with Essex it must be plain that, at this period, he would work with anybody who could advance him, and any suggestion that he brought back from England high patriotic designs cherished in the dark secrecy of a rebel heart, seems quite without foundation. During those years of '73 and '74 when English power was completely wrecked in Ireland: the new system helpless; when the Feudal south and the Gaelic north, and the half-Gaelic, half-Feudal west were ruling as they had always ruled; when England was in the greatest difficulties abroad—this young man was concerned only with feathering his own nest.

6

Political ambition thrives, clearly, on unrest. In a further breathing space of peace O'Neill's intrigues collapsed. He saw Sir Henry Sidney, the new English Deputy, come back again, and travel the country in state, unmolested, from end to end. He saw him come to Ulster and meet Turlough almost as a friend. Everywhere he saw men being told that they might henceforth rule in the ancient way, provided—the old subtle method of infilitration—that they promised formal 'obedience.' Turlough readily enough promised not only obedience but that if he were granted an Earldom he would adopt the English system—all the more readily so since he was simultaneously writing to Philip II of Spain for armed assistance against the English heretic. O'Neill further noted that James Fitzmaurice had left the country, though he must have known well what James Fitzmaurice was doing abroad—plotting also for a Spanish invasion, and guessed thereby that this outward-seeming peace and amity was the merest illusion. It was. The promise that men could rule and live 'in the ancient way' was soon broken by the newly-appointed Lords Presidents who began to administer English law, press the new religion, and levy rents as their need arose. The Burkes of Connaught were the first to find this out and when they protested were promptly cut to pieces. The Lord President of Munster, likewise, began to hang people by the hundred, including many whom the populace considered not only innocent but admirable, such as a friar whose only crime was that he was a friar, and a *brehon* (or lawgiver) who 'was much esteemed among the common people and taught laws repugnant to Her Majesty.' The Gaelic captains might not be interested vastly in international politics, beyond the new mythology of the King of Spain and the Pope of Rome and the harlot of England, but they understood the meaning of the gallows and that they were being threatened again with a hateful foreign system of life and law. The old growling began to be heard once more. It was only a matter of time before the storm would break as fiercely as ever.

England's foreign commercial treaties bore fruit for a time. For four years (1575–1579) James Fitzmaurice found himself hanging about the harbours of northern Spain, thwarted at every hand's turn by these treaties; and he might have waited for as long again if the deception and illusion was not broken by the sudden news that Drake was 'out' on the Pacific plundering the Spanish colonies, burning churches, and stealing Spanish bullion. On the winds of that revelation Fitzmaurice was able at last to sail with two ships from the port of Ferrol near Corunna. He left Spain in June (1579). With him were his wife, a bishop, some friars, and the Papal Legate Dr. Nicholas Sanders, an English Catholic zealot who was to be a pivotal figure in what followed.

For this invasion they had brought a mere handful of men. But they had more than the power of men, they had the zeal of the idealist; the cry *Pápa Abú* (the Pope to victory); a banner blessed by the Pope's own hands bearing the arms of Fitzmaurice, the red dragon and the Christ crucified and the great scroll 'IN OMNI TRIBULATIONE ET ANGUSTIA SPES NOSTRA JESU ET MARIA' —its length to be often after unfolded and spread on stakes in the Great Forest of Munster and as often folded up and hustled away through the woods, to be (as the Lord President, Malby, said sardonically) 'anew scratched about the face' by the thorns and lashing branches. With his arrival the peaceful interval of Desmond's life in 'Ashkeyton' ended. He was down in Kerry visiting his relatives, when in the afternoon of July 17th, 1579, the news came that his troublesome cousin had landed not forty miles away, in Dingle. He heard of the two ships from Spain, how the friars had first stepped ashore, followed by a mitred bishop, followed by an English priest with a great banner, followed lastly by Fitzmaurice, and a group of fighting men mostly Spanish, and English prisoners in chains.

Desmond, equally hesitant and conspiratorial, at once wrote to Her Majesty that he was at her service to expel the traitor, and did nothing beyond attempting to persuade his brothers to follow his example. He was a sick man, weary of all badgering and he was so far from being a religious zealot that he is put down even by antagonistic Protestant chroniclers as no Catholic. ('If he had been Romish Catholick the hearts and knees of all degrees in the Province would have bowed to him,' says Sir Thomas Stafford.) So that one can readily understand his exasperation with his cousin's new Holy War as set out in the long letter brought to him by messengers from Fitzmaurice who had now moved across the peninsula to Smerwick Harbour :—'After due and hearty commendation in most humble manner premised. For so much as James Fitzmaurice, being authorized thereto by his Holiness, warfareth under Christ's ensign for restoring of the Catholic faith in Ireland, God forbid the day should ever come wherein it might be said that the Earl of Desmond has forsaken his kinsman, the lieutenant of his spiritual father, the banner of his merciful Saviour, the defence of his ancient faith, the delivery of his dear country, the safeguard of his noble house and posterity. . . .' And after some awesome warnings based on the life of Henry VIII and Queen Mary, the main point: 'I cannot tell what worldly thing would grieve me more than to hear not only that your honour would not assist Christ's banner, but also that any other nobleman should prevent you in this glorious attempt. All that I write is spoken also to me good lady, your bedfellow, and to me good uncle, your brother, to all whom I commend myself, and also me bedfellow most heartily doth the like; trusting in Almighty God that as his Holiness has made me captain-general of this holy war, so your honour being head of my house will be the chief protector and patron of this no less your than me quarrel.' With this came a Proclamation in Latin and private letters in Irish whose promises and threats were lost on no one. While Desmond cogitated over this and dissembled as best he knew how, his younger brothers rose, and the friars set out on their crusade. Once more the rumour ran to the North. Turlough conferred with the friars, the O'Rourkes of Sligo, the O'Donnells of Tyrconnel, and his Scots, and again in the following summer with Lord Baltinglass who rose in Wicklow; that year he sent for more mercenaries to Scotland, using the galleys of the western O'Malleys to transport them to Ulster across the narrow seas from the island by the thousand. All this time Hugh O'Neill watched and waited.

Desmond already compromised by his inaction, unmanned by his knowledge of how much the Queen disliked him, and fearful lest the success of the fighting men, now led by his own family, might unseat him among his Gaelic, Catholic, Traditionalist people, was at his wit's end. He schemed and shuffled and dodged for as long as he could. He threw Bishop O'Healy and the son of O'Rourke, who had come from Spain with Fitzmaurice, as a sop to the government. (His wife, the countess, received the two guileless travellers graciously at Askeaton, on their way to Limerick, but sent before them her informer's message to the English.) He gave in his son Garret as pledge. He feinted with handfuls of followers on the skirts of the forest. He sent the English news of the doings of his brother. But it was all of no assistance to him: it did not even help when, one bare month after the landing at Dingle, the root and sap of the whole fight was cut off. For James Fitzmaurice was killed in a skirmish in the Forest by Theobald Burke—the inevitable internecine strife of the inchoate Ireland of the sixteenth century. Early as Fitzmaurice died he had done his work. The wheel had been set revolving too fast to be stopped. Besides, the English kept demanding action from Desmond—the only kind of loyalty that ever counted with them—and action was beyond his power; his people would not have obeyed him against the flame of spirit lit in them by Sanders and the friars. Still he held out. He even appealed to his old enemy Ormonde, who promptly passed on his letters to the English as 'from the lewd Earl and his traterous brethern.'

At that, he turned to Sanders—and thereby he was either saved or lost.

7

For Nicholas Sanders, was, as the Nuncio had written to the Cardinal of Como, a man of such 'prudence, judgement and religion' as to be more hopeful than an entire army. He was a cold, humourless, unbending zealot, a professor of theology at Louvain, a propagandist—his bitterly polemical *De Origine ac Progressu Schismatis Anglicani* was one of the most far-reaching anti-protestant tracts of all time; some say that it has influenced millions who never heard it—a man who was known and respected by all the greatest princes of the Church in Europe, a priest who had lived and travelled in France, Italy, Poland, Lithuania, Spain, everywhere stirring up the same fires of religious revival. So that now, at last, the sad dripping woods of Limerick, the wild kernes, the endless skirmishes, the despairs, the hardships of fever, of hunger, of the march were but a climax of a life devoted to the single idea of the overthrow of the new heresy and the establishment of a greater and finer spiritual Christian Empire on its ruins. The tone and temper of this man's life could have been the peace of cloister and library, their seclusion and security. But 'it was from just this life that Sanders turned; the too-great calm and order for one who was by nature a strong fighter, the slow rising from siesta, the heavy atmosphere beneath Janiculum, the burden of the hot, unmoving air. He was not made for this existence, guarded by the drowsy majorduomos, gazing somnolent upon their hot flagstones while he worked and wrote with His Eminence (the Cardinal Hosius Bishop of Ermeland), silent, untiring, as the Piazza di Santa Maria below him lay under the changing Trastevere sunshine. He had chosen the hardships of his Irish journey freely, and, considering the effect which the Fitzmaurice venture and the Desmond Rising had produced in bringing before the Irish the vivid remembrance of their Catholic Faith, he could rest contented.'[7]

Between the influence of this man's dominating personality and singleness of purpose, and the dread of a certain further imprisonment and possible death at the block if he came within the grip of the English, as well as because the whole momentum of circumstances was now gone beyond his frail control, Desmond found himself edged into revolt. The standard of a religious crusade in which he hardly believed was placed in his palsied hands. He was lifted to his horse. The kernes shouted the war cry before him, *Pápa Abú*, and all Catholic Munster rose behind him. By January 1580, though now to the English 'this mad-brained Earl, the only arch-traitor in all Ireland,' he had become the focal point of the entire secret Catholic league in Europe—the foreign refugees, the Highland Catholics, the English recusants, the authority of Rome, the court of Spain, the whole network of Jesuits and Franciscans continually stealing to and from the Continent as the Evangelists of the Counter-Reformation. His role was tremendous. If he had only been equal to the occasion he might have hammered himself into a great symbol. Poor, racked, doubting man, he was the most improbable, leaking vessel that ever held a precious idea; the most modest clay that Fate could possibly have chosen to be, for his moment, the chalice of Christ's blood on earth.

When he took the field in October (1579) the English lost their heads. Elizabeth would not spend a penny. Nothing was ready. Burghley told the Queen, 'You must conciliate Ireland; allow the chiefs to continue their ancient greatness, take away the fear of conquest lately grafted in the wild Irish, and wink at disorders which do not offend the Crown.' But Desmond was not effective enough. He sacked Youghal, threatened Cork, and then returned to the woods. Two more Italian ships turned up in Kerry. They had no effect. Then by March (1580), after endless angry haggling and squabbling, Elizabeth at last agreed to spend some more money on Ireland, and a greater force than the country had seen for a century sailed for Dublin, and the horror began—a slaughter which remains in the Irish memory with a sense of dread and rage exceeded only by that associated with the name of Cromwell. In the following campaign, if it can be called a campaign, a holocaust rather, Ormonde alone said that he put to the sword forty-six leaders, 800 notorious traitors, and about 4,000 common people caught in cabin and field.

The three captains, Sir William Winter, Sir William Pelham, and the Earl of Ormonde divided the army between them. Winter sailed about the coast of Kerry to Valentia. The others converged from Dublin and Kilkenny. There were no battles, they met with no opposition, as they harried their way to the farthest toe of the south-west. The *Annals of the Four Masters* record the purpose of the march by saying that they killed the old and the blind, women and children, the sick and the idiots—they spared none. 'We consumed with fire,' reported Pelham, 'all inhabitations and executed the people wherever we found them.' They began at the fortress of Carrigafoyle, where the Italian and Spanish who came with Fitzmaurice had secured themselves in an apparently impregnable position on a rock ninety feet high, cut off by water from the mainland. An Italian engineer, Captain Julian, had perfected its defences, filling every cranny of the rock with masonry so that it was smooth as a thimble. But the new weapon, the cannon, was brought up, and, say the Annalists with the hyperbole of awe, 'there was not a solitude or wilderness, a declivity or woody vale, from the Carn of Breas (the son of

Ealathan, the son of Nead), in the south-west of the Province of Desmond to Knockmaa in Connaught in which the sound and roar of these unknown and wonderful cannon were not heard.' The fort fell. Every man was butchered.

They nearly caught Desmond, Sanders, and the countess at Castleisland, but the three were warned and fled on ponies. They moved on to Castlemaine, at the head of Dingle Bay, and there divided. Pelham went down one shore of the vast bay to Dingle, and Ormonde went down the other shore to Valencia, burning and killing as they went so that at night each was able to check the course of the other by the flames of the cottages glowing across the bay. When Valentia bursts in clouds of smoke over the Atlantic their journey was completed. MacCarthy More and the two O'Sullivans of Berehaven, the first of many to follow, decided that all was up, threw in their lot with the English and were, for policy's sake, 'pardoned.'

The conquistadors now retraced their journey, lost in wonder at the beauty of Killarney—'a fairer land the sun did never shine upon, pity to see it lying waste in the hands of traitors'—and ravaged through the Earl's lands of Limerick. They did not leave a roof standing behind them. As more and more men came in to surrender Pelham invented a new horror: 'I do not receive any but such as come in with bloody hands as executioners of some better person than themselves.' Sir James Desmond's young brother, was thus betrayed by Cormac MacTeigue of Cork. When Sir John, another brother, and Sanders again escaped capture by the skin of their teeth at Kilmallock, Sir John was so shaken by the experience that he decided to betray his comrade, the Papal Legate. He changed his mind only because the secondary Baltinglass rising suddenly broke out in Wicklow. (It was largely due to the incitements of Sanders; most of the leaders, Plunkets, Dillons, Aylmers, Brabazons, and Nugents had been at Louvain and were staunch Catholics.) So, the two outlaws, the would-be traitor and his English guest, continued to move about together.

The Baltinglass revolt produced the one thorough victory the rebels enjoyed: that was a massacre in the recesses of Glenmalure where Lord Grey de Wilton's forces were ambushed and destroyed almost to a man. At the same time further hope shone in the west when the long-promised help came from Spain—800 Italians and a few Spanish—and landed at Smerwick. It was a feeble if gallant light, and it shone too late. That October, Sanders, Desmond, Baltinglass and two officers of the Italian-Spanish force wrote back to Philip that nothing could now be accomplished without 8,000 men, and ammunition and food for six months. By the same express Desmond confessed to Spain that every single thing he possessed was gone; not a roof remained in Munster to shelter his head. The province was virtually a desert. One can imagine Philip's cold reaction.

There was nothing to hinder Grey from marching down to face the Spaniards at Smerwick—so low had the embers of rebellion fallen that he did so untouched, although he had with him but 800 men. Winter went around by sea, and the two men met in the wild weather of that early November. A Captain Bingham had earlier come around in the *Swiftsure* to cut off retreat by boats. The bombardment lasted two days. Had there been even a score of armed kernes roving the country it could hardly have been sustained. But the peninsula was void as its rocks. The largest battery held by the garrison was destroyed on the second day by a fortunate shot and the men, persisting no longer, offered a surrender. There is evidence to suggest that the garrison thought that they had a promise of their lives. At dawn the next morning they opened the gates, marched out with lowered flags, piled up their arms and stood waiting. There were one or two laymen and some women, a few of these pregnant, who like the garrison had placed their trust in stone and mortar rather than take to the wilds before the enemy arrived. Grey set aside the officers for ransom, and packed the remainder together in their space. He sent in his bands among them, then, and the crowded Spaniards and Italians and the others were stabbed and slit before one another's eyes and ears. The women, he hanged. Then he stripped the corpses, had them laid down in rows on the sands, and surveyed their six hundred pale and red-streaked bodies—'as gallant and goodly personages,' he remarked, 'as ever were beheld.'

Among those held over for judicial execution two days later were Sanders' English servant, William Walsh, Father Lawrence Moore, and one Oliver Plunkett: (not to be confused with Blessed Oliver Plunkett). According to Sanders these men first had their legs and arms broken in three places at a forge, and were then left in agony for the night before being hanged, drawn and quartered in the following day.

'By the Queen, your loving sovereign, Elizabeth R.,' Grey was informed that Christmastide in her own hand-writing, 'the mighty hand of the Almightiest power hath showed manifestly the force of his strength in the weakness of the feeblest sex and mind this year, to make men ashamed ever hereafter to disdain us. In which action I joy that you have been chosen the instrument of his glory, which I mean to give you no cause to forethink.'

It is one of those incidents in history which though politically slight and unimportant in themselves will never be forgotten. It had no direct effect on the wars beyond intensifying their savagery, and in fact their angry backwash went on for years during which the Irish roved the forests and lived like the wolves with which the English constantly compared them. There they were either caught and lopped off one by one, or lived as rag and bone to tell the tale to rag and bone. If caught it meant another few heads in a sack, like those of the Eustaces, to be sent by courier to adorn the spikes of Dublin Castle, or the victim might be pressed to death in an engine like Oliver Burke in Limerick. Norman-Irish and Gaelic captains, Roches, Barrys, O'Tooles, Burkes, O'Rourkes, Eustaces, Fitzgeralds, O'Sullivans, and the rest, made their desert fires in the waste places, and reaved for food, and fed their last courage on the anger and hatred which they bequeathed to the generations.

8

Elizabeth, feeling that enough was done, and hoping to save herself further expense, now promulgated a general pardon. In the depths of misery, and hunted like a dog Desmond rejected it. When one of Desmond's cousins accepted it, Desmond's rapparees swept down on his land and burned thirty-six villages and took 7,000 cattle. Misery had given the man courage—even dignity; at his lowest ebb he wrote his defiance to St. Leger from his forest fire-side in the tone of a prince. English ruthlessness threw him back into the life-mould of the Gaelic captain. He havocked the Butlers from the recesses of the Knockmealdowns and dragged Ormonde into the field once more, and the country sank lower and lower under the weight of misery to the condition of sheer famine in which the people ate wild cresses against starvation. 'The lowing of a cow,' say the Four Masters, 'or the voice of a ploughman was not to be heard from Dingle to the Rock of Cashel'—an area about half the size of Belgium.

To the English it was all the madness of mad dogs. Grey had begged for a policy of utter extermination, neither the first nor the last to cry that nothing could be done with such a people. All the natural anger of the Irish at seeing their lands robbed from them, their rage at being humiliated, their stubborn refusal to see in the New System all the blessings of heaven, their adherence to their own religion, their affection for their own traditions, their thirst for revenge—all these are over and over again spoken of by English officials, soldiers, and travellers, with the infuriating complacency of the colonist, as 'treason,' 'theft,' 'mischief,' 'barbarity,' 'beastliness.' One official report to Walsyngham at this time declared that 'if hell were open and all the evil spirits abroad, they could never be worse than these Irish rogues, rather dogs, and worse than dogs, for dogs do but after their kind, and they degenerate all humanity.' And, complacently, another described the beaten men coming into the towns for pardon: 'If they meet an Englishman or two walking the streets, they shake their heads, they rouse themselves in their lousy mantles, and advance on tiptoe, as who should say, "We are those who have done this mischief, what say ye to us?"' If those creatures were captains they would be carrying in their fists, as Ormonde describes it, sackfuls of their brothers' heads.

The net closed in on Desmond. His chaplain was caught and hanged. His most loyal friend, MacSwiney of Kerry, was killed by a fellow Irishman. His great inspiration Sanders died in the Great Wood of fever, hardship, possibly hunger. He was attended by his companion in misfortune, Bishop Cornelius O'Ryan who, at his request, anointed him. 'Unge me illustris Domine extrema unctione olei morientium, nam hac nocte sum e vita discessurus, a creatore meo vocatus.' He was buried there. The wood is gone. Somewhere, never to be known, his bones have mingled indecipherably, with the rich fields of Limerick.

At last, down on the Dingle peninsula, in the woods of Glenageenty, Desmond's hour came. It was the cold winter of '83. 'His people,' say the Four Masters, 'were so much in dread and awe of the law and the Sovereign of England that they began to separate from him, even his own married wife, children and friends, so that he had but four persons to accompany him from one cavern of a rock or hollow of a tree to another, throughout the two provinces of Munster, in the summer and autumn of that year.' Then, it is said, a Moriarty, whose sister had been reaved of cattle by the Earl's followers, sought him out with some others 'in a hut in the cavern of a rock' about five miles from Tralee, near Ballymacelligot. In the morning twilight they rushed into the cold hut. It was a Tuesday, and St. Martin's festival. He had one woman and two men servants. A Kelly or O'Kelly struck at him and almost cut off his arm. The old man revealed his identity crying out, 'I am the Earl of Desmond, spare my life.' Moriarty took him on his back, but he was bleeding to death, so in the woods they finished him, and cut off his head. When he was dead, although it was deep winter, 'the cuckoo called at night at Ard-mic-Grainne.'

He died a far different man to that miserable creature who lived as a beggar in London, and havered as a weakling in Askeaton. Something had taken hold of him, and in spite of his natural mortality, had glorified him. He did not hammer himself into a symbol; but some force beyond and, indeed, literally outside him, did hammer him into a legend. National tradition, reaching above individual human weakness, translated him into one 'whose equal was not in nobility, honour, and power.' It is fantastically untrue, and yet it is not in another sense untrue, and in its truth is the power and the poetry of Ireland, and in its untruth her indifference to all her children whom she sacrifices ruthlessly to her needs.

The wars cost Elizabeth half a million. Munster was, in effect, a waste. And we must remember how easily this could happen since there had been no regular harvest for several years, and *three* years after the suppression, George Beverely the Crown victualler, reported (1586) that Munster 'was still destitute both of corn, beef, and other victuals for men and horses by reason it remaineth still waste and unpeopled, and the little corn which they have planted by digging and other shifts in tillage is destroyed by the late unseasonable harvest weather.' After all, even in normal times less people lived in Ireland than in modern Afghanistan. There were roughly twenty people to the square mile, if neatly arranged, which meant in practice that a traveller would meet nobody at all for mile after mile of his journey, and then he would see a cabin about every mile or so, and then come to a cluster of huts about a fort or a castle or some church buildings, which might call itself a town, all petering out again into the cabin-per-mile, and then the desolate mountain or lonely bog. When the people ran from the soldiery they ran into the death-traps of these uncultivated regions, and now—because a poet, Spenser, has described it, the image has stuck in the human mind ever since—in the winter cold and rain 'out of every corner of the woods and glens they came creeping forth, upon their hands, because their legs would not bear them; they looked like anatomies of death, they spake like ghosts crying out of their graves; they did eat of the dead carrions; happy were they if they could find them, yea, and one another soon after, in so much as the very carcases they spared not to scrape out of their graves; and if they found a plot of watercresses or shamrocks, there they flocked as to a feast for the time, yet not being able to continue there withal; so that in short space there were none almost left, and a most populous and plentiful country suddenly made void of man and beast.' There can be nothing exaggerated in the picture—unless, perhaps, the eating of corpses, although men starving at sea have been said to do this. As late as July 1587 Sir Edward Fitton wrote back to Burghley that 'there is not a pile or castle in any place but what is full of the poorest creatures that ever I saw, so lean for want of food as wonderful, and yet so idle they do not work.' Still later, June 1588, *five* years after Desmond had been killed, Sir William Herbert reported that the one hundredth part of Munster was not inhabited. This was because nothing effective could be done, or would be done until the five million acres had been bestowed on the conquerors; a slow, haggling business of measuring and surveying that went on for years and years. In the reports of the time we see the surveyors going their tedious round in a bunch—Norreys, Wallop, Jesse Smythes, Charles Calthorpe, Wilbraham, Alford, and Golde. We find them, for instance, down in Cork in the October of '86, shaking and shivering on the uplands over Youghal in the 'rain and foul weather,' finding it extremely difficult to tramp over the land which 'as we hear Sir Walter Rawley is to have,' because the fields everywhere have gone into a wilderness with weeds, heath, brambles, and furze. These pictures were etched sharply into the minds of the people as late as the time of Cromwell; even as in our time, to the ritual of 'I remember my grandmother telling me' the minds of small children were etched with pictures of the Famine of the 1840's.

The savagery of the suppression and its aftermath of confiscation were defended on the ground that an example was necessary. The example was, indeed, never forgotten. It served for ten years to quieten the country, and then its memory became and remained for ever an incitement. However, that ten years included the year 1588, the year of the Spanish Armada, and if it were only for Ireland's weakness in that year alone perhaps Elizabeth may have been thankful for the efficient workmanship of her 'appeasers.'

9

We have given a good deal of space to the Desmond wars and it is time we extracted from it its relevance to Hugh O'Neill. First of all, in all those years O'Neill did not lift a finger to assist the southern captains. He lay doggo in the north, purchasing the confidence of the English either by actively assisting them to butcher the south, or by his cautious inaction. It may be argued that he had no real power to assist. Yet Turlough and he were nearer to the eastern garrisons than Desmond was, and there were many times when an assault on Dublin (apart from its military value, to put it at its lowest, as a distraction), would have had an enormous moral effect. It would have encouraged waverers like Kildare, hastened the rising of Baltinglass, divided the English forces by a third, which would have been an important third, since Ormonde would have had to remain behind to protect his own territory. The fact is that he did not assist, and it may be best to agree that the probable reasons were that he knew realistically that, even if he wanted to, he was not strong enough by himself to face those powers whose solidarity he had had every opportunity of measuring when he cantered beside Sydney in the opening years of the war. In any case he and Turlough could not or would not co-operate.

Nevertheless the fact remains that here, in the south, had been a long-drawn-out revolt animated for the first time in the history of the island by an idea capable of welding disparate units together. That this idea did not fire the north means that the religious enthusiasm of the Counter-Reformation had not reached the north, and that in these things of the spirit Ulster still had a long way to go on the road out of the medieval Irish world which Fitzmaurice had had the imagination to reject at a blow. Here let us remember acutely that Fitzmaurice was Norman-Gaelic, and all the followers of Baltinglass still nearer to pure Norman, while the O'Neills and O'Donnells were pure Gaels; and, always remembering the important qualifications inherent in the threat of land-confiscation in the south, which had not yet begun to knock at the door of the North, we may draw our conclusions accordingly. But let us also remember that the followers of Fitzmaurice and Desmond were largely Gaelic. In other words Fitzmaurice showed that the old Irish world was capable of grasping an idea, and acting on it; the inaction of the O'Neills and O'Donnells showed that, lacking the spur of selfish interest, they were unable as yet to break through the tribal concept. Those southern wars show the tremendous power of the new system of centralization under a bond of obedience symbolized by the Crown. There were many occasions in England, at the time, when the people resented deeply the behaviour of Elizabeth. but the long Wars of the Roses had taught England its lesson, and time and again men choked down their anger; and resisted their impulse to assist rebellious men with whose ideas they agreed. They had come to realize that, though authority is constantly fallible, without it there must be chaos.

The turmoil of Europe had begun to weld the disparate element of English life into a forced unity. Englishmen had been through it, so to speak, while the Irish had equally evaded the pains, and missed the profits of experience. Fitzmaurice and Desmond and Sanders had thus opposed to the idea of a Nation welded by patriotic fervour the idea of the People informed by something midway between religious idealism and an intellectual idea. It was their tragedy that their idea came too late. For between the decay of the antique world of local rulers—the vulgarly so-called Irish 'clans,' mostly at one another's throats, or loosely bound by a scarcely practical adherence to the Christian code, and the rise of this modern world of central governments, binding men by the religion of patriotism, there had intervened something on which the Roman vinculum broke into pieces—but which strengthened centralization. That event occurred when Columbus stepped ashore in what was prophetically called The New World. At that moment modern international commerce was born. That tremendous adventure of Columbus came full circle—the riches of the New World corrupted the Old—when Elizabeth of England, 'whose symbolic virginity' (It is Froude who said this) 'had begun to replace in the minds of man the symbolic immaculateness of the Virgin Mary, whose fantastic dresses embroidered with monsters' ears and eyes symbolized the greater infallibility,' induced Philip of Spain, the ally of the Pope, the stamper-out of heresy, the same man whose transcendental vision of Heaven and

Hell we may see in El Greco's painting in the Escorial, to agree to kick out both the English and the Irish Catholics for the sake of that commercial treaty whose effects so hampered Fitzmaurice and which recompensed Philip for the gold stolen from him in the Indies.

For the next three hundred years the Roman vinculum stretched and stretched itself, in the effort to hold this gilded dragon of the new commercial world, but the more it stretched to bind, like elastic, the more it contracted in power. The Roman *Respublica Christiana* dwindled finally to the bounds of a public garden. In the disjunction of Church and State, Rome finally retired completely from all practical part in wars and politics. Only in small countries like Ireland, remote from the creaking, crunching wrestling of the great powers, the old informative idea persisted. In the Confederate wars for Charles, in the Cromwellian massacre, the fight for James against William of Orange, the 1798 Rebellion, the Resurrection under O'Connell, even in the days of the Land League and Parnell, the priests were always involved and sometimes even led the people with sword in hand, as bishop Mac Gowran did, to fall fighting on the great maghery of Connaught in those early religio-nationalist wars of the sixteenth century. The inaction of the North is therefore the inaction of men who did not see the point. There O'Neill the 999th was too busy watching O'Neill the 998th to have any time for Gregory XIII or Philip II or the plans of Elizabeth.

The Desmond wars have taken up much of our time but if that contrast is clear the story will have been worth while. It is worth while also in that its course was a great exemplar for O'Neill, and when his time came, he suddenly realised the lesson of it and it became his great aim to break through tribalism and establish a confederacy. There is one other thing that makes this southern campaign of Desmond's of first importance in the story of O'Neill. We might go back a long way for the origin of the final upheaval. We cannot afford not to go back at least to Desmond. For the fuse that finally exploded Ulster was lit in the south, crackled through the savageries of a later Perrot in Connaught, Sir Richard Bingham, crept up through the Settlement of Monaghan, until on the Great Lakes of the Erne the sedge burned on the borders of Tyrone. Then O'Neill saw the ghost of Desmond rising to warn him that the New System was about to engulf him also. He looked backward and forward, and made his choice. He knew from Desmond's example that in the end, the final triumph of the New System meant for him not the role of a petty prince—a role that he might, perhaps, have been willing to accept if he could only be assured of it—but an inevitable contraction to at best the role of a deputy of a deputy of a deputy, always suspect, always in danger, always on sufferance, trusted only when he brought in heads in sacks. That would be a role unworthy of so proud and ancient a lineage as his. Yet when he drew his sword to fling it into his great gamble he must surely have done it slowly, with a sidelong, backward glance into that mirror held up to him by that blood-boultered Geraldine against whom he had fought in his prime.

10

It is with something of a start that we realize, and it may have startled O'Neill also to realize that while all this was going on in the south he had imperceptibly slipped from his twenties to his thirties. It is a sign of the firm patience with which he nursed his ambitions that in these hottest years of a man's life, when his blood might be expected to control his brain, he kept quietly to his course. It is also, perhaps, one of the most startling illustrations of the disunity of that Ireland that he could live his life up there in the north as steadily as if all this turmoil in the south were actually occurring in another island. It must have seemed to him only two or three years ago since he first arrived back in Ireland, seeking after his prospects. As he looked back it must also have seemed to him high time that he reaped the reward of his circumspection. He had spent these intervening years, apart from his share in the Desmond wars, and the assistance he gave to Essex in '73–'75 in three main ways: in circumventing the ambitions of Turlough, in forwarding his own case with the English, and in privately consolidating his own power. All three interests come together in a letter of his to the Lord Justice in the winter after Fitzmaurice landed, in which he says that he observes an 'evil intent' in Turlough and asks for a hundred footmen to preserve the Pale, but that if Turlough breaks out into war he will need three hundred foot and fifty horse at the Blackwater. 'If my proffer may not stand you in stead, I shall desire licence to repair into England, hoping to have some maintenance of Her Majesty, for now I live but a miserable life, having spent all that my poor followers have.' To that Pelham replied, the same November, with a brief acknowledgement and a vague promise. A little later, March 1580, Pelham is more specific, and well he might be, for O'Neill had chosen the tactical moment when Desmond himself was in the field in Munster: 'I do like very well the course you have taken. . . . Preserve all the quiet you can on the border. When I may with safety condescend to your request I will devise upon it with your friend and mine, Sir Edward Moore.'

That Sir Edward Moore, incidentally, living at Mellifont in the Pale, is one of the first, and firmest, of the useful friends whom O'Neill gathered about him in the course of his life. He had, no doubt, already begun to nurse these important connections. He was the only Gaelic captain who, in this way, ever built up a connection outside his own local world, and the list of English and Irish gentlemen who were at one time or another on terms of friendship with him is remarkable. He started with Sidney and Leicester; he attached himself, as we saw, to the elder Essex, which stood him in good stead far later when he met the younger Essex; he married his daughter Margaret to the second Viscount Mountgarret; we find him mentioning, as friends of his, Lord Chancellor Hatton, Sir Francis Walsyngham, Sir Anthony St. Leger, Sir Robert Gardner; he writes as a friend to the Lord Chancellor Loftus; Sir Geoffrey Fenton is almost invariably on his side; he thanks Burghley for 'good turns received'; Palesmen who became suspects later, because of their friendship for him, were Sir William Warren, Sir Garrett Moore, Sir Lucas Dillon, Sir Thomas Bellew; so that it is not surprising that O'Neill should be spoken of, within another ten years, as having 'a great party in the English Pale'—and this is to take no account at all of the various people who, from time to time, came briefly under the mesmerism of his personal charm, such as those unimpressionable men Sir Nicholas Bagenal and Lord Deputy Fitzwilliam. From '80–'85, while the Desmond war and its aftermath was occupying the attention of everybody else in Ireland, he had been busy making useful friends like these.

As to his success in consolidating his local power the events which immediately follow show how his influence had begun to undermine Turlough. There was, too, in '84 the English report that the clansmen had elected him Tanist, or successor in Irish law to the title of The O'Neill. It may be to this period also, as well as to later years, for he would not have discontinued the practice, that the intimate picture of Archbishop Lombard refers: 'Whenever he used to go out hunting or fowling, or on some other exercise of business, he ever arranged that some guns should be carried by his company, and seized an opportunity of chatting familiarly with any of the people he met in the district, and used to ask them sundry questions as to their lives and habits . . . and when they replied that they knew nothing except spears, and bows, and arrows and other such primitive weapons of their fathers, he would produce a gun and having briefly explained its use bid them try if they could manage it. He would praise anyone handy and give him a piece of money and sometimes would bestow the weapon itself.' The people were so delighted that they would practice assiduously, scraping up bullets and gunpowder where they could. They even became anxious to discover how gunpowder was made, and having learned the science of it, made it themselves, and shared guns with one another. This was the nucleus of a rough army that grew secretly with the years to enormous size.

His first marriage, meanwhile, had not been a success. He had divorced his first wife before he was twenty-four. As she was the daughter of Sir Brian MacPhelim O'Neill, and as he had assisted the Essex who murdered this man and all his followers in '74, it must have been a bitter parting. His second marriage was on every ground happier. Joan, or Siobhán O'Donnell was the daughter of Hugh Duv O'Donnell, a family with which he remained closely bound until his death. Yet even that marriage seems to have had its ups and downs. In the winter of '79–'80 he had apparently put his wife away and was reputed to be living with, of all people, a daughter of his rival Turlough. At any rate in the January of 1580 Turlough was reported to be about to come into O'Neill's country to force him to marry his daughter. The sequel is lost; all we know is that Joan O'Donnell remained his lawful wife until her death in 1591 when, after a hardly decent pause he eloped with the daughter of his inveterate enemy, Marshal Bagenal.

II

So we find him, at the age of thirty-five, firmly rooted in Ulster, his ambitions ripe, clearly defined by his fifteen years of unswerving loyalty to his English patrons, riding down to Dublin to sit in the new parliament and participate in the triumph of law and order, as well as to help share out the Desmond spoils; but above all to claim his own wages. He was quite specific. He petitioned the parliament to grant him his title of Earl of Tyrone, and to fix the inheritance that went with it. The colonists had no option. Turlough's natural effervescence, his known sympathy for the Fitzmaurice-Desmond nexus, his persistent vacillations, all put him out of the running; and that carefully-built up connection of O'Neill's, and his well-established loyalty gave him an unanswerable claim. He was made Earl of Tyrone.

Then they looked at the map of Ulster, and to guard themselves they insisted that he must allow a fort to be built on the Blackwater River, which men called the Great River, the largest natural barrier that every force entering the heart of Ulster had to cross. The natural place for such a fort was either where Blackwatertown or the village of Moy stands to-day, both at fords on the direct road from Armagh and the coast. They chose the first as the nearest point to Armagh, and there, about a quarter of a mile down from the ford, on a tiny hillock, he built a wooden fort, known to the Irish as Portmore. They then considered his rivals, Turlough and the sons of Sean the Proud, and to keep these quiet insisted that he must not claim power over the lieges of Turlough and most give Sean's sons at least enough to stop them from being wandering outlaws. But these were small points. The crucial question was money, or its equivalent—territory. He wanted land, and plenty of it, all the power and prestige of it, its vassalage, its rents, its vast political influence.

He told them that he was beggared, and could not live like an Earl unless he got land. And, indeed, when he came back from England all he had found before him had been a comparatively small demesne around Dungannon: on the maps at the end-papers of this book a penny would cover all that he could venture to consider more or less his own, that is a region about fifteen or twenty miles square. And he held that little only by the grace of the Queen, the discretion of Turlough, and probably most firmly by the force of his personality and the gambling instinct of his own people who foresaw something of his future power. He put it to the Lord Deputy, and backed it with all the force of his most plausible arguments, and the upshot was that Turlough was persuaded, or manœuvred, into surrendering to the Earl all that the Earl held or could, from his centre, influence or command.

Turlough thereby abandoned a vast territory stretching from

Mullaghgara, at the foot of his own mountains of Upper Tyrone, down as far as the Great River; and he threw in the cess of Clan Brassilogh across the River, which he could no longer hope to reach. He agreed to allow Tyrone to extend his lands northward to the fastnesses of Glanconkyne and Killetra. As these were troublesome regions on the borders of O'Cahan's country, he secured himself sufficiently, for the time being, by retaining superiority over O'Cahan. There seemed only one possible danger to himself, that Tyrone, in spreading south, might eventually take from him the superiority which he held over the borderers down there, the MacMahons (of modern Fermanagh) and so threaten his own tail farther across on the Erne. He retained, therefore, his superiority over the alternative borderers on the Erne itself, the Maguires. To be doubly sure he made the whole agreement with Tyrone for a limited period of seven years. To be trebly sure he arranged that he could revoke the leases after three years. The rent was a thousand marks a year.

Thus, at a blow, Tyrone became one of the most powerful men in Ireland. He had an immense territory; he had access through Antrim to the Scots of the Isles; he had superiority over a host of lesser captains; he was in touch with Maguire; he could overawe Magennis down to the Newry; and it was a matter for himself to terrorize hesitant or refractory captains still farther afield. Ultimately his region of influence corresponded roughly to the modern Six Counties of Ulster.

Looking at this arrangement from the English view-point one is struck with admiration at the risk they took and the manner in which they held down so vast a territory; five-sixths of which either hated or barely tolerated the colonists. Only along the coast had they any footing, and even there the country was what the English called 'fast,' that is secured against them by its natural wildness and its nearness to Strathclyde and Galloway and the Scottish janissaries. The southern coast-districts of the Ardes, Lecale, and the rest, backing Iveagh and Orior, were held loosely by loyal Anglo-Irish, but the long wars of the barons had drained their best men, and either deputies held the country on rent, as Captain Piers held Little Ardes from Lord Savage, or the lands were farmed listlessly by debased successors of the gentlemen brought over by original adventurers like Sir John de Courcy—a degenerate string of Russells, Fitzsimons, Audleys, Jordans, or Bensons. Thus in Bagenal's report of 1586 the Ulster districts are dismissed despairingly one after another as quite unprotected. 'Monaghan—no buildings only defaced monasteries . . . Fermanagh—no buildings of importance. . . Armagh—Blackwater Fort, most needful to be repaired. . . Tyrone—Turlough has Strabane and New Castle; O'Neill has Dungannon. . . .' Only on the eastern coasts are there those English footholds, seven in a two-hundred mile coastline, and behind that all the mighty champaign was held for England by a superbly insolent outpost or two, remote from the coast and with long and dangerous lines of communication. Obviously it was not brute force, therefore, that counted with the colonists, but that old inability of the Irish to coalesce, and the policy of the balance of power cautiously measured—for their very lives depended on it—between the rival Irish. So that it would be the wrong metaphor to say that they put O'Neill in the saddle as Earl of Tyrone; they put him on a rocking stone and from time to time they shook the stone a little to remind him of his position, and occasionally steadied it to remind his neighbours of theirs.

That policy of the balance of power was not something vaguely apprehended by Elizabeth. She understood it coldly, and it was put to her coldly by the clear, rationalizing mind of her statesmen. This was something that the Irish nature took centuries to understand. For there, as in most small countries, remote from the European *haute politique*, personalities and politics were almost always confused, and ideas liable to become subsidiary to the human drama; as if international politics were a kind of folk-tale where any man acting with a cold-blooded intention becomes the Villian, and the Hero is all the more nobleminded for being a bit of a fool. In Elizabeth's day, as the State Papers show, men like Burghley and Walsyngham directed these deliberate policies every day as part of their job and Elizabeth studied their reports every day as part of her duty. Reporters on the spot regularly contributed invaluable data. The clearest analysis of the internecine disputes of Ulster, which the disputants themselves could not analyse—and suffered because they had not the wit to analyse them—comes, for example, from that before-mentioned secular primate, Myler McGrath, the Archbishop of Cashel, and may be found in the State Papers under the date May, 1592. It is a marvel of clear-headed dissection and is absolutely accurate.

To give one small instance, that proposal to make O'Neill Earl of Tyrone was put to Walsyngham for his opinion. He wrote across the proposal a qualified approval and added, 'If Her Majesty reserve to herself (to depend only on her) all the inhabitants from the Blackwater to the Pale (southwards, that is from O'Neill), such as the O'Hanlons, M'Cann, Magennis, MacMahon: and if the Fews (also south of Lough Neagh) be left to the government of some well-chosen men it shall assure the Pale from invasion, and cut off all dependencies of these urraughts, or principal persons (or vassals) from the O'Neills for ever.' The satisfactory thing about O'Neill, or Tyrone as we may call him from this on, is that he understood this policy perfectly, and repeatedly pleaded for a free hand to settle Turlough in his own way. There was the English suggestion, for example, to make Turlough a counter-balancing Earl of Omagh, with his son as Baron of Strabane. Tyrone fought strenuously against this, and whether it was due to his persuasions or not Turlough never was thus ennobled.

So, the Desmond wars ended as far as this man was concerned with the achievement of an ambition carefully cultivated for eighteen years. Lord Chancellor Hatton was bade in May 1587 to cause the Letters Patent to be made, under the Great Seal of England, granting O'Neill his title as Earl of Tyrone. But a man's private ambitions are one thing and the inevitability of a country's history are another: in the same year that the one story ended another began—the story of Tyrone's finest friend and final ally, Red Hugh O'Donnell.

PART THREE

THE PATRIOT MALGRÉ LUI: 1587-1595

I

IN OUR TIME a new word has arrived to describe an old military operation: infiltration. It is hardly more than a refinement on the antique method of establishing a position on, let us say, the coast of Madras and of then sending forward outposts to the hills of Mysore. To-day we have sometimes disguised our outposts as tourists; then, they disguised themselves as traders; in either case they ended up as soldiers.

Somewhere in 1586 a Captain Willis and three hundred of the scum of the kingdom made their way forward from Dundalk into O'Donnell country. If the O'Donnells had had any sense they would have butchered the men at once. But in these matters the adventurers gamble on the psychology of indecision. The people were lazy, slow to understand at first, suspicious of one another, it was all nobody's business, the newcomers had money, the O'Donnell had made certain obeisances to Elizabeth, become Sir Hugh Duv O'Donnell, was a friend of the Earl of Tyrone, and was considered loyal—and in any case there had been trouble before when the predecessors of these folk were set upon. The people did nothing.

Presently, however, Willis declared himself a sheriff, there was a measuring anew of lands, the soldiers' money ran out, looting began, and in the words of a contemporary 'the rascals did rob and spoil the people, ravished their wives and daughters, and made a havoc of all.' The people rose. Willis barely escaped alive, and appealed for help to the new Earl, who assisted him to escape. (Later on when Willis was moved south to Clones on the border the MacMahons slitted him.) It was all a slight and vulgar incident but the government at Madras-Dublin had to take serious note of it. O'Donnell was listed as a suspectable man, and the Lord Deputy and Council sat on the affair. But the Desmond Rising was not long over, and the Deputy was weary of warfare, and there was no money, and this was 1587, and the sails of the Armada could already be heard cracking in the roads of Corunna. It would take two or three thousand men to tame O'Donnell, as the Deputy—Sir John Perrot—pointed out to the Council, and altogether be a hazardous and a costly business. He bethought himself of other means.

'Give me leave,' he pleaded with the Council, 'to try a device I have in hand. I will quieten O'Donnell for you without the loss of a man or a penny wasted. If my trick fails then we can try force and see what else we can invent.' Perrot went his way, and somewhere on the Dublin quays he picked up a sea-captain named Skipper, and by bribes and threats induced him to take fifty soldiers on board and sail up the coast, around by the west, into Donegal with a cargo of sack, or white wine, as if he had come from Spain. Skipper duly drew into Lough Swilly, and anchored opposite Rathmullen Castle. Red Hugh O'Donnell, then aged fifteen, went aboard with some of the local

MacSweeneys and in the captain's cabin they sat and savoured the sack. The sack was good and they went on savouring it until they became too cheerful to notice what was happening. The next thing they felt was the wash of waves at their ears and the swaying of the ship under full sail before the north-wester, and the door locked. It was a matter of a couple of days before they walked ashore in Dublin as prisoners, and were marched to the Castle, examined, mightily approved, put in chains, and bestowed in the cells. They were to lie there for over three years, unwilling hostages, half-starved, anguished in mind, living on alms which they begged through the grate. With them there were some thirty others, youths and even children from ten years upwards, all pledges from the clansmen who had yielded them up, treated them as dead, and by neglect were now helping the anticipation to come true. There was no hope of escape. Every twenty-four hours the jailer came and examined their irons. Contact with the outside was virtually an impossibility. They were just another small fistful of the forgotten prisoners of the Renaissance world.

The kidnapping threw the North into a ferment. The father begged in vain for his son's freedom. Tyrone, who was married to Red Hugh's sister, and whose daughter Rose (by his divorced wife) was pledged to marry the boy, at once offered the government the ransom of a thousand pounds. He begged Leicester to act as go-between. He appealed to Walsyngham. Perrot said later that he could have had two thousand pounds, in our value nearer ten thousand, for the prisoner. But Elizabeth was not to be softened; not so much because O'Donnell was himself a dangerous man as that his second wife, Ineen Duv, was one of the MacDonnells of the Isles: and ever since Essex had butchered the people of her uncle, Sorley Bwee, on Rathlin Island, she had been one of the most bitter enemies of all Englishmen. The incident was passed over for the time being, but Tyrone, so proud of the influence of his new title, must have been a feeble man if he did not feel the smart.

It may be a mere coincidence rather than a consequence that from this on we begin to see him girding a little at his position. In the spies' reports we can follow his efforts to be compliant, the tug of old traditions, the sultry swell of ambition, the government's drag on the bit, his first resistances and his inevitable surrenders. It is embarrassing, even a little humiliating to watch him in the toils. Thus, three months after the kidnapping of

Red Hugh, in the Christmas of his 'nobilitation,' a spy named Ambrose Lacy sent information to Dublin Castle that his behaviour, government, and religion were not all that they should be. He was not, for instance, allowing sheriffs or Englishmen into his country; further, he had had messengers from Scotland and was in a confederacy with the Earl of Argyle for four thousand Scots. Another spy, evidently one Hugh M'Edeganny, reported that the Earl was dealing with MacMahon, his new neighbour and vassal down in Monaghan, and even across country with the Maguire who was supposed to be the vassal of Turlough, and that he was assisting O'Donnell in his local raids. Indeed, the general gossip was beginning to spread that his Lordship was trying out his fledgeling wings. One David Powes declared in the streets of Dundalk in the presence of many men that the Earl 'will climb so high as he will break his neck.'

This is the beginning of that long and, no doubt, deliberate policy of espionage with which the government consistently tried to keep a check on his power. He had to take note of these stories, and in fact it was he who reported Powes's gibe to the government as a libel. Nevertheless Perrot himself remarked, two months later, 'there has been some hard bruit of him.' Dublin on receipt of these reports at once rapped his knuckles and bade him come to the capital immediately and explain. For the first time Tyrone tried to hedge. His letter deserves close reading.

> 'It may please your Lordships,' he wrote, 'to be advertized that I dealt not with MacMahon as was declared to your Honours. Neither went I further than the borders of both our inhabitance as ourselves did appoint, with which I made the Commissioners acquainted, and took not so much as a sheaf of oats from him, so as now we are thoroughly agreed, without that, that I demand any horsemen of him, but am able of myself to defend my inhabitance if your Honour would permit me; and am not desirous to deal with those people whom your Lordship hath named, if they would desist from working my annoyance.'

The only meaning this can have had was that Tyrone had already come to a friendly arrangement with MacMahon, the very thing that Turlough had feared; in other words Tyrone was already spreading out beyond the territory on which he and

Turlough had agreed. More, Tyrone was taking it on him to protect O'Donnell; for, in another part of the same letter, speaking of O'Donnell he said, '*I would not suffer him to sustain any wrong by such as now continually annoy him.*' Years later when the Royal Proclamation was issued against him it mentioned as one of his chief crimes that he had 'allured O'Donnell by matching with him in marriage.' So that if a man might not marry where he needed assistance, what can have been thought of a man who gave assistance where he had married? This was proud talk from the newly-appointed Earl and the Lord Deputy may well have growled that the Earl was strangely innocent of the limits of his power. '*I* would not suffer him,' indeed! But when the Deputy came to the rest of the letter he was aghast:

> 'As for my going to Dublin at this instant it is so that my inhabitance is continually annoyed by the said Turlough's people and his sons, as in my former letters I have declared to your Lordship, in so much as I am now constrained to make a fortress six miles beneath Dungannon and encamp myself there. . . . And withal I humble beseech your Lordship not to send for me to Dublin upon every information of my back friends. . . . And this request I desire the rather for that since my coming from England I have been at Dublin thrice, twice at Dundalk, and once at Drogheda to my great charges wherein I am not able to continue.'

The letter concluded by pointing out that if he could not defend his country where he stood, he was much less likely to do it from Dublin.

The Deputy repeated his orders and rattled his sword. 'I proclaimed a general hosting and provided men as though I would have done great things.' Tyrone, boiling inwardly, had to come down to Dublin with his tail between his legs, and at this time left behind him two of his best pledges to lie with Red Hugh in the Bermingham Tower: his guarantee that he would keep the peace in Ulster, and towards Turlough. Turlough chuckled and, thus encouraged, naturally became saucy again. Tyrone, enraged, harried Turlough's country to the walls of Strabane in defiance of his guarantee. Turlough enually enraged, collected help from the rivals of O'Donnell whom Tyrone had assisted, caught Tyrone on the hip and trounced him. The Deputy now began to chuckle, and wrote gleefully to Walsyngham that this had 'done as much good in the north as anything that has happened in these nine years. It hath abated the Earl's edge much.' The policy of the balance of power, the technique of the rocking-stone, was working out perfectly.

Multiply that incident by a hundred; realize the extent of the pride of an O'Neill—the family that once had held the High Kingship of Ireland unbroken for six hundred and fifty years; and we have the combustible materials of explosion.

2

The spring moved in quietly. The bodachs tilled the fields. The kernes and horsemen rested after the winter's raiding. Tyrone could lie and eat in comfort out in the green-sprouting fern with his children and their tutors, his poet and his harper. He could see from the hill-rise the great moving cloud-shadows of his creaghts slowly passing before the cowmen from pasturage to pasturage down in the green plain sloping to Lough Neagh. The air, drowsy with floating pollen, would induce after-dinner sleep and full content. This was his centre and perimeter; it was his everything—his ritual, his morning, noon, and night, his yesterday and his to-morrow, the life that had always been and that he was satisfied to think would always be, essentially unchanged from what it had been when an O'Neill ruled all Ireland from Tara. It would soon be twenty years since he left Penshurst. That memory was fading.

We, of a restless age, and read in the story of the world's restlessness, find it hard to imagine a time before men accepted Change as the only changeless part of the scheme of things. Only by going back to the poetry of the time do we realize how solid, even for a man of the Renaissance, was the common feeling of permanence. The first gently troubled thoughts of the men of letters at the portents of unrest are still wholly lyrical in the slightness of their regret and stately in their moralizing; as in Spenser. It is a poetry far removed from the tossed and often harassed pain or anger of those later centuries that experienced the bitter fact which these Elizabethans foresaw with such a delicate melancholy. Elizabethan literature is, of course, full of terrific passions and rages; but these are a passion with the permanent and unalterable torments of life, the great evils and emotions, like jealousy and hate and ambition, unlike our exasperation at being subject to the Unpredictable and

Unintelligible. Their very intensity, as if arising from their certainty, shows how far removed they were from our concern with the insecurity of constant political and social change. Apart from local satirists, men like the earlier Langland, who wrote for the people, stirred by their oppression, this modern sense of instability was not in the temperament of the century. In Ireland Gaelic poetry, so wrapped up in local, or can we say national affairs, could not evade for ever such upheavals as they saw disturbing the old regime in every part of the country, and when the poet saw his patron decline and his own mode of life becoming more and more endangered he could not fail, from time to time, to reflect his feelings. But it is not until the last years of the sixteenth century and the beginning of the seventeenth that poetry in Ireland really shows any full awareness of what is happening and in O'Neill's time it reflects a general indifference and blindness to impending ruin.

Tyrone would have understood the drama of foiled ambition which was such a favourite theme with the Elizabethans

> *To have thy Princes grace yet want her Peeres ;*
> *To have thy asking, yet waite many yeares ;*

and he would have understood any love poem, or the lyrical quiet of

> *No other noise nor people's troublous cryes*
> *As still are wont t'annoy the walled towne,*
> *Might there be heard ; but careless Quiet lyes*
> *Wrapt in eternal silence farre from enimyes.*

But he could have had no idea as to what Spenser, the only poet of the century with any power of prophecy, was aiming at in his cantos on Mutability which foretell the great coming social changes in which the 'raskall many' will make themselves felt and kingship be no longer inviolate. His whole upbringing, his racial memories, his atavism protected him from any such disturbing ideas. The only unrest in that balmy sleep among the ferns would be the unrest of every ambitious heart like his that thirsts for the juice of life.

That unrest, with him, would be like a mountain stream in which one can swim and think it calmly warm, only to find, when one dives, that the bottom is flowing with a strong icy current. It is typical of this apparent sloth and actual activity that it is not until long after that we discover the things on which he has been quietly working all the time. For example, this is around 1586: nobody mentions or appears to know until 1594 that he possesses an extraordinarily powerful army, for his rank and for the time. He was collecting that army section by section in these quiet years during which he attracts no particular attention from anybody. He was, of course, not supposed to keep more than a fixed number of men under his command but it was generally accepted, *after* he showed his hand, that he had constantly changed the garrison permitted so that over the years an excessive number was trained and disciplined. Likewise, he was not supposed to import an inordinate amount of ammunition; but there never was any trouble in Ireland about smuggling it in, and the English merchants never had the slightest objection, even in times of war, to supplying the Gaels with all the guns and ammunition they wanted—provided they could pay for them. So that in explaining his secret strength there is no need either to rely on, or to question, the popular story that he ordered a great quantity of lead to roof his castle and turned it into bullets.

At the same time he has been pushing his personal influence wider, east beyond Lough Neagh, south below the Great River, south-west into Monaghan, establishing trustworthy captains or taking tribute from those who already ruled there and were willing to acknowledge his sovereignty. That was the most exacting as well as the most important part of his schemes; for at every step he met his enemy, Bagenal, the Queen's Marshal, and all that he represented. It was often disappointing as well as exacting since he repeatedly found that the Marshal, on seeing these districts made secure by the Earl, promptly sent in government officials and the Queen's writ.

Clearly, that balmy sleep among the fern would have been troubled by many ambitious dreams. It bore no resemblance to the torpor of the milk-fed clansmen who would wake from it merely to repeat the familiar pattern of raid and rest—raid and rest as men like them had done on the Persian uplands for two thousand years.

3

The horizon began to darken. Suddenly the thunder-cloud burst. In July, 1588, on the 12th day of the month, a Spanish fleet sailed out of Corunna, bent for the English coast. England gasped and feared the worst. There was a general atmosphere of panic. On the 20th the British Navy left Plymouth. The day after, a Sunday, they fell in with some stragglers of the Spanish and the guns began to belch. From that on to the end of the month an intermittent and indecisive sea-battle went on up and down the Channel. The Spanish fleet was enormous and, as usual, Elizabeth had stinted her navy. But little by little the English plucked their feathers and all the time the south-westerly wind drove the Spanish relentlessly leeward in heavy seas. On August 5th a great storm blew up and by the 7th the invaders were being hurled up the North Sea, past Scotland, and even past the Isles; but the English were still badly frightened; their losses were serious and if any further action had taken place they could not have met it. Indeed, the Lord High Admiral, Lord Charles Howard, was writing to Walsyngham that if the Spanish put in anywhere such as the Orkneys to refresh themselves and return, things would be very bad indeed. 'A kingdom is a grand wager.'

The news of the appearance of Spanish ships off the coast of Ireland, therefore, produced a series of frantically frightened reports to London. The rumours begin with three great ships from the south-west that have drawn into Killybegs, out on the far-west corner of Donegal. Then six more have come into the open bay of Aringlass in Sligo. Next two have appeared at the Blaskets: later the two became four. Seven off Limerick become eleven over night: two days later this eleven becomes twenty-four. One Spanish ship has come across the horizon at Tralee. The Mayor of Limerick tells the Mayor of Waterford that he reckons that 140 ships have been driven on the coast of Ireland by the weather. The Mayor of Waterford reports in terror to London 'a great fleet of Spaniards on the coast.'

Next comes the fear of what the Irish may do. Sir Richard Bingham writing 'at one o'clock from Athlone' reports that Rickard MacRickard Burke, better known as The Devil's Reaping Hook, one of his bugbears of Connaught, whom he calls 'a notable malefactor,' has come into the Mayo Islands, presumably for an assignation. He further reports, 'after dinner at Athlone,' seven more ships off Limerick and a scare-story of '600 Scots with shirts of mail, and 300 English, landing in the North'; while, up there, Bagenal loses his head completely and wails that there are not 750 foot in the whole realm, that the horses are unshod, and that they all expect to be overrun. The Munster

Bands are called out. 'We the forces of Thomond were all every day and night watching seven ships (at Kilrush, in Clare) until they were all gone, which is a great loss for us in this Barony.'

All that first fortnight of September the panic spread and spread. It was groundless. The crushing failure of the Desmond war (the last time that Spanish ships came to Ireland) had cowed the people. There was in any case the old weakness—the Irish were as scattered as the Armada itself, and the few English officials, though outnumbered a thousand to one by the Spanish alone, did what they liked because they did it in concert. Nobody, naturally, saw things in that perspective then, and in these first excitable reports it is the fabulous Armada that looms up before us like Boney grinning like a devil in the firelight of the Wessex Inns. All through September the stories pile up as the ships are reported off Tirawley, Erris, the Isles of Aran, the Galway Roads, Lismore, Loop Head, Clare Island. There is no way of checking their number. They were probably, in large part, the same ships seen by a lot of people. Secretary Fenton, summing up on the 9th of September speaks of sixteen ships lost. There is no way of estimating accurately the number of Spaniards drowned, or dispatched; just as there is no evidence at all for the traditional Tudor story that the people murdered them indiscriminately in their thousands.

We have seen how the first rumours as to the number of ships swelled day by day, and it is the same with the size of the crews and the casualties. Carew estimated in the end that 3,000 who came to land by swimming were slain, and 2,000 drowned, Secretary Fenton raises that figure a little to 5,394. Bingham, but he was a notorious braggart, raised Fenton to 6,000 or 7,000 'at least,' and these of course perished only on the coast of Connaught where *he* was Governor. Modern historians have gone as high as 10,000. To this day, on the side of the people, the folk-legend still lives in the Blaskets and about Dingle where the King of Spain's son—so ancient a figure in Gaelic legend—was drowned in the bay 'with 500 tall men.' (A rude stone still marks the place where he is said to be buried.) He was the King's illegitimate son, the Prince of Asculum, who had embarked in the galleon of St. Martin with the Duke of Medina Sidonia; he had gone ashore at Calais, and come back to the quays to find that the Duke had cut his cables when Drake suddenly appeared from the north. By that fatal chance, so mariner John Anthony of Genoa tells us, Asculum boarded the *Santa Maria de la Rosaria* with Don Pedro, Don Diego, and Don Francisco, struck the rocks in the Blasket Sound and sank. So too, on the side of the colonists, George Woodloke in Galway sends his runner to Waterford to tell how at Borris there came striding out of the waves sixteen persons '*alive*' with their chains of gold. Another sent to Gerry Comerford of Galway a man with tokens—to wit, a hat, and a pane, and other things from the ship, and on the sight of these wonders Comerford jumped on his horse and rode off hell for leather with—'Other news there is none but there is great fear in these parts.'

That fabulous atmosphere may in part explain, if it cannot palliate, the killings that followed. When the same Boethius Clanchy who stared in awe at the 'small board, the red anchor, and the foreign prock ' saw the strangers come clambering in their hundreds out of the sea he must have slain his share of Spaniards in a horrible orgasm of sheer terror before the Unknown. When Don Pedro de Mendoza's crew was cast away off Clare Island and Dowdary O'Malley's kernes fell on the poor wretches limping ashore exhausted, battering them down on the rocks or slashing their blood into the sandy shorewater, they were all as much maniacs as murderers. Certainly these hideous things are of a psychology beyond normal understanding—unless we dismiss them complacently in the English fashion as the work of 'savages,' than which, in truth, for those hours they were no better. But, what of all the official government killings? The government's orders were that no quarter must be given to any Spaniard who escaped the seas, and Bingham in Connaught proclaimed throughout his province that anyone who sheltered them for more than twenty-four hours would be at once treated as a traitor. 'My brother George,' said Bingham, 'executed seven or eight hundred or upwards, first and last, *one way or another*.' And what does that ominous phrasing mean? Three hundred were executed formally in Galway city. Norreys took a score in Tralee and killed them merely because there was no prison in which to put them. These executions must, no doubt, be laid at the door of long-sustained anti-Spanish, anti-Catholic propaganda, in revenge for Alva, and for the thousands of St. Bartholomew's Day—wherein we may see propaganda as the manufacture of a myth, the inducement in the minds of simple men of the psychology of the homicide.

There were only one or two incidents which might have in any degree justified this general panic. These were the landings in Donegal, at Killybegs and Loughros, and at Glenganivey in the north of Inishowen. Three ships tried to land at Killybegs; one was lost, the second battered on the jags of the rocks, and only the third escaped serious damage. Twenty miles across the boggy ridge of the same peninsula, at Loughros, Don Alonso de Leyva, Lieutenant-General of the Armada, was cast up in the *Santa Anna*. His leg being crushed by the capstan, and his ship stoved in, he came ashore and set up a regular camp. When he heard about his compatriots across at Killybegs, who were trying to float their third ship, the *Gerona*, he joined them and presently sailed away with as many as the *Gerona* could carry. She ran on the Rock of Bunboys and was wrecked with all hands.

In that tense atmosphere of hysteria what did Tyrone do? By all the laws of his life, as hitherto lived, he should have played the part of the obedient English feudal earl, intent only on building up his local power and his reputation with his superiors. He did something rather different. In fact it is evident that he was beginning to regard himself as something quite different to, and perhaps more powerful than any of his English exemplars. Standing on his own right as an independent noble and a civilized man he came with a great herd of cattle to feed the castaways of Inishowen, to his North. Whether that was an act of defiance, or an act of common humanity, the import of it cannot be exaggerated, nor can the risks it involved be over-emphasized. When a lesser man, O'Rourke, with equal humanity apparelled, armed, and refurbished castaways in his territory of West Breffni, Bingham pursued him, smashed him, and levelled his country by fire. O'Rourke had to fly to Scotland. James VI handed him over to Elizabeth, and the poor devil was hanged as a common criminal in London. In short, Tyrone's suppressed natural passions were roused by the plight of the wretched Spaniards. When O'Donnell, heartbroken for his son stewing in Dublin Castle tried to barter thirty unfortunate castaways for his release. Tyrone blazed out at him. He told him that he and his posterity might one day have to seek a refuge in another country—as these castaways had done—and that it would be a fitting revenge of Fate for betraying these poor creatures in their only refuge: a prophecy that came true.

That speech and a record of his general behaviour at the time was, of course, duly carried hot-foot by the informers to Dublin Castle. They are the first few words that have come down to us from the private heart of a generally most reticent and cautious man. They are all the more precious for being recorded beside other words calculated for the public ear, i.e. the messages he dispatched simultaneously informing the Queen's Deputy of his war-like preparations against these very same Spaniards. The natural upshot of the incident was that the English, in their panic, suddenly begin to feel that they could not trust Tyrone in any crisis. So that in the same two or three days that Tyrone is praying the Deputy for munitions and a commission of martial law to go against the Spaniards, and offering a month's victuals for the expedition, Bingham very naturally feels that he 'doubts the Earl of Tyrone more than all.' And a month after the storm, on October 12th, a joint report to the Privy Council in London, signed by the Deputy, the Archbishop of Dublin, the Bishop of Meath, the Lord Chancellor, and the Chief Justice speaks of 'a special distrust of the Earl of Tyrone.' He might have had to pay dear for his humanity to these Spanish castaways had the times not been in utter disarray, and had not other matters come to his assistance in the nick of time. Those other matters are woven in with what may seem, on the surface, a tedious and dry question —the old dispute over land with Turlough. No land-dispute in Ireland has ever been merely tedious and dry. This one here takes on a new twist and tangles into a story with a typically sinister conclusion.

4

This new story opens in the wintry weather of '88 with the Lord Deputy, Fitzwilliam, an elderly, avaricious, but urbane man, riding along the western sea-coasts to see the tail-piece to the great adventure—enough great baulks on the beaches of Tyrconnell alone to build fifteen ships, tangled cordage, cables, 'great mighty boats,' masts rolling in the surf fit to make any normal two. And perhaps he saw the mounds of the one thousand and two hundred bodies reported to have lain along the shore a while before, or perhaps the tides had carried them and only the sad inanimate wreck remained, greening and rusting in the storms. Having seen his fill he turned inland across the sodden Croaghgorm mountains to Turlough's castle at Strabane, and then southward beside the wooded mountain range of the

Sperrins, with Mullaghcarn rising on his left, and so down the uplands to Tyrone's castle at Dungannon. He received such cheer and refreshing at the Earl's house as left him, and he gratefully acknowledged it, without a desire unfulfilled, and then, in the main room, over the (probably Armada) wine, with the storm outside, and the door rattling in the wind, and the smoke vacillating in the gusts to its vent, the two earls bartered.

The fact was that for over two years the Queen had not got a penny of rent from the Tyrconnell country that he had traversed. She was 'owed' more than seven times three hundred cows, and he had been able to collect nothing. Not a single carcass. Nothing but the usual promises soft and thick and unreliable as the rain and winds under which they were made. Tyrone understood all this and he was apparently quite ready to assist. But . . . there was his wild cousin at Strabane standing between him and Tyrconnell? The Deputy thrust on. Why should he not take pledges for the rent, that is adopt Perrot's trick—Did a frown pass over O'Neill's face at this tactless reference to Red Hugh?—and then Tyrone could raid Tyrconnell for the rent in the Queen's name if it was not paid?

Tyrone did not baulk at that; there would be no difficulty about pledges; in fact the Lord Deputy held O'Dogherty the chief of Inishowen, and O'Gallagher—or rather, for it was difficult to remember these ill-fitting foreign titles for the long-glibbed clansmen, 'Sir Owen (O'Toole) O'Gallagher'—and the Deputy might, if he wished, take him for security. (Though that meant, as he must have known when he offered this pledge, that they would very possibly never again see the free light of Ulster day. And sure enough O'Gallagher was stewing in the Castle two years later for that rent which was never paid.) But, again O'Neill intervened, raiding was another matter. He could not raid without men, munitions, money—in short without the land which meant all these things. Perhaps the Deputy knew. . . . ?

Fitzwilliam knew only too well. . . . (His ruminations need little guesswork: the necessities condition them rigidly.) And he had been getting letters enough about the accursed land-squabble from the Privy Council to bind him to the conditions. Turlough had laid it down that the lease could be revoked after three years, and here was the third Michaelmas come and gone. He had heard Turlough swearing, back in Strabane, that he would rather die than lose his lands. 'Bid Tyrone give up his claims,' had been the Privy Council's advice—remote from the deadly insistence of the thing in their rooms at Whitehall, or deciding at their leisure with the Queen in that cosy little palace on the river at Richmond. 'Make him if he will not. But compound if you can.' Make him? No doubt that could be done, though it would be costly. The man was powerful. And supposing they did cut him off they would have the same story to settle with Turlough, thereby become equally great. Besides what of those angry, landless men, the sons of Sean, shivering out there in the woods with their 'addicted and affectionate followers,' all of them behind Turlough and against Tyrone?

Meanwhile Tyrone prompts—the beeves? Yes, the beeves. . . . The land: the beeves. Possibly treason: certain money. Certain power; possible resistance. And there was no alternative for the one but to trust this unusually gracious red-bearded Irish captain. And the other would risk anything (even the life-imprisonment of poor O'Dogherty and O'Gallagher) so long as he can get a firm grip on Glanconkyne and Killetra, and the lovely champaign stretching to the Loughside, and the rich alluvial plain across the river; enviable miles and miles of it spreading out there in the dark to the gates of Newry; its thousands of men; its scores of thousands of beasts. . . . So they argued and argued, until Tyrone ended it with a sudden, seemingly gracious compliance. Let him only have the land until May, and then he would willingly give it up. Well pleased at the bargain he had won the Deputy agreed and simply added to the twenty-one hundred cows already due another thousand by way of fine. He took O'Dogherty and O'Gallagher with him in his retinue: he fixed a final reckoning day: and he laid it on his host that he must raid and harry the O'Donnells for the rent if they still refused to pay. ('His friends?' O'Neill might have murmured secretly. 'His blood-relations?') The cavalcade moved off. God knows what O'Neill said to encourage his two hostages: possibly that he would buy them out: and sure enough, though the news of O'Gallagher is bad, O'Dogherty—if one of the secretaries to the Exchequer is to be believed—was released later because the Lord Chancellor received so many hogsheads of salmon from the rivers of Ulster. The charge is neither unusual nor incredible. The Dublin government was wormy with corruption: its officials had to live somehow. From Dublin the Deputy wrote happily to the Privy Council of his success. Not only was the old land-squabble settled but thereafter he would be well able to compound all future matters between the two O'Neills—and all 'matters of like or even greater weight.'

Three months later Tyrone was declaring in his turn that he would rather lose his life than give up his lands to Turlough. This time the Council did not in the least know what to reply—less even than Fitzwilliam knew that night in Dungannon. For they had since been rightly or wrongly informed, indeed only that very month, that the Earl of Tyrone was now in communication with Philip of Spain. Fitzwilliam's dilemma was at fester-point.

The patent fact is that Tyrone's power had already quietly crept far beyond the limits intended by his patrons. The policy of the balance of power was beginning to crack. He had out-influenced Turlough, and his strength was beginning to be serious. They knew well that no Irish Deputy of theirs, no matter how loyal, ever could behave as if he ruled in Warwickshire or Devon since, whatever they pretended, the law and tradition which his people respected was Gaelic law and Gaelic tradition. They might, indeed, pretend to be severe about such matters, and stickle for every single point; in private they recognized the essential fact about infiltration—that it had to be very gradual. They may have disliked his methods but they had to trust him, and trust to the power and enmity of Turlough and the sons of Sean to keep him in check. They favoured him, once again, in the land-dispute. But they underestimated his arrogance and his ruthlessness: as the sequel revealed.

5

Let us follow this new sequence of events. In February (1589) one of the sons of Sean, Hugh Gaveloch, that is Fettered Hugh—because his mother bore him in prison—suddenly came out of his lair in the woods as yet another common informer to sting at the pride and power of the Earl. His action has all the appearances of a gesture of despair. He said through one Captain Nicholas Merriman that he had 'weighty matters to disclose.' What they were we may guess because it was in March that the Deputy reported that Tyrone was said to be plotting with Spain. On hearing of this new informer's treachery Tyrone's fury boiled again; but he said nothing for the moment. For the moment he was intent on settling the land-question and would not fall out with the colonists. Instead, in May and April, he suffered the humiliation of having his affairs once more dragged before the Council, and though he must have hated these endless questions and probings he persuaded them (and this time it was probably the bare truth) that the whole thing was merely part of a family feud, that sort of stupid malice of simple, jealous men which is so infuriating to their betters. The Council accepted the explanation. On the very day that they drew this breath of relief their lawyers were concluding a nine-days session on the land-question at Drogheda. Turlough, realising that he was discredited, agreed there and then to compound in Tyrone's favour once more. The plotters fell back.

Through the spring and summer there was quiet. Then, in November, Nicholas Merriman comes forward again, and it seems a fair inference that he is once again passing on information collected from some native informer. He now reports that Tyrone is plotting with the Scots, that he and Angus MacDonnell had been making merry at Dungannon, and the two even slept in the same bed. This, to O'Neill, was even more exasperating than the earlier story. Long after, in 1603, he cried out that he was so dogged by these spies that he could not get drunk in his castle without some cur running with the story to Dublin—and he was then in low fortunes: what he felt now, in his growing pride and power, we shall see from what resulted. The spy went on to say that when MacDonnell was leaving he gave Scotch plaids to some of Tyrone's men, and Tyrone gave him seven of his best horses. The general idea, of course, was that in the darkness of the night, and the privacy of the bed, the two whispered treason across the pillow into the dawn. Merriman summed up by saying that 'if Turlough were gone Tyrone would be as bad a member as ever came of his name.' Now, we are not given the name of Merriman's informer, but the sequence reveals it. O'Neill asked permission to go to London; far-seeing man. Maguire caught Hugh Gaveloch in a raid. Tyrone bought him from Maguire. The common, but incorrect tradition, is that he then took him and in his rage swung him with his own hands off a thorn-tree. At any rate, the man was dead and buried by the following January: (1590).

At once the hurly-burly began. The Deputy stormed. Reports poured into London that the Lord Chancellor had ordered Tyrone to stay the execution, and that the Deputy likewise had bidden him to forbear. They believed the story that Tyrone had hanged the man on a thorn tree with his own hands. More than that, the countryside had offered three hundred horses and five thousand cows in ransom for Hugh—he had been a great favourite with the people, a wild, reckless, raider, one of their own temper and tradition whom they understood perfectly—so that, they said, with all, the country was seething at Tyrone's arrogant defiance of native opinion. 'Ireland,' Perrot was told, 'will shortly be so ill as it will hardly recover again.'

Once more Tyrone had to chase down to Dublin and defend himself before the Council. He had not hanged the man. Melaghlin M'Murrehey and his brother Cormac had been the executioners, and a hundred of the best people of the land had stood by and seen it done. He had hanged the fellow because he was the son of a traitor and himself a traitor; because he was a murderer and the son of a murderer, a spoiler, and a killer of women and infants; a man of whom he had complained more than once to the Deputy and 'my honourable good friend, Sir Thomas Cecil.' In short he had done nothing but good, in the best interests of the Queen. As he said all this, standing bare-headed before the Board of the Council in Dublin Castle, he began to bawl like a child. He made such a hullabaloo that he embarrassed the Council, and nobody could quieten him. He took old Fitzwilliam aside and, overcome with emotion, wept aloud to him that he could not rest until he had thrown himself down at Her Majesty's gracious feet to attend her pleasure in judgement or mercy. They did not know what to make of him, and indeed they can never have seen the like before. (Some were to see it again; Tyrone was always liable to floods of tears.) Old Fitzwilliam finally soothed him by giving him permission to visit the Queen, and wrote him a covering letter which he probably expected him to open and read before handing to Burghley.

> 'The bearer, Earl of Tyrone, hath overshot himself in doing execution upon Hugh Gaveloch. I find him so much grieved that he cannot be quiet. If the fact were to do again I am persuaded that he would never do it and I think he is sufficiently warned now to incur the danger of any more such hereafter. He desires to submit himself at Her Majesty's feet. This makes me hope well of him that he will increase in his dutiful endeavours to make amends for his fault. . . .'

But a somewhat less benevolent private letter went simultaneously from the Dublin Council to the Privy Council:—

> 'Albeit we disallow well of his fact as well as of his answer, yet in respect as well of the time as of his calling in this State, we forbear to make any restraint of his person. . . .'

And even Fitzwilliam, in another letter, while admitting that the Pale felt 'great good and security in his neighbourhood' and that as long as Turlough held he was not really dangerous, agreed also that 'when he is absolute and hath no competition then he may show himself to be the man which now in his wisdom he hath the wit to dissemble.'

He crossed in March (1590) to London on that permission—so strange a return for one who had left it so slightly. But although he could apparently count on the friendly support of Sir Christopher Hatton, the Queen would not look at him. Instead he was put under arrest in Sir Henry Wallop's house—Another reminder of the fate of Desmond?—and bade report himself to the Privy Council. There, attuning himself to the more deliberate atmosphere of London, he argued circumspectly and cautiously. 'I acknowledge,' he said, 'that by my education among the English I am not altogether ignorant but that in the strict course of Her Majesty's laws I might be reprehensible for this execution. Nevertheless I humbly desire that consideration may be had to the place where this fact was done and to the person—a notable murderer—and to the ancient form of government among us in Ulster, where there is neither magistrate, judge, sheriff, nor course of the laws of this realm; but certain customs by which both O'Neill and I and others of our sort do govern our followers; neither have we been at any time restrained from execution of evildoers, nor of such as be invaders of our country, or professed enemies to the same.' And he went on to plead that unless Turlough and O'Donnell and others like himself were allowed to use their ancient customs they could never defend their country at all. Later, he agreed, when the whole province was governed by English law as in other reformed parts of the realm, the situation would be different. He concluded by begging for Her Majesty's grace and favour, 'which is my greatest comfort and the chief cause of my coming over.'

These claims and admissions are interesting even after making every allowance for a large admixture of disingenuousness and for that 'profound dissembling heart' of his and his 'high, dissembling, subtle and profound wit' to which contemporaries like Moryson and Camden pay unflattering tribute. In sum, he was speaking already for all Ulster, and claiming openly the rights and needs of Gaelic law and tradition, while admitting that in time they must yield place to the New System.

Turlough, hereupon, came up again. He sent Conn MacSean, brother of the murdered man, to the court to plead against Tyrone. But he spoiled the dramatic effect by pleading at the same time for his arrears of rent. His charges were numerous and, doubtless, repeated in substance what Gaveloch had communicated, or been about to communicate, to the Irish authorities. Among other points he declared that Tyrone had sheltered a Spanish nobleman named Don Antonio Mancicio, whom he afterwards got out of the country. (It is an entertaining detail that while old Fitzwilliam had been bargaining with Tyrone, that night of 1589, in Dungannon about the rents of Tyrconnell, this refugee was lying low somewhere in or near the castle.) To cool Tyrone they kept him there all that spring into August (1590) and then sent him back with orders to behave himself properly in future. He accepted all their conditions quietly. What he secretly felt we may guess. For Perrot's notes as to what he must henceforth do indicate what he had hitherto not been doing. He must cease to press his authority northwards into O'Kane's country and southwards into the lands of the Archbishop of Armagh. He must stop taking black rent from his vassals. He must try to bring his people to adopt English habits, wear English dress, cut that long Gaelic *glibb*, or fringe of hair, to which they looked as through a vizor. He must stop communicating with the Scots, and he must allow his land to be shired like any English county. The Gaelic lord must toe the feudal line.

Tyrone had, incidentally, whiled away this trying period in London by doing some shopping; he brought back with him rich furniture for his house, bedding, arras, carpets, and the like. He also got a license, during this visit, to import lead for the roof of his castle. He had shown his purchases to Burghley, saying, 'A few little things I've been picking up?' Burghley approved mightily. It would all help to civilise Ulster. The lead did not go on his roof, however, but into his guns, as bullets.

6

The autumn of his return passed quietly. He was worried by his wife's health which suffered in that cruel winter of sleet and heavy snow. She pined in it and did not outlast it. He was worried, too, by the state of the country to his south-west—across the great lakes of the Erne, down in O'Rourke's country in Connaught. He could see trouble coming, and whereas he once throve on trouble he was now eager for peace in which to consolidate what he had won. To understand that atmosphere of unrest, which gradually inflamed the whole of the North we must go back a little to the autumn of '88, after the Armada, and cross westward to Connaught, where the power of the colonists was creeping up to Tyrone's borders.

The key-figure is Bingham, the English governor, a man who understood no other rule than the sword and the hangman, and had been for years badgering the West into madness by his savage, bullheaded methods. In self-defence, O'Rourke, who was still sheltering the remnants of the Spaniards and refusing to give them up, raided, burned, and preyed where and when he could, until between the two of them the people were ground as between two mill-stones. It illustrates the state of the country, and the necessity for a central authority, that in the end the people saw that there was nobody to whom they could appeal except Bingham's masters—O'Rourke now powerless. The sequel illustrates also the weakness of the authority to whom they did appeal. The Bishops of Meath and Kilmore were sent by Dublin to the west at the head of a Commission. Bingham straightway flaunted and insulted the Commissioners. His soldiers even dressed up as clergymen and mocked the Commissioners to their faces. 'Why,' howled Bingham, 'are these men sent into my province? It is a hindrance and a disgrace unto Her Majesty that she should seek unto a race of so treacherous and beggarly a nation, and of so little estimation as these are!' He despairs of doing any good while such namby-pambys hang about his door, and begs to be sent back to England, 'seeing the good days so few I can enjoy in Ireland.' And then he cools himself (his own phrases again) by chasing the fastnesses, marching along the greatest mountains, driving the rebels from hill to hill, though—as another said—because these 'wild wolves kept to the woods and mountains,' and drove their creaghts far into the islands and along the seaside, he could never catch any prey, and nearly always comes back unrewarded if not unblooded.

It appears to have been a kind of Black-and-Tan rule all over Connaught under Bingham. The wretched Burkes and O'Rourkes were so scalded by it that they dreaded even to approach the Commissioners. They had to be lured in like chickens with little grains. And the more the hardworking Commissioners lured, the louder Bingham swore at the disgrace of it and egged his man at the 'malefactors.' The Commissioners gave up the ghost, and on the day they rode away to Dublin they were followed by horsemen from the Burkes pleading with them to come back, to wait a little longer, even one more day, and perhaps the captains would then dare to come in and settle. The Bishops refused. They were sick of the timid Irish, the brutal colonists, the crude country life. They left the vast wooded Brenny—it covers most of modern Leitrim—to burn behind them to the shores of the Erne, and Bingham, black with smoke and powder, now in his element, crying that not a sinner remained but young Brian Oge O'Rourke, the son of the chief rebel, who was now and again seen prowling about the charred edges of his father's country with a few affectionate men: another little handful like the Desmond rapparees or the remaining sons of Sean, landless, outlawed seed-carriers of hate. So did the plague of Munster spread across the Shannon to the west, and lick the Ulster marches.

The Ulster clans, hearing this rumble from below the Erne, were even more distracted by another annihilation much nearer at hand. The whole of Monaghan was proclaimed overnight, and the chief, Hugh Roe MacMahon, was taken and executed. This event more than any other woke up the northern clans out of their daydreams. For between the burning of the Brenny in the west and the settlement of Monaghan in the east, there was now left hanging downward into the open jaws of the English crocodile the great salient of Maguire's country of Fermanagh. It was obviously merely a matter of time, and very little time at that, before Bingham would turn his troops on Maguire. A glance at the map, especially some contemporary map whose exaggerations are always significant, will reveal at once the absolute importance of that salient. For it includes the Great Lakes which stretch half way across Ireland and whose only narrows at Enniskillen formed the Gap of the Erne. Whoever held that gap did for the west what Bagenal did for the east by protecting the Gap of the North from Newry. The net was closing on the last outposts of Gaeldom.

Nor did Bingham hesitate to attack Maguire and that vital salient of Fermanagh. Maguire first tried to buy off his sheriff and then appealed to the Privy Council which, as usual, was a little more accommodating than the local governor and bade him hold a while. But this produced no effect at all on Bingham; for it is the way of empire-building that there are always adventurers ready to risk a reprimand from home, knowing that if they win out they will be upheld and rewarded. Bingham went on marauding Maguire. On the east Henshaw, Seneschal of Monaghan, likewise preyed and slew indiscriminately. Maguire fought back east and west and was thereupon proclaimed a rebel, which was satisfactory for everybody except Maguire and his neighbours—who knew that if Maguire fell the same disaster would soon visit them. They could no longer doubt the course that history was taking under their noses. Desmond was gone. Bingham was tearing through the west. O'Rourke was gone. MacMahon was gone. Maguire had his back to the wall. Whose turn would come next? How long more would the antique world into which their mountains had so far comfortably lapped them resist the crumbling effect of the tide? Was there any man among them big enough to roll it back? If any of them thought of appealing to Tyrone in that crisis they would have found him otherwise engaged. He was playing the passionate fool with a woman.

7

The girl whom Tyrone wanted as his third wife was, of all the desirable women in Ireland, Mabel Bagenal. She was the daughter of his bitterest enemy Sir Nicholas Bagenal, formerly the Queen's Marshal, and the sister of the present Marshal, Henry Bagenal. He had begun to court her only four months after the death of his second wife (in January, 1591). He had often seen her, when he visited The Newry on business, watching her with interest grow from a slip of a child into an attractive young woman. He was now forty-one and she was twenty, but women married early in those days, and the men early and often, and only the toughest women like the pirate-queen Grania O'Malley reversed positions with the much-marrying men. Mabel was attracted enough by Tyrone to trouble little about the difference in their ages; he offered, in any case, what youth could not, the flattery of his rank and the suavity of his greater experience, and she might well be allured by him, who allured many women in his life time, and could hold himself nobly before her as one far better born and bred than she. He was now at the height of his physical powers, and when he put on his courtier's costume, his crimson jazerine gold-studded jacket, and his lined cloak, or if she saw him in glinting mail, with his scarlet spade-beard and his broad shoulders on horse-back it is no wonder that she was fascinated. And when he played on her that charm to which so many succumbed, and she thought of herself as countess, and taking his gift of golden chains thought of herself as rich, it is no wonder that she felt also that she would be cherished and happy with him. As she ought to have been, and would have been had she been as intelligent, experienced and cultivated as he.

He was absurdly indulgent to her at first, and agreed to marry her according to the rites of her own Church, and although he was a Gael and she was an Englishwoman those early years with Sidney and Leicester seemed likely to bridge that difference of outlook also. But how can she have understood what it really meant to live according to Gaelic ways, and may he not have begun to forget how rude they were? She, poor girl, can only have understood when she found herself among his kernes and gallowglasses, his churles and mistresses, and all the rough ways of the wild-wood. The girl was, one must presume, numbed at first, and then horrified, and then furious. But to expect them both to foresee all this is to expect the sort of considering wisdom that does not thrive in the atmosphere of a wild infatuation. He had no doubts. He spent money like water to add to the comforts of his castle, ordering things direct from London to deck his home to the taste of his future English girl-bride. When it all broke into pieces he was pained and at a loss, and so bland about the reason for it—merely 'because I affected two other gentlewomen'—that it is plain that he had simultaneously begun to fall in love with the native life without in the least realizing it. (It is a curious detail that Turlough O'Neill had once been an ardent suitor for Mabel's aunt and came with offers of twenty English servants and six gentlewomen who would wait on her. He had gone back to the hills with a flea in his ear when her father told him that he would rather see her burned.)

Henry Bagenal did not, naturally, dare to speak like that to the Earl of Tyrone, although he hated the very idea and when the thing happened and she was irrevocably married he swore to high Heaven in his rage to think that his 'honest blood,' that had so often been spilt in repressing this rebelly race, should be mingled with a pack of traitors like the O'Neills. For the moment Bagenal put him off with fair words. But Tyrone was impatient and came again and again. He came six times in his eagerness to have the girl until in the end Bagenal had to be open about his dilemma.

Marriages of this sort were almost within the Royal benefice to allow or disallow. The Queen might object strongly to such an alliance between a colonist and a Gaelic noble. He declared (at any rate so Tyrone alleged later) that he himself liked the idea but that he must consult the Privy Council. Tyrone agreed so far; but then, for precaution's sake, Bagenal had Mabel shifted away from the Newry to the house of his brother-in-law, Sir Patrick Barnewall, some nine miles from the city of Dublin. The separation aroused all Tyrone's passions. He rode to Barnewall's house, swept away the girl's remaining defences, left the house secretly betrothed to her, and then kept constantly writing to her to elope with him. It was midsummer, and in the warmth and colour and quiet of it the romance flowered. In June, like any medieval lover parading his power before his lady, he took one flying foray at Turlough, whom he sent limping home with a bullet in his shoulder and a wound in the small of the back from a horseman's staff. Then he could wait no longer. He had been a whole six months without a wife, he had chosen his bride—and only this stupid lout of a brother stood in the way. It is possible that the sister enjoyed the romantic wooing, and may even have connived at it. If she did not she made an exceedingly poor duenna.

The lover rode down, first week of August (1591), to Barnewall's house to dine. With him he took six English gentlemen; close friends of his. It was a pleasant dinner, and Mabel was there, smiling and glancing across the table. After dinner his friends amused the company, and he encouraged them with his laughter. Then Mabel went aside to chat with one of his friends, named William Warren. They walked in the courtyard, in the pleasant coolness of the August night, and then she was suddenly gone—on a pillion behind Warren, and they were hurling at a gallop through the night to a rendezvous. Later Tyrone followed them with two serving men and the four men and the girl were off again galloping south along the coast road until they had come, at Drumcondra, within view of Dublin, to the house of his fellow-conspirator, Warren. Drumcondra, now a suburb of the city, was then three miles outside the walls. From there he sent one of his men to the palace of the Bishop of Meath, Thomas Jones. Jones, who was of course a Protestant Bishop, was thrown into dismay by this entreaty to marry 'in honest sort' an eloping couple with such influential connections. He finally agreed for the sake of the girl's reputation which was, in any event, thoroughly compromised by now.

At once the despatches began to fly to and from London, and it was not Papa Bagenal who had to be appeased now but Papa Government. Tyrone carefully told Burghley all about it, begging him to believe no sinister stories he should hear, especially such as he was likely to hear from the Bagenals. And Bagenal duly sent in his charges on the very next day. The Earl had taken advantage of his sister's youth; he himself had had no complicity whatever in the affair; he could not describe his grief; he would, for the future, hold a far more vigilant eye on the Earl than ever before; he made it quite clear that he was not allying himself with the Earl; and to prove it he refused to give the girl her dowry—that precaution was to breed more bad blood between the two families; lastly he declared that the marriage was bigamous since Tyrone had never been properly divorced from his first wife, the daughter of Brian MacPhelim, so that in effect his sister had been seduced. Indeed Bagenal expressly asserted at one point (August 13, 1591, to the Lord Treasurer) that the girl was pregnant when married. Tyrone counter-asserted (October 22, 1591) that, at the time of the abduction, he 'did not once touch her' until after the marriage. On this what are we to make of the statement of the Bishop of Meath (Oct. 22, 1591)? 'I resolved chiefly in regard of the danger wherein the gentlewoman's credit and chastity stood, to perfect that knot which they themselves before had knit, and did accordingly . . . celebrate that marriage. . . .' It is to be noted, in passing, that after her marriage, Mabel became a Catholic.

The government need not have doubted Bagenal. He pursued his sister's 'seducer' all through that autumn of 1591. He had the Lord Deputy up to Monaghan for a formal enquiry. He entered his enemy's country with horse and foot and forced him to attend. He kept him cooling his heels outside the town while the Deputy inquired thoroughly into the alleged bigamy. He made him bring in the official from Armagh who knew of the earlier divorce; 'a silly old man of ninety-seven.' He made him bring in the Archdeacon and Registrar of Armagh and they cross-examined these men. And however Tyrone fumed and cursed he had to obey. He was still fuming eighteen days later, because Bagenal was still unsatisfied. He was not permitted to go until he produced the actual sentence of divorce, confirmed under its seal, and proved beyond argument that both the legal divorce and the annulment by the Church were in order. Back in his castle, beside his bride, he might well write to the Privy Council of 'the discontentment which I feel and the wrongs which I endure at Mr. Marshal Henry Bagenal's hands.' It was just another of those prolonged interferences with his private life that finally drove him beside himself.

The young Countess was happy that winter in the first thunder of his passion and her own astonishment at the apparent triumph of her adventure; and while the furnishings were coming in from London, and she was arranging them, and he watched and admired, she must have felt the innocent illusion of every woman who marries a great man—that his desire is her sufficiency, and his sexual weakness is her intellectual power, and that the brilliance which she reflects from his adoring love is her's alone. She was bringing a new grace into his life, and all through it she would exercise a happy influence and an unflagging power. It is the largesse of greatness to give to everybody it touches this sensation of an increase of personal strength. Anne Boleyn must have felt with Henry VIII just what Mabel Bagenal felt with Tyrone during the first few months of their love-making.

Then, whether suddenly or gradually, she must have realized her isolation in this foreign world of Gaelic Dungannon; seen the slighting looks of the hardy fighting-men; pined in the routine of a life that became more and more uncouth as she became mistress only in the kitchen, and had to prove herself by qualities that she apparently did not possess in any abundance. A woman of tremendous character and intelligence could have made a success of that marriage, so full of incongruity in race and rank and religion. This poor child cannot have brought any great experience of life from that close-fisted, prudish, petit-bourgeois house at the Newry. And he, although he succeeded better than any Irishman before him in disciplining his 'wild Irish' nature, was at bottom a man of gusty passions and hot blood out of the epic world. He could hardly be expected to give up his high-born women living in the same house as his wife, manners old as the lovers of Queen Maeve and the courtesans of Brian Boru, and all the swift life of the border-raider; and this inexperienced English girl may finally have seemed to his humiliated eyes nothing but a silly little weakling when he realized that his passion had betrayed his pride into a mesalliance, and he saw the contemptuous looks of his own full-blooded women and heard the sniffs of neighbouring amazons like O'Donnell's Ineen Duv—she whom the Four Masters describe as a woman 'like the mother of Machabees who joined a man's heart to a woman's thought.' On her side his wife must have been utterly broken when she saw at last, quite clearly, to what a rude life she had surrendered herself, with its lapses into cloaked assassination and plain murder; so that when she refused to countenance his mistresses any longer, acknowledged to herself that she hated him, fled from him to her brother and laid public complaint against him before the Council, the humiliation was bitter and mutual. Nevertheless it was at Dungannon that she died, so that they must have patched up some kind of reconciliation before the end.

Apart from his own reported words admitting this, we have one clear, sinister glimpse of the girl's life with him. It takes us forward two years to the early summer of 1593, when he was trying to keep Maguire out of serious war with the English: (see page 134), and concerns the murder of a clansman named Phelim M'Turlough O'Neill. Phelim was under the Queen's protection at the time, and Tyrone had demoted him in favour of certain O'Hagans. In his trouble Phelim came up to the Bann river where Tyrone was encamped at Crannock and sought an interview; but Tyrone was conferring with Maguire during that weekend and would not speak with him until after Mass and dinner on the Sunday. Then they met, and apparently came to no agreement because they parted in an unfriendly way—the Earl stepping into his cott beside Mabel, and Phelim saying piteously, 'Well, God be with you, My Lord,' and Tyrone turning his back on him and saying, ominously, 'May God be at defiance with you until night!' The O'Hagans who had been watching this conference with a natural uneasiness now came about Phelim

M'Turlough. They stood and watched the Earl being rowed up-river, and put their arms about him, and soothered him, and coaxed him away into their camp at Crannog, and there at the gate they suddenly fell on him. One slashed off his arm. Another struck him down. Together they finished him off. One of his men ran for the river but they drowned him in it. Two more escaped into the woods and lived to tell the story of the murder.

Tyrone and Mabel had meanwhile reached Portglenone, five miles away, and were followed thither by Hugh O'Gallagher with some evening food.

'Why have you been so long?' asked Tyrone.

'I was seeing the doing of an ill deed,' said Gallagher dourly.

'What is that?'

'The killing of Phelim M'Turlough.'

'And is he killed?'

'Aye.'

'And is Donal Oge killed too?' asked Tyrone—meaning the son of Phelim.

'Aye, both killed and drowned.'

'What became of my shot that went over the river?' then asked Tyrone.

At that (whatever the question may mean) Mabel became excited, and began to weep, and clapped her hands—'sorry, as should seem, of that which happened' said Gallagher, who could not understand the altercation that followed between herself and her husband, for they spoke in English. Tyrone silenced her hysteria with some vehement speech, and the two rowed away into the dusk. It is the last glimpse we get of Mabel Bagenal. She died two years later, in December, 1595.[8]

8

Tyrone had abducted Mabel Bagenal in August, 1591. The honeymoon was well over and the two were settling down to the routine of life when something happened in Dublin that snapped him back sharply into the stress of political affairs. Red Hugh O'Donnell escaped from his prison in Dublin Castle on Epiphany morning, or as the Gaelic chronicler called it *Nottlaic Stell*, or Christmas of the Stars, 1592. It was his second effort to escape. He had been recaptured in Wicklow on the first occasion and brought back to his cell. This time with two of the sons of the famous Sean O'Neill, Henry and Art, he crept through a privy—

one of those chutes which blandly opened on the outer walls of the castles of the day—and slipped down a rope into the castle ditch, or moat. There he was met by one of those O'Hagans who were so close to Tyrone—the O'Hagans had fostered him; the closest bond known in Gaelic society—and the four slipped into the city streets. Without difficulty they passed through the gates. Henry O'Neill went his own way. The others struck off towards Blessington, west of the snow-covered Wicklow mountains, and there they began to climb. They were making for Glenmalure, that deep cleft in the heart of the mountains held by Tyrone's friend (and later ally) Fiach MacHugh O'Byrne.

From Dublin to Glenmalure, even to-day, over good roads, is a very heavy march—by that route it must be forty miles or more. Then, in deep winter, with the snow falling heavily, over rough bye-roads and slight goat-tracks lost in the snow, it was a superhuman test and Art O'Neill failed under it. He had grown fat in jail, and had hurt his leg in dropping down from the privy, and was soon being dragged along by Red Hugh and O'Hagan. After a night and a day of this agony they finally managed to reach a *col* under the mountain now called Table Mountain: beyond, to the south, was Glenmalure. The final stage would be down an impassable declivity into the Glen where only the sheep had ever gone before. Red Hugh and O'Neill could struggle no further, lay down in the snow to sleep, and sent O'Hagan forward to bring help. When Fiach MacHugh O'Byrne's men arrived they found the two bodies with shrouds of melting hail about them, their scanty clothes frozen to the skin, and every limb apparently lifeless. When they lifted Art O'Neill he died. Red Hugh's tremendous constitution barely saved him. With Tyrone's assistance he was smuggled stage by stage to the North, where he was under the care of his father's doctors until April—he had to have his two big toes amputated. Then his father resigned the chieftainship in his favour (May, 1592); he drove the colonist's garrison from his country, brought back the friars, and defied the Queen. He had suffered unforgettable and unforgiveable miseries in jail, and his heart was blazing for revenge.[9]

9

All men were at the time satisfied that Tyrone had engineered this escape: and there is every reason to believe that he had done so, that it had been in his head a long time, and that he finally managed it by bribery, cunning, and influence. But men were not, as usual, certain as to his motives. It was natural that he should wish to help his relatives and friends, the O'Donnells. It was natural that he should enjoy showing his power. It was even natural that he should relish the discomfiture of the Dublin government which had refused his most earnest appeals to release Red Hugh. But it was also suspected that he had a selfish motive in the affair; that he was as eager, that is, to get hold of the two sons of Sean O'Neill as for the release of Red Hugh O'Donnell. For the sons of Sean had always been his enemies, and it was therefore also natural for him to fear that the Dublin government might some day set them up against him, as he had been set up against Turlough Luineach and Turlough Luineach against him. The death in the snow of Art O'Neill would accordingly have caused him no sorrow; and when Henry O'Neill, the third of the escaping prisoners, arrived in the North he at once seized him and imprisoned him. If these were his motives they rebounded on him—through Red Hugh. In releasing that fiery particle he created for himself a powerful ally, but when a man is working, as Tyrone was all his life long working, with highly combustible materials, the presence of a ball of dancing fire so close to him is embarrassing.

Red Hugh did not, indeed, create any fundamentally new situation for Tyrone. The westward and northward drive of Bingham in Connaught, the whole forward-pushing policy of the colonists, had already created the situation. But Red Hugh accelerated matters so much that the year 1592 threatened to become crucial to Tyrone's career. Neither did Red Hugh 'influence' Tyrone. Intellectually and politically Red Hugh was a babe in arms beside Tyrone, so that one may as easily say that some brilliant soldier like Raleigh influenced Elizabeth, or that any one of his admirals influenced Philip of Spain. But Red Hugh represented Gaelic resistance at its most obstinate and inspiring, fired the imagination of the clansmen as a soldier, and gave the people what the more cold and aloof Tyrone could never give them—the image of a popular hero as rooted in their own traditional life as some flashing figure out of the sagas. They seized on him with delight. They wove him into a legend. They revived old prophecies to dilate on him and their faith in him. They remembered that St. Columcille had been the patron of his people and his family. ('Dearer to me are all the Gael than the men of the world, and dearer the race of Conall than the Gael, and dearer the Family of Lewy than the race of Conall.') They passed around among them the ancient prophecy: 'When two Hughs lawfully and lineally succeed each other as O'Donnells (i.e. Red Hugh and his father Black Hugh) the last Hugh shall be a monarch of Ireland and banish thence all foreign nations and conquerors.' That rise in popular emotion, combined with Red Hugh's lust for revenge, had a practical effect on Tyrone. It brought him directly, by friendship and marriage and alliance, into the heart of a fight which he had hitherto succeeded—at least in outward-seeming—in handling as a matter of great importance, quite impersonal to himself and quite detached from his own affairs. Everything that follows shows him trying to get control of Red Hugh, and to cool the popular feeling which the escape had aroused.

He observed at once that the colonists were already beginning to play upon the hot-headed young man their old policy of Divide and Conquer. He set out to turn that policy to his own ends, by making Red Hugh cognisant of it, and by advising him that the only way to circumvent it was by playing a cautious game in reply. The English plan is stated clearly in the State Paper, i.e. to put his step-brother up against him: 'There is no readier way to cross Red Hugh than . . . to countenance Sir Hugh O'Donnell's son by his *first* wife. For these are the opposite faction against O'Donnell's *second* wife, being Scottish.' (That was Ineen Duv, Red Hugh's mother.) For months Tyrone worked along those lines to awaken Red Hugh to his danger.

At this point the hand of God moved the Catholic bishop Neal O'Boyle to come sailing into Ulster in a fly-boat laden with salt and sedition. At once the clans began to sharpen their swords, Bingham began to roar, the government became proportionately tentative, and the Lord Deputy feeling a little less influential than the Lord God appealed most opportunely to Tyrone to see if he could do something with his kinsman in Tyrconnell. One cannot help being a little flippant about all this because the situation is a juicy morsel of the *Comédie Humaine*. Here is the cautious Tyrone in the middle of his marriage brawl, flanked by his hot-headed kinsman on the west, an angry brother-in-law on the east, an importunate set of officials badgering him on the south, and to his north the tipsy Turlough—one sighs at the mention of it—once more pointing out that the fourth

Michaelmas has come and gone and that he will assuredly die this time rather than give up his beloved lands. The thing might be a French farce of the nineteenth century if so much were not at stake, for the classical figure of the cuckold, though only a cuckold by proxy, plotting revenge for his sister's seduction, now comes forward like a minor character out of Balzac. The month is July. During those long summer nights when Tyrone is wondering how far Red Hugh O'Donnell is going to complicate life for him, Henry Bagenal is poring over the exemplification of Tyrone's grants—listening betimes to the mocking voice of the cuckoo? He appears to the mind as one of those unpleasant supernumeraries to a tragic drama, those slight figures which are necessary only in so far as they pull the lever. As he sits there he is trying to twist the meaning of the grants, plucking at the net to see if he can find revenge in a flaw. Suddenly he believes he has it, and writes joyfully '*In Strictest Secrecy*' to Burghley disclosing a plan whereby 'the service whereof we formerly advised you may be effectuated.' If he is right and, as he thinks, Turlough has the better claim he can 'set down such a plot as may advance both a good revenue to Her Majesty and enlarge the borders of the Pale even unto the very heart and strength of the rudest parts of Ulster.' What the crafty young fox proposed was that when Sir Henry Sidney granted certain lands to Turlough it should be understood that what he granted was a freehold for life, so that as long as Turlough lived Tyrone's patent was null and void. Even if the London lawyers were stupid enough to disagree with him, Bagenal palpitated, the grant was at any rate a Royal promise unless 'other composition can be made between them for the best advancement of Her Majesty's service.'

How beautifully the plot of this farce fits together. Assuredly, at any other time, the Lord Deputy might have listened to Bagenal. At this particular moment he needs Tyrone's assistance too badly, and Bagenal is brushed aside. Identically, Turlough, who had been complaining against Red Hugh, and has now begun to complain against Tyrone, has the ground cut from under his feet by both, when Tyrone apparently succeeds at last in persuading O'Donnell to peaceful and loyal ways. Even Bingham is discomfited, and after raging against the 'beggarly Burkes,' and the 'bagging sept of the Burkes,' and crying that they will now have Red Hugh's Scots to assist them, has to growl his hopes that Red Hugh is going to 'make a show of dutifulness' and keep them all obedient. At the centre of the stage, Tyrone tantalizes us with every kind of suspicion as to his true motives and secret thoughts. He is, indeed, only just beginning, this summer of 1592, aged forty-two, to take his rightful place in the centre of the stage—and that we should be mystified by him when all the others are so clear-cut is the apex of the comedy.

Listen to him. 'I travelled into O'Donnell's country at the hazard of my life . . .' (Note that O'Donnell was his kinsman and was son of his best friend and ally.) '. . . and have brought him hither to Dundalk to submit himself and do duty to Her Most Excellent Majesty and I promise you I will do my best to persuade him to allegiance and duty. And if he shall not be directed by my counsel and advice herein I will be as ready to serve against him and scourge him as any man shall be in this kingdom, beseeching you so think of me and not believe every report that is written against me, before it is examined and found true. For I acknowledge myself most bound to Her Majesty for her great goodness and bounty extended towards me, so will I never do anything that may offend Her Highness.' Heaven knows what heated arguments went on at that meeting between Tyrone and this young man less than half his age. Ineen Duv would have been there, with her red-hot tongue and her relentless hatred of the English who had murdered her kin on Rathlin Island. The father of the two rival lines of sons would have been strongly on Tyrone's side—all for peace and postponement. Hot blood, racial hate, the thirst for revenge, the desire for power, all the pride of youth were against the Earl—and yet . . . he won out. On the very next day (August 1st, 1592), in the afternoon, he made good his word. The Deputy and a great assembly of the townspeople waited in the church at Dundalk, in the afternoon, and to them Tyrone led in this other red-headed captain from the mountains. O'Donnell delivered his humble submission to the colonists; he spoke of the misdemeanours he had committed—chief of which, no doubt, was his insolence in escaping from jail; he made a great show of sorrow over it all, swearing that he would in future live a more dutiful life; and when the Deputy asked him if he would promise all this on oath he most willingly allowed himself to be sworn. 'All of which,' said the Lord Deputy, 'I pray God he may faithfully perform.'

That submission crowned the farce. But even then, when it is virtually impossible to believe that O'Donnell meant a single word that he spoke, Tyrone leaves us in considerable doubt. We may be certain that he definitely wished O'Donnell to remain overtly loyal, and there is no reason for deciding that he did not wish him to remain explicitly loyal. For the first, even if—in the face of the absence of all evidence—he were at that very moment contemplating throwing off all English support and connection, the one word in his mind would be Time—and his hand on young O'Donnell's arm; so that it would be natural for him to wish O'Donnell wise enough and patient enough to keep for some years close to his promises. But may he not have wished much more than that? May he not have wished that O'Donnell would follow his own course and become the makings of a powerful Anglo-Gaelic Earl?

The fact is that this is the course which the O'Neill who went to England as a child and returned from it as a young man has followed *for twenty-five long years.* Which is, indeed, why his story has so far been so reticent, matching the quiet with which he has pursued his own personal ambitions. There have, indeed, been many incidents calculated to discourage him from loyally following the course marked out for him, but no man in his position could hope to avoid such checks entirely, and there can hardly have been a week in the life of any of the English or Anglo-Irish lords when they had not to bear some such snub or discouragement, and he had so far suffered nothing that one can describe as unbearable.

That, however, raises the whole question of the kind of life that any such proud and gallant young man would have visualized for himself at the beginning of his career, and from time to time weighed in the balance. He had seen the example of Cecil, Leicester, Sidney, Burghley, Essex, and others, and thought, no doubt, that to be as they were must be a great deal; and even after he surmounted the chilling experience of the realization that rank circumscribes as much as it bestows, those examples would still inspire him. Unfortunately no Anglo-Gaelic earl could ever live quite as these men did. For the model of *his* life could not be Burghley, or Leicester, or Essex, or Sidney, but every badgered harassed, exhausted, petty tool of imperial expansion from Bagenal to Bingham, or Baltinglass to Desmond. He could never be a true earl. He would always be and live like some provincial Mayor. Leicester's people were content as he was content, because he was a symbol of the greatness of England and her traditional ways of life. A Sidney could be admired and loved. An Anglo-Gaelic earl would always invite some suspicion both from his own people and from his English masters. So that, as he must ultimately have discovered, the choice was not a clear one between office and dignity on the one hand, and on the other the risky, attractive life of the old Gaelic raider, king by the ancient law and his own muscle, admired of his people, sung of his poets, part of the ancient, affectible, beloved Irish world whose thousand and one familiar touches would caress from dawn to dark like the softness of the rain and the balm of the wind and the damp, cosy moss of the mountains. Yet the very dubiety that such a weighing-up of pros and cons would provoke in him could not have tended, without greater cause, to do anything except postpone decisions indefinitely; and knowing how miraculously long the conspiratorial Irishman can refuse to admit consciously that which his soul intends, that which is his appetite, his motive, his passion, his unacknowledged law, we do right to be especially slow to suspect any decision in this most cautious and secretive man.

That holds even though it is also true that Tyrone came nearer than almost any other Irishman in history to the cold pragmatism of the Renaissance mind, and was miles apart from that other sort of Irishman who is all impulse and instinct, full of capricious genius, brilliant at improvisation, but constantly oscillating between the definite Yea and No. It holds because his caution offset his deliberation, and his decision was constantly checked by his prudence, and in the end it was his instinct rather than his intelligence that threw the dice. And whatever we may decide about his secret intentions, their nature and their hour, this we must always remember with the greatest sympathy—that the agent, whether it was Maguire advancing to meet Tyrone's fate on his borders, or Red Hugh eagerly rushing to embrace it, were blithe in their irresponsibility, whereas he alone took the tragic sense of the drama forced on him. That distinguishes the behaviour of Tyrone and of Red Hugh in this ceremony of submission at Dundalk in 1592. O'Donnell, with his loyalty on his sleeve, was patently buffooning; only by buffooning could so young and inexperienced a man have gone through an otherwise profoundly humiliating performance. For Tyrone the thing was a matter of life and death.

10

In Gaelic legend the 'King of Spain's Daughter' is a phrase as evocative as The Sleeping Beauty or the Queen of Sheba. It was appropriate that she should turn up in a spy's story just now, when the air was filling with legends in which rumour about Spanish aid freely amplified the reality of increasing contacts with the Spanish King. This year (1592), according to the Irish spy James O'Crean, she was travelling into France 'in a wagon,' to her marriage with the Duc de Guise. The king, her father, was with her, and in his company was the Irish Catholic Primate, M'Gauran (later to fall fighting on the Maghery, or Great Plain of Connaught), and as the cavalcade rumbled its way through Languedoc—so the story develops—the Primate and the King conversed. How much of this is somebody's imagination running wild we cannot precisely tell. Certainly the King of Spain did not visit France, and the King of Spain's daughter did not marry the Duc de Guise. Possibly either O'Crean or the Primate embroidered fantastically on the fact that, in the autumn of 1590, the League had offered the throne of France to the Infanta, who, it was proposed, should marry the young Duc de Guise: actually, nothing came of the proposal. All that is certain is that Primate M'Gauran did make his way, by the usual secret routes, into Drogheda; that he was in Ulster for the Christmas of 1592; and that he was soon in conclave with seven bishops, composing letters to Philip and the Pope. He told his eager clergy how two armies would be sent the next summer, one to England, the other to Ireland, and how the Irish army would land in Scotland and cross to Ulster, so that all that was needed was some great man to be the leader or general of the Rising that would naturally follow. The full report of this secret meeting of a new junta of the Catholic League was carried hot-foot to Ballymote to George Bingham, and passed on from 'my brother George' to Richard Bingham, who passed it on to the government. Rumours and reports followed pell-mell. Monaghan spoke of 'a monstrous exploit intended.' Bingham cursed O'Donnell and Maguire as his province's worst neighbours. The Lord Deputy definitely reported that a 'combination' existed in Ulster, and Bagenal inevitably declared that the Earl of Tyrone was about to revolt with O'Donnell and Maguire. Tyrone was summoned to Dublin, and he refused to come.

It may be a mere coincidence that we hear, just at this point, the second unguarded sentence from the secret heart of Tyrone. (We overheard him, at the time of the Armada, upbraiding O'Donnell for betraying the Spanish refugees.) The English pursuivant appeared so frequently before him with messages from Dublin that he cried out in Irish: 'By the Son of God I'd rather be dead than be looking at you running to me every second day in your cursed little jacketeen of red.' The pursuivant dutifully reported this 'traitorous' speech and the Dublin officials, in passing it on to London, remarked with a bland surprise that as this was the regular uniform of all messengers they could not quite see the Earl's point. However Tyrone, true to his methods, and whatever his exasperation, took no chances with these spies and informers, for he wrote to Essex of his grief that anybody could possibly suspect him, begged him to present his letters to the Privy Council, and asked permission to visit London, where he might have a better hope of clearing himself of these constant, ridiculous accusations of disloyalty.

The spies had reported accurately enough in general; if not in regard to him. The priests were on the march once more, and that new enlarging ideal of national service, under the only Roman tradition that Ireland ever knew, was beginning to weave its spells again, to bind the broken parts of Irish life into the double crusade. For one, James O'Hely Archbishop of Tuam went all through the country consulting with the chieftains and the Catholic bishops, speaking sometimes in public, sometimes in secret. Nowhere did he meet with a rebuttal; the chieftains had exhausted themselves in trying to appease the English; the bishops looked only for Spanish aid; the anger of ten years of suppression broke like a lanced boil. But the country was feverish. It needed more blood-letting. The Binghams in Connaught, the suppression of Monaghan, the threats to Maguire, the pitiless aftermath of the Desmond revolt had all created a fever; and that was the picture of Ireland given by Bishop O'Hely, as from the Primate and Red Hugh, to Philip and the remnants of the Desmond exiles in Spain. More—they were warned that if there was to be a confederacy 'it would be of much importance if the King would order a friendly letter to be sent to the Earl of Tyrone, called O'Neill, *that he may enter into the confederacy publicly, seeing that he belongs to it already in secret*, assuring him that your Majesty's aid will not be wanting.' The English got all this from the dubious spy O'Crean. A much more circumstantial account came from Patrick M'Art M'Mahon, the English-appointed sheriff of Monaghan, who reported that in the presence of Tyrone several men of the MacMahons, Maguires, and O'Neills took an oath to aid the Spanish—incited thereto by the Primate M'Gauran. M'Mahon had this from his own uncle, the Earl's own son-in-law, Henry Oge O'Neill, married to Tyrone's daughter. Yet a third report, that of Patrick McKenna, spoke of a secret confederacy, but he did not incriminate Tyrone, and he declared that some of those whom M'Mahon gave as present at the meeting were not there at all. Bishop O'Hely meanwhile failed to bring back the King's reply. His ship foundered on the return journey in 1594, while the conspirators waited for him in vain.

It is impossible to believe that Tyrone really did conspire with the priests and his neighbours as the spies alleged. No doubt he was constantly meeting them, and was privy to all their thoughts and most of their plans. But that he would trust himself to a clear conspiracy is a very different matter. Nobody could trust, or even credit these men. Take their charges one by one. The spy Crean's report is dated January, 1593. On June 30th, after they had had ample time to sift his charges thoroughly, the Lord Deputy and the Privy Council admitted that they had not sufficient ground to proceed against Tyrone for being in any foreign conspiracy. The other reports are dated well after the event—in April. M'Mahon had his story at second-hand; at the examination was contradicted by two of his main witnesses; had had a quarrel over the stealing of hogs with his alleged informant—whom he names as one of the conspirators; was a rival for power to another whom he also named as a conspirator; and is finally contradicted by the third informant, M'Kenna, as to the presence of Tyrone at these meetings. Even if Bishop O'Hely actually did tell the Spanish exiles that Tyrone was secretly part of the new confederation the long, long hesitations and distrusts of Spain are alone a warning to us against being any more credulous than Philip II when confronted by optimistic accounts by eager Irish ambassadors. The chief interest of the incident, coming so soon after Tyrone's good offices with Red Hugh, is that it emphasizes again the increasing insecurity in which he lived.

II

But, whatever about Tyrone, Maguire and the other border-captains had no choice but to fight.

And here it is not entirely pointless to consider what Tyrone would have done with his life had he been born a minor chieftain like Maguire. He was, it is true, a man who was, if not the creature of circumstance, certainly enlarged by it, and if we remove him from his circumstances we are simply dealing with another man. That is always the futility of the 'If I were . . .' hypothesis. But the point in putting the question is, first, to emphasize the inevitability of Maguire's resistance to the aggression coming up from Connaught, since Tyrone, or O'Donnell, or Desmond would have done the same in his place; and, secondly, to annotate the difference between Tyrone's dilemma and that of every other man in Ulster.

These men were driven—they had no choice but to follow their instinct, even if it shipwrecked them. The whole course and composition of their blood, their natural passion, led them where they were and there was no alternative to deflect their headlong drive—or no practical alternative, since any composition that they might have made with their enemies could not, in the nature of things and in their own nature, have worked. 'They went out to battle and they fell,' but there was no 'revolt against the despotism of fact' in their fall. It was a recognition of the actual nature of things, and the impulse was not something factitious, or trivial, or wilful; it was a tragically heroic impulse since the alternative offered them by the English would have been not merely foolish since it could not work. but base. Their tragedy lay in the fact that each one of them fought a hopeless, isolated fight, however courageous, and none of them had the intelligence to hammer out the native alternative of a Confederation. Whereas Tyrone, with just as powerful an impulse as they, had in addition the stature of the man to whom chance gives just barely sufficient opportunity to rise above the blind fatality of less intelligent men if he has the strength of will to exploit it. His dilemma, then, was between his arrogance and his prudence, since for him there was an alternative of sorts; between self-confidence and self-interest; between his belief in himself and his intelligent knowledge of the magnitude of an English war. How restless he must have been with all these neighbours of his, how irritated, even how angry, since they were all the time pressing his final decision on him!

He must have felt that way about Maguire's gallant defence of the Gap of the Erne. There Maguire was not merely holding

Bingham but driving him back into Connaught. At Tulsk near dawn on midsummer-eve he came up on Bingham out of the mist over the plain of Roscommon, routed his horse, took a great booty, and burned his brother George's town of Ballymote to the very door of the castle. Bingham, who always exaggerated his victories and the wickedness of his enemies, blamed the defeat on the Lord Deputy who had guaranteed a general safe-conduct to Maguire; that 'outrageous traitor and notorious faith-breaker.' He further complained that he had been prohibited from raiding across the Erne into Tyrconnell after Red Hugh and his gang of traitorous bishops. Elizabeth loyally backed up her bulldog and decided to let her Deputy go as soon as she found a successor. The result was a feud, typical of the times, between the Deputy in Dublin and the soldier in the field—just the sort of situation that a more astute and influential man than Maguire would have been able to exploit. For the Deputy (it was now Fitzwilliam), here began to play soft with Maguire through sheer spite for Bingham, and if ever after Bingham even dared to mention the difficulties of his campaign Fitzwilliam would scrawl across the despatch such satirical remarks as, 'This is written with less confidence!' or, 'How little he is able to perform the offer he made to overthrow Maguire!' And here again we see clearly the difference between a Tyrone and a Maguire, for Tyrone did seize on this rivalry between the two English officials and began to exploit it. He agreed to act as an intermediary with Maguire as he had previously done with Red Hugh. What followed illuminates his critical position at that date, July 1593.

The proposal to bring Maguire to a parley arose for the first time on July 10th. On the 27th Tyrone said that he had persuaded Maguire. On August 1st the Lord Deputy gave Maguire twenty days to come in, and he ordered Bingham to be ready to attack him if he had not come in by then. At the end of July Tyrone wrote that Maguire had now sworn that he would come in by September 15th. The Lord Deputy leashed Bingham and waited. On September 1st Tyrone wrote that Maguire was now saying that he was afraid that some of his men might remain behind him undispersed, and if they raided while he was with the Lord Deputy his safe-conduct would lapse. Could he, therefore, have yet until November to gather in his outlying bands?

Now the traditional explanation of this sort of thing is that Tyrone was employing delaying tactics; an explanation which is part of the old theory that Tyrone had decided years before to throw off his allegiance. Yet when a general employs 'delaying tactics' the implication is that he intends to attack when he is ready, and in this case it should be presumed that Tyrone was proposing to attack either the Deputy or Bingham. Tyrone did attack, but the man he attacked was Maguire. The explanation on the surface of the facts is sufficiently satisfying. For reasons best known to himself he was trying to hold back Maguire, and in all probability at least a main part, if not the whole, of his reason was that he simultaneously wished to keep in good odour with his masters and to save that general peace without which everybody, including himself and Maguire, was likely to lose. Now, three days after Tyrone had promised the government that his man, Maguire, merely wished a respite until November, Maguire had begun to raid again. We may well imagine Tyrone's fury. He hurried down to Dublin to defend himself for the hundredth time against the medley of charges that naturally followed, with Bingham at his heels roaring out that 'Ulster has for many years been the sink of all revolts: the Earl of Tyrone is the chief rebel and Maguire himself might be suppressed with two hundred men.' To prove it, within a week of Maguire's contumacious raids, Bingham ordered a general hosting of all loyal men to meet east of the Erne and attack Maguire. Tyrone cursed but had to obey implicitly. At the foot of the mountain of Slieve Beagh, on the Fermanagh side, Tyrone found himself shoulder to shoulder with Bagenal and Bingham, driving westward along the east of the lake as far as Assaroe against Maguire. There is no need to exaggerate his tempest of emotions during that march, but the annalists understate them almost comically: 'It was not pleasing to the Earl of Tyrone to go on this expedition. However he had so much dread of the English that he was obliged to obey them.' One thing he must have pondered bitterly —how hard it would be for any man to control these undisciplined sub-captains, to canalize their courage, to weld them into any really unfriable combination.

The *comédie humaine* declares itself here once again, as it so often does when Tyrone is in a particular dilemma with his associates or neighbours. Conspiracies and conspirators always have that element of the sub-comic, the derangement of the normal, the atmosphere of the masked ball where nobody knows anybody else. Here is Fitzwilliam grinning sourly at

Bingham's honest promises to 'put against the traitor Maguire, God assisting me, what force I have,' and his appeals for the money to do it; and as he grins he scrawls on the margin. 'But he promised to do it without further charge!' There is Maguire, driving his cows before him into the wilds, and entreating peace. Here is Tyrone choking down his angers and playing all his charms on tough old Bingham, not without some effect. 'I see no reason,' growls Bingham, 'but to hold a very good and honourable report of the Earl of Tyrone.' But that it is uphill work is patent from Bingham's qualifying remarks on that 'good opinion.' 'Her Majesty and the State hath set him up and the State must uphold him or he will fall. And besides he is wise and well-experienced in the course of things. But all men of judgement here and such espials and beggars as I emply into Fermanagh do wholly assure me that Maguire doth nothing without the Earl's advice and consent, and that the Earl may at his own pleasure rule both Maguire and Red Hugh O'Donnell. This is so common and avouched with such ground of knowledge that I wish it to be foreseen and you to have care of it. . . . And yet,' he concludes characteristically, 'they are all together but a heap of ragged beggars and their numbers exaggerated by untrue reports!'

The comedy develops a few days after that report, behind which we may see Tyrone, Bingham, Maguire and Fitzwilliam all watching one another like spies, flattering one another like courtiers, and betraying one another like trollops; for Bingham now sends off a courier post-haste to report that Maguire, Red Hugh, and Tyrone have been seen conferring (of all places) on top of a mountain. 'Great treasons are like to follow!' Tyrone, just as eagerly on his side, is warning the Lord Deputy, for his life, not to trust Red Hugh, and the Lord Deputy, on his side, and on the very same day, writes a most polite and loving message to the same Red Hugh to the tune of 'We greet you well . . . our very good lord Tyrone . . . we perceived how clear you stood . . . we thought it not amiss to signify . . .'—and so on. The rage that this sort of thing produced in Bagenal's mind we shall see in a moment.

In this welter of mutual deception and suspicion all that is clear is Bingham's straight-cut fighting attack. He met Maguire's men at Belleek and won what he calls hopefully if not with accuracy, 'a splendid victory.' Tyrone also eagerly reported his own share in the battle against the 'enemies,' how he put them to flight, slew a round three hundred of them, and was himself wounded: though, as he says to his Queen with gallantry, 'glad it was my chance to have a print upon my body of this day's service.' It might seem that no man could do more than spill his blood for his friends to prove his loyalty. But no Gaelic lord was ever lightly trusted The spies' reports continued to accumulate against him in Dublin.

A lieutenant of Sir George Bouchier picked up a talkative trull who revealed, or alleged to reveal, what lay behind those earlier tactics of Tyrone; she said that Tyrone had been telling Maguire to avoid war until the Queen's forces were dissolved. Unfortunately the lady, in the traditional mode, vanished during the night, and could not be produced in proof. A loyal Maguire, Conor Roe, repeated the story of the meeting on the mountain. One James MacManus said that he had asked Maguire why he had gone to war, and that Maguire said that Tyrone had pricked him on to it. Bagenal also got busy, infuriated by Dublin's credulity; he sent in a private report to Bingham, marking with a shamrock-leaf, for Bingham's benefit, every point in his public report where a suppression was annotated by these secret notes that only Bingham was to see. Here he declared that all through the night before the attack at Belleek Tyrone's men had sat on horseback close to his camp; and, whether it is on this information or not, even the Lord Deputy reported to London that Tyrone had made every possible excuse to be gone the day before the battle. In vain Tyrone protested, repeated his great services, proclaimed his eagerness to do his duty, cried out in his grief at being suspected. The Lord Deputy and Council formally rebuked him for 'lingering the service.' It was one more snub to be added to the long list that his pride was finding it increasingly hard to bear.

12

Tyrone's destiny was now at his heels, and it becomes increasingly plain that men felt generally that he would sooner or later be dragged into the conflict. Maguire was still in the field and more and more Scots were coming in weekly to assist him. The English were pressing hard since only Enniskillen now remained between them and the open road into Ulster. If they pierced this Gap, O'Donnell would have to fight, and then, Tyrone realized, he would come face to face with his final choice. His messengers brought him constant reports from the Lakes of the Erne. There, in downpouring rains, fowlers, falcons, and falconets of brass were on their way to clear the islands lying in the jungle and swamp about Enniskillen, and boats were building for the assault on the island castle. Captain Dowdall was in charge of the colonists; with him were Willis, Sentleger, and Fuller. They rowed past Enniskillen until they knocked against the stakes driven in the river. They landed, placed their guns, entrenched themselves, and nine days later they opened the assault. Their main boat was large enough to hold a hundred men, and it was covered over with hides and hurdles against the old-fashioned javelins of the defenders. One of Maguire's own men, Connor O'Cassidy, guided them under the walls of the barbican which rose out of the water. Using their great picks they breached it. The ward of the barbican retreated into the castle, which Dowdall now mined. There were only thirty-six defenders and these quickly surrendered rather than be blown up. The Gap of the North was in English hands. It was a fine, resolute piece of work and the Gaelic captains had made a poor show. They never mastered the art of attacking or defending fortresses, being so sold to the old traditional methods of guerilla warfare that they always abandoned whatever castle or sconce they held at the time of an attack, hating with a claustrophobic terror to have to sit still inside walls and be fired at. So, when Enniskillen fell, O'Donnell immediately wanted to destroy his castle at Ballyshannon, a good twenty miles away. He was only stopped from doing it by 'the Mother of the Machabees,' Ineen Duv.

Enniskillen Castle was taken on February 2nd 1594. Somewhere between that and March 8th Tyrone received a peremptory message from the Lord Deputy to come in with O'Donnell to Dundalk. Both demurred. From that undefined date, probably in February 1594, until February 1595, when there could no longer be any doubt about his intentions, Tyrone carried on a public struggle against his destiny. The first scene in the first act of this drama of irresolution is marked 'March 10th, Sunday.' The Commissioners from the Privy Council were at Dundalk—the Lord Chancellor, Sir Robert Gardiner, and Sir Anthony St. Leger. They had finished dining when Harry Hoveden was announced. Hoveden was an English gentleman with an estate in Ulster, a foster-brother of Tyrone, and his life-long and loyal friend. Tyrone had sent him to explain to the Commissioners that neither he nor O'Donnell dared come to Dundalk for fear of arrest. After all—he developed the theme—Sir John Perrot had been a greater man than he, and where was Sir John Perrot now, thanks to the machinations of the Deputy and Bagenal? (Perrot had died in prison two years before.) Hoveden asked finally on behalf of his friend what the government intended to do against Connaught-men like O'Rourke who were still in the field? The Commissioners were abrupt. They said they would answer all these questions when Tyrone and O'Donnell came in to ask them, and not until then. Hoveden went away. Tyrone chewed on his report.

On Monday morning, (scene two) the Chancellor, Loftus, who was friendly to Tyrone, sent another mutual friend, Garret Moore, to persuade him to his sensible duty. Tyrone received Moore, but he was evasive, and the only tangible thing that Moore brought back was the remark of one of Tyrone's men who had been standing by—the thrust of the usual fatal supernumerary: 'When Sean O'Neill was overthrown Tyrconnell was an enemy but now we are all united together.' But Tyrone sent a milder message after him and the Commissioners spent that evening and most of their tact over it, and sent out Moore again that night to ply his persuasiveness once more: they even authorized him to say, if everything else failed, that the Commissioners themselves would go out to meet Tyrone and persuade him to come in. This showed a virtuous and commendable eagerness to avoid a conflict but took no notice of the fact that it was they, as representatives of the Queen, who were exercising the pressure on Tyrone. It is a sardonic example of the at once comic and tragic helplessness of men beside the monstrous machinery of international politics for which no man is responsible, which none creates, which each man supports, but whose origins in human appetite and ambition so few recognize, not even when in humanity they attempt, as these three men did, to assuage or deflect its more brutal consequences. Accordingly the three write to the Privy Council of the 'great mischief' of a break with Tyrone, the 'great fear of the country,' its 'unwillingness to serve,' the lack of 'preparation to resist his incursion,' and the size of his army, in a characteristic jumble of humanity and opportunism which touches nothing of the first causes beyond their control. On his side Tyrone seemed just as eager to avoid a clash, if it could be avoided; but to retain one's neutrality indefinitely when one is surrounded by warring groups, and when a principle is at stake which deeply affects one's own life is possible only to men of great strength or of slight conscience.

Moore came back at nine in the morning of Tuesday the 12th saying that Tyrone would meet Sir Robert Gardiner at Castletown, Sir John Bellew's house. Gardiner prepared himself, took six others with him, and in the early morning stole secretly by back lanes out of the town. As he rode up to the gate of Castletown he saw no sign of the Earl, until lifting his eyes he saw, about a mile off, a large number of men standing on the hills overlooking the house, and Tyrone with about twenty horsemen, and sixty others running by the stirrups, galloping down towards him—but not towards the house. The cautious Tyrone was taking no chances of an ambush. Gardiner spurred on for a half mile and there halted on a hilltop in full view and sent a messenger forward that he was waiting for Tyrone. The Earl halted his company, and galloped forward.

At once he launched into an attack on the Deputy and Bagenal who, he declared, were plotting for his life. He went off then into a long discourse about his services to Elizabeth. Then he assured Gardiner how much he trusted in him, but as for the Deputy and Bagenal, they were liars and deceivers, and at that very moment, he even declared, they had a secret warrant for his arrest that the Commissioners knew nothing at all about. He began to cry as he recited the great goodness of the Queen, and how kind she had been to him, and he wanted nothing but to be faithful to her, and spend his blood for her, and he would even leave his whole country to her and go away and trust his life to her. Then back to the wickedness of the government officials—saying that the execution of MacMahon of Monaghan five years before, and the invasion of Maguire's country by Willis showed that the same thing was going to happen to all of them. (That at least was true). Then more weepy lamentations began and more protestings until Gardiner grew utterly sick of it and told him bluntly that he had not come to hear this sort of rigmarole but to persuade him to come in to the Deputy. At that Tyrone bade him wait, spurred off and returned with young Red Hugh. He left the two together, watching from a little distance.

O'Donnell could understand English but he spoke very little

of it, so that this interview was not so garrulous. He even suggested that he had better write to the Commissioners, which did not please Gardiner in the least. However Gardiner finally made out that Red Hugh would be advised by Tyrone, and at that a new conversation with O'Neill began and went on for two more solid hours on that windy March-weather hilltop until Gardiner, exhausted, retired to Sir John's house for his dinner.

After dinner, looking out towards the gate he saw a great company waiting, and went out on his horse to meet them. There—all these names should really be heard in their resounding Gaelic forms—were Tyrone and Red Hugh, Cormac O'Neill—Tyrone's brother, Turlough M'Henry O'Neill—Tyrone's half-brother, Sir John O'Dogherty, Sir Art O'Neill, his brother Henry Oge M'Henry O'Neill, the Earl's son-in-law Ever M'Mahon, and many others. The double cavalcade set out in the direction of Dundalk with Tyrone and Gardiner side by side, repeating everything that they had already said and the Gaelic captains watching and trotting in a sullen bunch fore and aft. But into Dundalk Tyrone would not go. He cried that he dare not. He said he was afraid of his life. The horsemen raised their voices and shouted that they would not let him go. In a bunch they halted and argued, and Gardiner shouted to Tyrone:

'I understand you, I understand that Her Majesty is being fooled, I see that all the favours and bounties that you have been prating about are wasted on you. And then I think of the blood of innocent women and children that must be spent because of you. If you have no care for your own duty, think of them at least. Remember that you and only you will be the cause of all their misery.'

Tyrone cried back that it was a question of defending his own life, and at that some of the captains began to drag him away. Gardiner said solemnly,

'I am sorry to perceive your end. And,' turning to the horsemen, 'I have no doubt that when some of these forward fellows see the miserable state to which you will be reduced they will very soon forsake you.' Then he put out his hand, and said good-bye, with 'I am leaving you, now, and *for ever*.'

But at those words 'for ever' Tyrone broke into a fresh wail of tears and besought him not to go,

'Don't let me lose you, Gardiner,' he begged. 'You're my best friend.'

'You won't lose me, Tyrone, until you lose yourself!'

Then they shook hands again, and the horsemen began to growl to Tyrone to hurry away, and Tyrone plucked Gardiner's sleeve as they dragged at him and whispered,

'Send Tom Lee back with me.'

'Very well,' said Gardiner, and told Captain Lee and Moore to go back with Tyrone. The two groups whipped their horses away in different directions.

As the Gaels rode west the whole argument started again with Lee and Moore;[10] Tyrone began his protesting; the two began their persuading; in the end even Tyrone's friends became so disgusted with his behaviour that they beat the two messengers with their staves and told them to be off and that if they ever came back they would be killed. Tom Lee and Garret Moore galloped back to Dundalk and said that all hope of peace was gone.

13

Now, are we asked seriously to believe that all this was a put-up job, an 'act' played out by all those men for the benefit of the English? Or may we not accept, even though with certain reservations, what appears on the surface—that Tyrone, the Commissioners, and Tyrone's lieutenants were pulling in three different ways? Or even, though it oversimplifies Tyrone's state of mind, that the Commissioners and the Gaelic lieutenants were engaged in a tug of war in which Tyrone was the rope? It is, at any rate, out of the question that Tyrone did not sincerely mean some of his protestations, and it is certain that he did want to come to some kind of terms, for that very same evening he rode back into Dundalk under a safe-conduct. He spent the whole of the next day writing out his complaints, and when the Commissioners objected to some phrases he spent a further day on a second draft. When the Commissioners again objected to the phrasing he flew into a temper and, with what seems like a lack of humour, actually told them that if they did not accept his draft he would complain to the Queen.

His complaints boiled down to one main grievance—that his power was being undermined by Bagenal and the Lord Deputy. He had, he pointed out, brought a number of districts under subjection, such as Clandeboy, Kilwarlyn, Killultagh, Orier, Monaghan, and McCartan's country, and what was the result? Immediately Bagenal had put 'base and servile fellows' in charge of these districts and ejected his officers, soldiers, and servants. In short the Deputy and Bagenal were 'knit against him' and they had friends at Court, whereas he had none since the death of Leicester, Sir Francis Walsyngham, the late Lord Chancellor Hatton, and other English friends who would once have taken his part. So he could only humbly beseech that 'it would please Her Highness to remove these base, covetous, and cowardly persons who seek his overthrow.'

Was this approach absolutely frank? If not it was an extremely clever one since it reduced everything to private grievances, ignored the general political unrest, did not touch on Red Hugh, or O'Rourke, or Maguire. If he intended to rebel, the settlement of these grievances would give him time, and might even give him more power. If he did not intend to revolt they cleared him of worse suspicions. One thing is evident. Had the bunch of Gaelic captains back at Castletown known what Tyrone was complaining of in Dundalk they must have scratched their heads to know what all this about Bagenal had to do with them. The Commissioners decided, seemingly, that it had nothing to do with them since they readily concluded a kind of truce with Tyrone.

Whether this list of grievances was a manœuvre or a genuine document it put the government in a quandary. And the thing would be so neat as a manœuvre that one is sorely tempted to regard it as such for the pure delight of analysing its possibilities as a manœuvre. For the government, like us to-day, had no real evidence as to Tyrone's mind: all they had was a profoundly uneasy suspicion. He was holding aloof, and here were his reasons, but that did not make him disloyal; and there could not be a worse situation. As Sir Geoffrey Fenton pointed out from Dublin Castle, on seeing the report of the Commissioners, 'So long as the Earl of Tyrone stands aloof, as he does, he will be a sponge to suck unto him all doubtful parts'; and Fenton's annoyance may be measured by his afterthought about the number of high crimes that have to be passed by without full examination 'for want of a rack in Ireland.'[11]

And others, such as Sir George Carew, Fitzwilliam, the three Commissioners, and more besides, began to send in tremulous, querulous, or furious reports against him. One says that he has 700 horse and 3,000 foot; another that he can command 1,000 horse and 7,000 foot. One day the Deputy asks for a force of

1,500 men to meet him. The next day the figure rises to 2,000 men. A month later it rises to 3,000 men. The most impressive report was Sir George Carew's to Cecil warning him that if Tyrone were driven beyond himself the rebellion would 'cost the Queen more crowns than any that had yet been attempted. . . He is the best man of war of his nation, having had had his education in our discipline and being naturally valiant. . . .'; and having spoken of 'the great desire of the Irish lords to keep justice out that they may tyrannize with absolute power, confiscating both goods and lives at pleasure' he ends up with the well-known passage: 'Like Desmond he should be prosecuted to the utter extermination of himself, his adherents and followers, that the land may be divided amongst the English Colonels. He has evermore had a thirsty desire to be called O'Neale, a name more in price to him than to be intituled Caesar.'

We have become so accustomed, in the history of the English conquest of Ireland, to seeing everything as part of the Patriot myth—with each new Hero rising against the ancient Tyrant—that we are liable to forget that there existed in the sixteenth century an alternative myth, that of the ancient Hero rising against the new Tyrant, or the local feudal knight against the king. These alarums about the great ambitions of the Earl of Tyrone are from the point of view of Elizabeth, just as much part of that general struggle of the monarch for absolute power as part of the conquest of Ireland; and she may well have regarded his subjection entirely as a matter of discipline, seeing the Earl primarily as part of the entire system of which she was the head. This was an aspect of the situation which—as is evident in the wording of his complaints and self-justifications—was quite clear to Tyrone. It was beyond the understanding of his Gaelic followers because it was outside their experience. And it was equally outside the experience of all the native annalists who therefore naturally recorded Tyrone's life in terms of the Patriot Myth, without reference to that other myth which is at the core of so many of Shakespeare's historical and patriotic plays and about which they knew nothing. To remember that is of paramount importance.

Whether a patriot or a feudal knight in revolt against his lawful Queen, what strength could the Earl, in fact, command in this year 1594? There are two estimates of the forces of Ulster which may be quoted, the first drawn up in 1586 by

Bagenal, the second in 1592 by an un-named Irishman for Sir George Carew. The comparison is a striking testimony to the swift growth of Tyrone's power during the years of peace. The total for 1586 is 1,160 horse and 5,780 foot, or a sum of 6,940 men. Six years later there are 2,398 horse and 15,130 foot, or a sum of 17,528 men—an immense force for those days.[12] To these must be added an indefinable number of Scots mercenaries, and Spanish aid remained, as always, incalculable: when it finally arrived it numbered an effective force of 4,000 first-class fighters. The insubordination of Tyrone was, therefore, a serious matter and had he been an English earl his contumacy would have sent a shiver through the Court in London.

14

Further disturbing reports began to tell of the movements of great troops of men by day and by night, and everything pointed to Tyrone although Tyrone himself never appeared. His brother Art raiding about the Newry one night in April (1594) 'in the most cruel manner burned men, women, and children in their houses.' Captain Thomas Henshawe reported a great company of horse, shot, and kerne passing in the night into Maguire's country, where they met Cormac, another brother of Tyrone, and preyed and burned the lands of the loyal Maguire, Conor Roe, sheriff of Monaghan. 'The fort is weak. We have one cask of powder, no match, and little lead. I beseech your Honours to have care of us.' Another relative of Tyrone, Henry Oge M'Henry, his son-in-law, was also reported in command of troops. So was Con Mac-an-Iarla, one of his bastard sons and so were the sons of Turlough McHenry, Tyrone's half-brother. O'Reilly of Cavan complained that Maguire and O'Rourke threatened him on one side and all Tyrone on the other, 'except the Earl's own person.' The trail comes a little nearer home when Shane M'Brian M'Phelim O'Neill informs the government that an O'Hagan came to him in Belfast village to have him become Tyrone's man against the Queen. It comes still nearer when Bagenal reported that Tyrone had now finally possessed himself of all Shane's sons who might have impeded him. And still nearer when Brian McFertagh O'Neill from Castlerea complains that Tyrone has threatened to take his country and make Owen M'Hugh M'Neill lord of it unless he became his man and forsook his prince. (On June 20th Tyrone actually did this, and Burghley dryly commented on the margin of the report, 'A busy officer without warrant.') Worst of all there came to hand an alluring letter from Tyrone to the Earl of Kildare offering to aid him with 2,000 men well appointed if he cared to come up north against their mutual enemy the Marshal.

What, in certainty, did all this amount to? The Lord Deputy's opinion, and he was on the spot, must be respected: that Tyrone and O'Donnell 'have made a strong combination either to remedy the Earl's private griefs, or to have a force in readiness to answer any occasion of the foreigners.' As to which of these Tyrone aimed at the Deputy could not make up his mind, and we are not certain that Tyrone was able to make up his own.

Maguire and O'Donnell proceeded to force the pace. The first warning came from the loyal Maguire, Conor Roe, who declared that the whole of Fermanagh was desolate and all the people fled. But, as with so many of these stories against Tyrone, could he be believed? It was one of the curses of the Deputy's job that the Irish were always exaggerating, if not lying, and this Maguire was notoriously a man without discretion of any kind. But for once the sheriff was not exaggerating. A week later James Ecarsall, the constable of Enniskillen Castle, reported that he was now beseiged. Maguire and O'Donnell had decided to take back the Castle. There was not a scrap of food within twenty miles, for Maguire turned the cows into the corn, and O'Donnell swore that he would not raise the siege until he had eaten the last cow in the country. The two chieftains kept up that siege for two months, from June 8th to August 10th, with 3,000 men, of whom 700 were fusiliers. The colonists could do nothing. They had no army ready. Their northern deputy Tyrone was quarreling with them for those alleged private reasons of his—and once again that excuse of Tyrone's for remaining aloof is so convenient that it might have been expressly designed for the purpose.

O'Neill still refused to be pushed from behind by Maguire and O'Donnell. He continued to keep in touch, however ambiguously, with the government. He informed them loyally in July that Donal Gorm MacDonnell had arrived with 3,000 tartaned Scots. He informed them that these mercenaries had come 'by no local procurement,' which was a lie since he well knew that they came for Red Hugh. He informed them in August that Red Hugh was now craving pardon for his offences. He assured the Lord Deputy, furthermore, that he himself was going to the relief of

Enniskillen, which he did not do and which he had no apparent intention of doing.

Three days later his spies informed him that the Deputy was no longer Fitzwilliam but Sir William Russell (August 11th, 1594). That was bad news because it removed one half of his private griefs: Bagenal was the other half. Worse news followed. By superhuman efforts Russell collected a force of 2,500 foot and 400 horse and decided to send it north-west to the relief of Enniskillen. O'Donnell appealed to Tyrone, and that must have been for any other man the final crisis. If Enniskillen was relieved by such a force as Russell's, at such a juncture, Ulster was prone. ('It was most meet,' said Russell, 'to serve a turn to pierce further into the north.') He was in bad odour. If he assisted O'Donnell, or if he failed to assist Russell, he exposed his hand. And in either case the tide from the west would flood through Tyrconnell and his land would be like the ark on the last remaining rock above the flood. Even yet he did not take the final step.

His brother, with 100 horse and 300 foot came with guns to the help of Maguire and O'Donnell. Maguire and Cormac O'Neill drove south until they saw the clouds of smoke rising from the wasted land where the English were driving northward. They intercepted and harassed the generals in command, Sir Henry Duke and Sir Edward Herbert, to prevent them from wasting the country further, and to see to it that they would not be fresh for the attack on O'Donnell. They followed them relentlessly, harassing them in the typical Irish way, until they came near Enniskillen to a ford on the Erne thereafter called by a Gaelic term meaning the Ford of the Biscuits because all the food that Duke and Herbert were carting with them was scattered on the ground after the battle which ensued there. Duke and Herbert fled with the remnants of their forces west into Sligo. The Gaelic captains could not keep their men from plundering and there was no pursuit. The news of the battle went far and wide; it reached even to Spain, and its moral effect was out of all proportion to its military importance.

15

In all this danger and disaster Tyrone had not lifted a finger to protect the Queen's cause, and no other proof of any Irishman's loyalty had ever been thought worth a penny piece by the English. Their mood was murderous. The year was gone as far as any real fighting was concerned, since no large force could be collected for several months. Tyrone knew that as well as they did, but he also knew that a large force would inevitably come north in the next summer. The tension had reached breaking point. Still Tyrone concealed his hand. Instead, on August 15th (1594), he voluntarily rushed down to Dublin, without even asking for a safe-conduct, and presented himself to the cold glares of the Council.

The man's effrontery, as well as his courage, was colossal. What he hoped for Heaven knows. Did he hope that he would wheedle them into setting him up as undisputed king of the North? It is fantastic. Did he hope to win useful time? It was, for the moment, unnecessary; and he cannot have hoped to deflect them indefinitely from directing a new attack against O'Donnell and Maguire. That clash was, sooner or later, inevitable. Or may we believe that even at that later than last moment he still had some faint, wild, despairing hope to avoid the doom that he saw in the darkening skies? He knew what war meant. He had seen its horrors in the south years before. He was a man of mature experience, nearing fifty. He knew that if war burst there would be no halting it, that he must carry it through without pity, without mercy, without hesitation. The decisions of such a man are real decisions where every hesitation is to be honoured for its courage and humanity in that it springs from a profound knowledge of the consequences of the final choice.[13]

He persuaded the Council to believe that he had had no part in the recent disasters. His attitude was clear and direct. For sixteen years he had served the Queen: his reward had been suspicion, humiliation, interference, distrust, 'false accusations and corrupt practice.' If he had stood aside now, it was because his spirit was wounded by the treatment he had received from the Bagenals and Fitzwilliams, and he could 'endeavour nothing else but the preservation of his life only.' The Council debated his case, and as always happened when Tyrone faced men in person they were impressed. Besides what he said was true; as far as it went. 'The opinions of men are much divided' was the sum of the Deputy's report to Cecil, and the upshot of it was that Russell over-ruled a proposal to clap him into the Tower. Secretary Fenton was strong on his side, protesting that Bagenal was the 'villian of the piece,' and even Ormonde was not averse to him. But his main ally was the fact that the only alternative to the Earl of Tyrone would be those who in overthrowing him must themselves in turn be overthrown. There O'Neill reaped the reward of his patient consolidation of power. Old Turlough was now on his death-bed. He held the sons of Sean. He had won Magennis and the O'Hanlons away from Bagenal. He had deposed Brian McFertagh as he had hanged Hugh Gaveloch and murdered Brian McPhelim. He had removed, murdered, overawed, outmanœuvred, or persuaded every possible rival.

They let him go on August 19th with orders to control his people, call them back from O'Donnell and Maguire, expel the Scots, and send in his own first-born as a pledge. On hearing of this decision Elizabeth flew into a rage and cried that it was the most foul oversight that had ever been permitted in the Kingdom; and it so rankled in her mind that, three years later, when Russell came to her with a present of the heads of some poor Gaelic captains in a basket, she taunted him for his vain parade and sent him flying from the Court. There is a story that Tyrone was warned that August 19th to run from the city because Russell had secret orders to arrest him, and that if he stayed his fate would be like Red Hugh's, seven years before—to sit in irons in the grate begging for food. Some said that it was Ormond who warned him. Others said that it was Captain William Warren, who hid him in the house of one Westall, a merchant, and smuggled him to the quays at dark aboard a ship bound for the north. However that may be, when he faced from Dublin that August, he was facing his decision to fight and the only joy that can have been in his heart was that the suspense was at an end.

16

When Russell followed Tyrone northward, and on August 30th again manned Enniskillen Castle he reported back that the North was in a 'staggering condition.' He found the muster roll dismaying. The old garrison bands were decayed and largely made up of Irish, which was wholly contrary to the rule that not more than five Irish should be in any one company of a hundred men. He bemoaned the usual lack of money. He had borrowed from the port-towns all the money they had to lend him, and the towns were, in fact, already owed the last £1,200 levied on them by Fitzwilliam. As to Tyrone, he felt that he could not be relied on. He begged for instructions, and said that if they were to be positive instructions they should be accompanied by the cash to put them into action.

The North, as represented by Tyrone, was no longer compliant, although he still continued to parley. Safely back in Dungannon he had refused to send in his son as a pledge, offering the weak explanation, which nobody could credit, that their foster-parents had stolen them away from him. (The Deputy naturally termed this 'a frivolous excuse.') He also declared that his people had sworn fealty to O'Donnell; which Russell described angrily as 'an undutiful and loose answer.' O'Donnell did indeed offer peace but only if the Queen's officers were withdrawn and the 'poor exiles' were restored. Maguire also offered peace, but he added that 'otherwise he and his must be regarded as hungry and rapacious wolves.' All Russell could do was to reply softly to O'Donnell and to order Tyrone sternly to come at once to Cavan with his son. Whereat Tyrone exasperatingly replied that he could not come down to Cavan because he was expecting Angus McDonnell to land 'next Wednesday with a great number of Scots.' The patience of the government now began to run out quickly. On September 12th Russell told Burghley that they could now hope for no good from the Earl; while Fenton wrung his hands and cried that if they must fight it would be a 'grievous consumption of treasure and a perilous inconvenience,' and complained, too late, of the amount of gunpowder they had allowed Tyrone to engross in one year. Old Fitzwilliam reported from Aldersgate, from where he was still keeping in touch with his former officers, that Tyrone had sent an English messenger to Spain, but would keep his own person free of absolute disloyalty until he received an answer from Philip. But the air was thick with rumours from Spain, and men heard on all sides of secret importations of ducats, powder, and men into the western creeks.

By mid-October Russell was definite that Tyrone was now determined. Still the parleying went on—chiefly because nothing else could go on but war. At the end of October he was nevertheless again inviting Tyrone to come in for a general discussion on how best to pacify Ulster. Tyrone refused. As late as November he again commanded him to come in. Again Tyrone refused, declaring that he had no more to say. At that Fenton threw up the sponge. 'If he publish himself as a Protector of the Catholic cause he will shake the Four Provinces.'

Yet in the next few months, over the end of 1594 and the

beginning of 1595, Tyrone behaved in the most puzzling fashion. And the observers who believed that the man was a wily diplomat, long resolved to fight, but practised in the tactics of delay, as well as the observers who believed that he was truly reluctant to fight, must have been equally astonished. Nine days after the Deputy's apparently irrevocable decision—and we may be sure that Tyrone knew every move taken in Dublin Castle—he wrote to his friend Sir Edward Moore of Mellifont that 'if he had security of his life, lands, goods, and tenants, he would serve against the rebels.' Now, if this is to be considered yet another attempt to gain time by a man committed, for years, in his heart to rebellion, what follows? It follows that the man must either have been tormented out of his mind, or one of the poorest possible judges of character and circumstance. For his behaviour all through that winter of 1594, ever since his last-minute ride to Dublin, had been tantamount to a challenge to fight, a final and irrevocable decision to fight; and anybody but a ninny must have known that it was that, and would be taken as that by the government. If, in spite of that, his letter to Moore is to be taken as a genuine effort to avoid war he must be considered either a completely indecisive character or a near-coward. And since the whole run of his life equally rejects all those conclusions, it can only have been that his nerves were in flitters. He was on the brink, and he knew it. He was the race-horse shivering at the tape. He was any soldier taut with the drag of wild terror and wild courage at the last second before zero-hour.

17

Whether he was hoping to deceive or to parley the colonists had made up their minds. They attacked his best southern ally, Fiach MacHugh O'Byrne, in January (1595)—'unkennelling the wolf from his den' was their savage phrase. Even then, around February 2nd, Tyrone wrote feverishly half a dozen letters to the Lord Deputy, to Sir Robert Gardiner, to Moore, all to the one tune that the North was bursting with eagerness to come in and receive a general pardon—his own amazing words are 'impatient of further delay.' Possibly the attack on O'Byrne explains these demarches, since they included a petition on his behalf; but it is better to see this fresh extraordinary incident in the round and note that even now Tyrone does not involve himself. He says so clearly: 'I pray that I may be favourably conceived of and that what is amiss in them may not be imputed to me.' And the articles of petition were duly signed by O'Donnell, by Tyrone's brother, by Tyrone's son-in-law, by Turlough's son —in fact by everybody concerned except Tyrone himself, and they do not include mention of him. Further than that, when he spoke of how eager 'the gentlemen of Ulster' were to come in and ask for pardon he said that he himself would not come. What was the man trying to do? The most common explanation, that he was playing for time comes up again at this stage. Or was he deceiving his allies? Did he not trust them? Was he leaving loop-holes for himself? Did he genuinely think of himself as an innocent and wronged man? Was he trying to deceive everybody about everything? But there are some human problems too complex to be answered in a simple and straightforward manner and Tyrone's tumultuous state of mind in these desperate final weeks is beyond normal experience or understanding.

For the last time circumstances drove him on. The government decided on January 8th (1595) to import 2,000 of their best veterans from Brittany. Russell got the news late in February. Tyrone got the news before Russell, through his own excellent secret-service—when, exactly, we do not know. When he heard it, in spite of the impatience of the 'gentlemen of Ulster' to come in for the pardon referred to in his letters of February 2nd, he sent his brother Art to attack the Fort of the Blackwater on Sunday, February 16th. Art took it and gutted it, and demolished the wooden bridge. The clans who must have been chafing furiously at the bit all through these protracted parleys, for which they had neither taste nor trust, burst out at once. Cavan was burned flat. Louth was ravaged as far south as Drogheda. The colonists fled to their towns and every gate and door was barred. After that there could be no retraction.

The war was to have many pauses, but it did not cease finally for eight long years, and not until all Ireland was blasted by blood and fire. In the opening years of the war Tyrone was, as he had always been, tortuous and diplomatic but he also was, as he had always been, four-square as to his objects. He had not wished to fight. Now that they had forced him those objects narrowed down to one main object—to make Elizabeth and her counsellors, both in London and Dublin, live to regret the day they drove him beside himself. The irony of the thing was that by the time he had battered England into a more sensible frame of mind, something had lit in him and his that neither he nor they had foreseen—a religious idealism which, it is more than probable, he at first began to exploit dispassionately but which, as the war went on, ended by consuming Ireland as fire consumes smoke, consumed him, consumed and burned up every personal or political minor reason for the war, and was to remain lighting behind him down the centuries.

I do not think that it is possible to exaggerate the fury of Tyrone at having to fight this war—fury with his immediate enemies like the Bagenals and the Fitzwilliams, fury with the Queen and her counsellors whose stupidity drove him mad with wounded pride and outraged common sense, and above all fury with his own people who, he well knew, were unfitted for war. Once he was in it he fought with fury—and his Gaelic fellows felt the edge and weight of his temper, for he knew, too, that he must take them by the scruff of the neck and make proper soldiers of them, discipline them, control them, change them from raiders into an army and from a rabble to a people. He was a silent man, and a determined man, and if there is any modern parallel to him in Irish history it is to Parnell who had to do almost exactly the same thing with the democracy by which O'Connell had replaced this 'aristocracy' of the sixteenth and seventeenth century clansmen. The late-nineteenth century invented a myth about O'Neill—the usual romantic patriot myth, all enthusiasm and glory and idealism and trustfulness in Ireland's cause. The truth is almost at the opposite pole. So little did he trust his people that he surrounded himself with Scotch bodyguards and English secretaries, like Nott and Weston and Bermingham and Hoveden, some of whom proved no more reliable. Weston was the brother of a paid spy. Nott was bought by the English and constantly forwarded secret copies of his master's letters to Dublin. It is, surely, no fanciful legend which declared less than a year after the war began—'The Earl is oftentimes vexed in his sleep with the Devil, and when he awakes he falls into a great rage with his people.' Through the silence of the man's own naturally reticent temper, through the silence with which the centuries have secreted his private mind from us, we must hear that rumbling of his determination and his anger, like the rumbling of a great boiler generating power.

PART FOUR

THE WAR : 1595–1601

CHAPTER ONE

THE CAMPAIGN OF 1595–1596

'Tyrone will cess the three Furies of *Penury*, *Sickness*, and *Famine* upon Her Majesty's armies that are to assail him in Ulster.'

—*Calendar of State Papers*: 1599: p. 69.

I

THE IRISH WARS were wars of the frontier and the forest. The frontier was wherever a fort or castle stood as a spearhead into the wilderness. Everywhere else was the forest. The English colonist relied on the frontier. The Gael relied on the forest. The colonist set up forts for defence and attack. The natives' defence was the wilderness of mountain and woods: they had no art in fortification—in that they were as primitive as the Bible—so that, as we saw, a handful of English soldiers took Enniskillen Castle in three days, and Red Hugh O'Donnell with an army of men then sat under it for two months without ever once daring to approach it.

In sum, the strategy of the Irish wars, thus centred on the frontier, was conditioned almost entirely by food. The governing fact of the wars was that the colonist had to revictual his outposts. He did this in two ways: while waiting for supplies from Dublin the garrison raided outward from his fort for cows and corn: it was revictualled ultimately from some nearby centre larger, safer, and more powerful; which centre itself depended ultimately on Dublin and the sea. The clans kept the outposts out of food in two corresponding ways. They resisted the outpost's local raids for food by destroying the crops like locusts for miles around, and they ambushed the in-coming stores. Most of the battles of the Irish wars, therefore, were strategical perforations of the enemy's lines of communication. They were never formal pitched battles and they were not of large dimensions, and they were all invited by the colonist who was, perforce, always on the offensive.

The Irish, apart from occasional raids, fought a defensive war. They rarely if ever attacked gratuitously: they let the enemy wear himself out. So that it is fair to say that when the

English ceased to take the initiative they suffered a defeat, and the whole fighting policy of Tyrone was to reduce them to that impotency. For inanition was costly; it meant that food had to be bought for cash and transported from England; which, in turn, because of natural delays due to wind and weather, meant that an army was always in danger of starvation. And, sure enough, the English came to that pass within eight months of the outbreak of the war. To defeat the English colonial troops in open battle, full man-power against full man-power, was physically impossible. Their resources were too vast. Tyrone only once in his life attempted it—and lost the war.

A complete picture of the military situation, however, must include Great Britain as well as Ireland. Men and supplies, arms and money, many minor and all major decisions came from London and came slowly, subject to all sorts of hesitations besides those of wind and sea. For example, on March 3rd, 1595, Secretary Fenton asked whether Tyrone was to be proclaimed a traitor and, if so, on what limitations—a mere matter of a Council decision and a despatch of letters; yet the Earl was not proclaimed in Ireland until either June 21st or 23rd. Men and munitions suffered the same delay. It had been decided somewhere in December '94 to send 2,000 veterans from Brittany into Ireland. In March 1595 the men were still detained by rain at Plymouth; only 1,616 having arrived. They landed in Waterford around the 20th March, now reduced to 1,553 men. It took them a week to reach Wexford, still 'very weak in the legs' from the long sea voyage. (They had not been allowed ashore at Plymouth—an obvious precaution against desertion.) The corn they brought with them had then to be made into biscuit, bread, and beer; and the usual army complaints about bad food are soon heard, such as that the hot biscuit has been spread to dry on damp floors and became mildewed, or that Master George Beverley, the sutler-in-chief at Chester, is wilfully holding up further supplies. Meanwhile, powder and match and arms are lumbering in the rain along the Chester road from London, nineteen carts of it, with their spare axle-trees and their half-starved hackneys, a wearing sixteen days journey, with the horse-boys piteously begging high officers of State in London for more than four-pence per day for their 'tender' underfed horses. These Breton forces were not in action until May 26th and the next report about them, in July, was that they were 'in great decay' and 'deserting as fast as they can,' so that the whole process of collecting an army had to be gone through all over again seven months after the original decision to collect it.

In addition, the government of these troops was not, as now, that of a regular standing army. Shakespeare's picture of Falstaff, Bardolph, Nym and Pistol gives us a good picture of how loosely these things worked in the sixteenth century in England; and Ireland was merely an accentuation of this natural looseness into a chronic indiscipline. Seven or eight companies of men, that is to say, were employed there in normal times, but only for six or seven weeks in the year. During the remaining ten or eleven months the men hung around town and tavern, chalking up the score, content to wait as long as three months at a stretch for their pay—an idle, uncontrolled militia, either brawling and thieving or well-behaved, as might happen. But in disturbed times there might be up to fifty companies of men in the country, and town and tavern became the centre of a spoiled and famished countryside. The men could not now wait for even fifteen days without pay—the shopkeepers could not afford it—and in the words of one of their own commanders, Sir John Norreys, they had to 'live upon what they can catch, by which licence the country is wasted, the towns unpeopled, and all discipline subverted.' The men were soon miserable and their complaints pitiful—penniless, starving, in rags. No wonder that Chester had a proverb, 'Better hang at home than die like a dog in Ireland.'

The complaints of the people against these soldiers were even more pitiful and they never ceased; with good reason. Many of these ragged fellows were unwilling, angry conscripts picked up God knows how or where. 'Poor old ploughmen and rogues' was what Sir John Norreys called them, and a report of that very first April of the war described the losses as 'some sick, some mad, some in prison, and some run away.' The Mayor of Chester complained that some of 'the last levies are in very bare and naked way, some taken upon the highway, and some out of their beds without shoes or doublets'—an extraordinary picture of a mob of sleepy-eyed, barefoot fellows shambling in their shirts before their armed conductors through the Welsh night-hills, forced to fight in a country as remote to them as the farthest Balkans to us.

These wretched conscripts were supposed to get what they

called 'coat and conduct' money but their conductors frequently cheated them of even these few shillings, so that they became an immediate burden on the towns which had to feed them. The complaint of the townsfolk of Cavan that June was that 'no poor man can escape from the market but his goods are taken by the soldiers.' They were, thus, less an army than a gang of freebooters, and when a Bingham or a Bagenal talks of the beggarly rebels one may wonder what word is left to describe the troops that opposed them. Norreys, by August, was calling them malefactors and hanging some to keep all from deserting, and in dismay watched them straggling to the coast in search of a ship, or even going over to Tyrone, or wandering about the land in their rags, the looting Nyms and Bardolphs of the Irish wars. Perhaps it is not inept to call them the sixteenth century forerunners of 'the loosed khaki cut-throats' of *The Playboy of the Western World*. Incidentally, of the remainder of Norreys' army twenty men of every band were on the flat of their backs with disease, which they often took back with them to Chester to kill their own innocent people.

As for the fighting strength of these companies, young blades took Irish commissions partly for adventure, partly as an investment (some of them were to create famous Irish peerages like the Wingfield who founded the house of Powerscourt), and it was inevitable that these men should become more eager to draw their full salaries than to command full companies. They sold leave of absence to their men, they neglected their roll-call, they filled up blanks with Irish 'sepoys' who were willing to serve for the mere chance of loot, they were so insanely corrupt that they actually took in Irish 'rebels,' they did not buy powder and ball, they did not pay their men, and the final wonder is not that they lost battle after battle but that so many of them escaped with their lives.

For tail-piece add the greed of the profiteers 'who care not how long the war last so they may make their profit'; as well as the self-seeking of men in even the highest offices who kept a keener eye on their own fortunes than on the fortunes of the war. Small wonder that Burghley should ask sarcastically why this Kingdom cost so much and brought in so little to its Prince, or that Elizabeth should be so stingy about investing money in it. There is hardly a single aspect of the colonization of Ireland in the sixteenth century which has not the air of what we can only call a dirty business. And yet the generals in command were almost invariably reporting great victories, so that if the war-bulletins from 1595 to 1600 were to be credited the whole of that struggle, in which Elizabeth lost army after army, money by the million, and honour every day, was one long dazzling success.

That picture of the Irish wars is repeated over and over again through the years. The fog parts to show us a straggling army of English and Welsh plucking their feet out of the bogs as they march to the relief of some garrison in an outpost like Armagh, or Fort Monaghan, or Portmore on the Blackwater. They arrive and return, almost always scarred from Irish ambushers, but invariably thinned in numbers through desertion or sickness. Now and again as at a Tyrrell's Pass, or a Yellow Ford, or a Carrickfergus they are decimated. Then the fog settles down and we wonder what has happened to them. The fog lifts and in some muster-master's figures, or captain's complaint, or the rage of the Privy Council at the expense of the war, we see the whole story. We see the remains of the army of the previous campaign wandering in twos or threes towards the coast. These men have sold their guns to the rebels, are in rags, bearded, sick, bootless, and eager only to get aboard any smack that will carry them back to the Welsh coast away from the stink and rain and hunger and danger of this rebel-infested and ague-infected island. Or we see the shreds of the army quartered here and quartered there, receiving no wages, extorting food and even money from the harassed people, bickering with their captains for their back-pay, looting their friends, and annoying everybody but the enemy. There is one vivid picture of a wretched paymaster arriving in Newry where these toughs have been for months waiting their money. It is a snowy day. The street, the roofs, the fields are deep in white. The infuriated men bombard the horseman with snowballs, tear him from his nag, roll him in the slush. The captains and lieutenants have to rush from the taverns to save the man's life, and save the treasure from the fury of their men. When he finally succeeded in taking refuge in a house he never dared for sheer terror to leave it while in that village, and stole away down the river at night and so to Dublin by water.

Men not only deserted to the rebels. Men died by the thousand of want. After the 'victory' of Portmore in 1597 a thousand men were 'famished.' There was no military hospital from end to end of the island. Where the wounded fell they lay. Disease ran through the troops like wildfire. For lack of beer they drank water from the rivers and streams and caught all kinds of fever. Their food was unreliable. A shipload of cheese is found to stink beyond use. Half the beeves sent to a garrison are carrion. In May 1598, long after a 'clean sweep' had followed the famous report of Maurice Kyffin as to the rank corruption within the army, the captains themselves reported that 'it is well known and of truth to be avouched that there have been divers garrisons in many places which have lived without the taste of bread or drink, but with relief only of "beef-water," some the space of six months, some eight, some more.' Thus armies decayed and vanished as fast as they were created. Ireland swallowed them up as if they had sank into her bogs. Commanders loathed the country, and men who had won fame and been hardly practised in the wars of the Low Countries, such as Sir Callisthenes Brooke, begged for God's sake to be removed. To them it was not war. The Gaelic clansmen were, as Brooke said, better hunted with dogs than men. There was no fighting in the classical sense of the word. They faced wraiths and fogs and not an army. They squelched over bogs and tore through plashed woods and flung a few hundred cows into a scurvy fort which had already cost the Queen an army to establish, and they returned pricked from the woods, and poisoned by disease, and demoralized by want, and found within a month that another army had vanished in the process.

Thus when the troops were mobilized from their various billets and had to march to some central destination the men took their ease, perhaps not covering more than three or four miles a day, extorting meat and drink of the best as they went along. The officers would violently force their 'hosts' every morning to give them three, or four, or five shillings apiece; to every soldier twelve pence or two shillings; to every one of their women as much; to every boy sixpence or eightpence at least. And if the wretched civilian did not have the money, or pretended not to have the money, these rascals would take garrans, coverlets, mantles, sheets, until we shape a very strange picture of these freebooters of the Queen straggling along with their loot in a white bundle on their backs, from cabin to cabin over a terrorised countryside.

All that goes back to the rank corruption of the officers, muster-masters, commissaries, quartermasters, the treasury, the whole Civil Service up to the highest officials in Dublin Castle. Kyffin took the lid off this gigantic swindle in 1597 but, although there was a general 'clean sweep,' the thing was too deeply rooted and went on just as badly as before. Captains still faked the numbers of their companies. If inspected, they still got Irish to stand in the line and fill blanks. They continued to bribe the inspectors. They still took on Irish who asked no pay at all—having no intention of fighting but content to be mere passe-volants, with liberty to spoil the Queen's subjects in the Queen's name. Still they sold their men their liberty, they took their horses and 'furniture' and filled the ranks with Irish who rode pillion behind the remainder and carried for arms, perhaps, nothing but a stick. Still they wilfully kept from the men their imprest and diet money, spent it on their own backs, their drink, their pleasures, their pipes and tobacco, and the men—unless, as naturally happened, they rose in mutiny—either fed on roots, boiled nettles and the like, or as before, looted for their bellies' sake.

Not all the captains, of course, behaved so. Some were as needy as the men themselves, and these were hard put to live. Thereby more peculation followed. The shopmen, victuallers, merchants, gentlemen, craftsmen, came into possession of the captains' bills of reckonings—which the corruption above them refused to meet. The merchants, that is, bought a bill-of-reckoning for twenty pounds when the bill was for, say, £100, and relied on getting, say, £50 from the Treasury for it through the influence of friends in court. The Queen, of course, paid the full £100, and the dishonest officials pocketed the balance. Captains were known to fake their bills to treble the rightful amount, sharing the swindle with the inspectors. No wonder the privates, being swindled themselves, swindled the Queen. Thus they had to buy their weapons and powder out of their pay. It occurred that armies marched to fight the rebels with no powder at all, or with but little, as Ormonde found when in a skirmish with the rebels in June '98 and his men's guns were silent in the very first attack. Conyers Clifford ran out of powder after his first battle on the retreat from Ballyshannon.

The deceit was not confined to Ireland. The conscripts were robbed in England in just the same way. At one time only 5,000 uniforms were reported available for 9,000 men, and when the lists were checked it was found that the 5,000 uniforms were, in fact, 2,500—and this in the depth of winter so that the Council feared 'a dangerous mutiny.' Lord Brough, as he died, in harness, summed it all up with: 'O gracious Queen, how art thou cozened!'

Bearing all this in mind one glance at the map shows the complexity of the English military problem and suggests those opportunities for the Irish which Tyrone was so adept at exploiting. The colonists had several forts, some small, some larger, across the actual Ulster frontier. Beginning at the east coast, their line of communication ran from Dundalk for about eight miles to the Newry, Bagenal's centre. From there a long march of thirty miles took them to Armagh. That long line was later broken by the erection of Fort Mount Norris half way to Armagh. A shorter march of some eight miles more took them on to the Blackwater Fort, to the north-west. Or another long march of thirty miles took them down to Fort Monaghan in the south-west. Behind Fort Monaghan and the Blackwater Fort was the wilderness. There was nothing, then, until the Great Lakes of the Erne which hung half way across Ireland in from the Atlantic. On these lakes Belturbet was at the hither end; Enniskillen at the centre; and Belleek and Sligo at the farthest west. There were also a few minor posts, satellites which depended for their existence on these major points, as well as store-houses in the coast towns.

The distances mentioned may not seem very dismaying to our eyes, but distance is a relative matter. How long is one mile on a dark night in enemy country? When, that summer of the opening of the war Bagenal was at Newry with 2,000 men, he dared not make the eight-mile march to Dundalk and had to send a special messenger for help. He suffered the abject humiliation of being taken off, i.e. from his own home-town, by sea. It was that or be destroyed. It would have been a folly for the clansmen to fight pitched battles where everything thus encouraged the strategy of an endless cut-and-come-again. So long as each invading army left no permanent mark behind it, such as a new settlement, the tactic was rather to invite their frequent visits and let 'the three Furies of Penury, Sickness, and Famine' finish what a constant guerilla warfare began. It took the colonists a long time to realize this; meanwhile they taunted the Irish with being cowards and crowned their fury by calling Tyrone 'The Running Beast.' When they did realize it they saw that the solution was simple—more forts and shorter lines of communication. But they also saw the obstacle to the solution, namely, Money, and so went on wasting money, in futile armies, in the effort to save it.

2

The war had begun in February (1595), with the destruction of the Blackwater Fort and bridge. Within four months the English communications were cut to pieces. Having lost Enniskillen, and retaken it, they lost it again in May to Tyrone's brother Cormac MacBaron. They retained Newry, but the Irish ate the country for miles and miles about it and away down into the next county, to within forty miles of the gates of Dublin. After that second loss of Enniskillen the main line of communications was reduced to Newry—Monaghan—Sligo. That virtually was all. The colonists decided that the centre must be preserved at all costs and thereby came the first direct conflict with Tyrone.

Fourteen colours and some horse, so he was informed on May 24th, had been drawn from various garrisons and put under the command of Bagenal. On the 25th his spies reported that Bagenal had left Newry with horse, hackneys, and waggons, for Monaghan. Late that evening he came, with a hundred horse, to overlook his enemy's force. Bagenal sallied out and Tyrone, starting early to invite his nickname, hopped back from hill to hill until Bagenal abandoned him sourly and returned to camp. The next day the Irish saw the enemy break camp and march forward towards Fort Monaghan. They raced ahead and laid in wait for him on the borders of that country, but after about three hours of hot fighting Bagenal pressed through the ambush and got safely to the fort with his supplies. He had won the first round. On the next morning, the 27th May, he set out at ten o'clock on the return journey and had come back about three miles of the way, almost to where the first ambush had occurred, when his van and rear suddenly found themselves again under fire from the bogs on either side. This place was known as Clontibret.

This time Tyrone's men were more successful, probably because they had meanwhile made themselves familiar with the terrain. Horse and foot rushed in to stab at the enemy's flanks, the foot sometimes running by the stirrup for greater speed, in-fighting, whirling, flying at a flying stirrup like acrobats, then whirled out of danger by the horsemen as their store of weapons or their explosive energy gave out. As they fled they lured the enemy to the skirts of the fastness where fresh companies lay in wait to trap them. Thence, as the English drew back out of gun-shot range fresh horse and foot burst after them, hacked and cut and again whirled and fled. This time the scrub would not look so innocent to the English, and their interrupted ranks, however firm, would stand at a loss. Their line of march was long. They had not chosen the ground. There was no clear front. What Bagenal said after the battle about the alleged Irish dead was also true of the living—'They were so scattered in wood and bog that we could not see them.' No English commander could do more than reform his ranks and press onward with the march, leaving his horse to skirmish as best they could, left and right; though that kind of retreating battle could go on devastatingly, and often did, from morning until night and it would be badly decimated force that would finally arrive in camp. This time Tyrone did not allow Bagenal to move from the spot. It was dark before the fury and plunging and shouting died away. Some said that the fight lasted for six hours, some for eight hours, and Bagenal himself said that it did not stop until it was 'very late.' Then Tyrone drew off his men, satisfied that he had taught his enemy a lesson.

He might well be satisfied. In his first open meeting with his enemy he had shown himself superior; and he knew that the consequences of that were, succinctly, that everybody would begin to 'think again.' They did, We can see it in the words and behaviour of all concerned. Bagenal reported that he lost only a mere 140 men. But the muster-master, Sir Ralph Lane, wrote privately to Burghley that there were 'more hurt men in the late service than was convenient to declare.' Again, Bagenal generously guessed that Tyrone's strength in the battle was 800 horse and 5,000 foot, but the Lord Deputy, in passing on the record to London, transformed these figures into 1,000 horse and 14,000 foot. Sir John Norreys, the Commander-in-Chief, wrote in dismay of the skill, arms, and numbers of the Irish. Secretary Fenton spoke of the 'overcrowding forces' opposed to them, but by withdrawing that in a cooler moment revealed how much he had been shaken at the time. Lane went so far as to tell Burghley that Ireland never seemed in greater danger of being utterly lost. Elizabeth declared her 'grief at the loss and death of so many good soldiers.' The general feeling was one of panic, and these misgivings increased when it was found that Bagenal had had to resume the battle with Tyrone in a flying retreat all the way to Newry, and was so demoralized that he had to be taken off by ship down the river and around by sea to Dundalk. From the practical military point of view he was ham-strung in his fort at Newry. His lands were burned, his tenants dispersed, and he himself was soon reduced to a living of five shillings a day. From this on his complaints as to his own lot are persistent.

The moral effect of Clontibret was staggering. It exposed the mental thing behind the whole military strategy of colonization. The English had ruled by moral influences driven home by a comparatively weak sword, so that had all the Irish at any given time risen up in simultaneous wrath they could have swept them into the sea by sheer avoirdupois—even as the American Indians could have done with the European colonists in the days of Chingachook and the wars of that frontier. Any defeat was therefore a serious threat to their influence, and from that, actually, had arisen their policy of constant pardons. For they were always ready to pardon and even to reward the casual 'rebel,' knowing that the moral effect of a victory by any clansman was nullified by the demoralizing effect of his subsequent surrender.

It was not, therefore, necessary for Tyrone to follow up his victory in person. Bagenal found life impossible outside Newry because his Gaelic tenants, excited by the news of Clontibret, turned on him. The same sort of thing was liable to happen everywhere as the news ran like wildfire through the country that so powerful a Gaelic clan as the O'Neills were 'out' again. And of course the news did run everywhere. It went as far as Spain where there were processions and *Te Deums* in the streets of Lisbon for this first rebuff to English power since the Desmond rising.

Simultaneous news from the west confirmed all this. The two Binghams, as we have seen, had been ruling there like Black-and-Tans. They had hammered the Irish and the Norman-Irish into virtual outlaws and they had finally done with them what all colonists do sooner or later, they had paid them the final insult of believing that they could now be trusted as faithful servants. They had made sepoys of the noble Clanricardes; one of them, Ulick Burke, had actually become ensign-bearer to George Bingham of Sligo Castle. These men, in common with all their like in the west, had already been excited by a raid which Red Hugh had led into the heart of Connaught. Very little was made of this raid in the English reports—a bare sentence referred to it—and they obviously underestimated its effect. The Irish chroniclers saw it in a better perspective. This is how it is recorded by Philip O'Sullivan Beare :—

> '1595. O'Donnell, remembering the cruelty with which the English had thrown women, old men and children from the Bridge of Enniskillen, with all his forces invaded Connacht, which Richard Bingham was holding oppressed under heretical tyranny. In his raids extending far and wide he destroyed the English colonists and settlers, put them to flight, and slew them, sparing no male between fifteen and sixty years old who was unable to speak Irish.
>
> 'He burnt the village of Longford in Annaly, which Browne, an English heretic, had taken from O'Farrell. He then returned to Tyrconnell laden with the spoils of the Protestants. After this invasion of Connacht, not a single farmer, settler or Englishman remained, except those who were defended by the walls of castles and fortified towns, for those who had not been destroyed by fire and sword, despoiled of their goods, left for England, heaping curses upon those who had brought them into Ireland.'

The further exciting news of Clontibret awoke in these cowed Irish and Norman-Irish of Connaught all the memories that despair had crushed down into that corner of the heart where every slave hides his sullen, lurking hatred. A few days after the battle the ensign-bearer and some twenty others of the Clanricards fell on George Bingham as he sat writing in his chamber in the castle and murdered him. They dug out seven Englishmen unlucky enough to be in the castle at the moment of their sudden, savage joy and killed them also. They spared only two nephews of Bingham, the Martins and their wives, and with these as hostages they held the castle and began to treat with Sir Richard Bingham, who likewise had in custody two brothers and the mother of Ulick Burke. He agreed to an exchange and O'Donnell, who came down into Connaught with 800 men to make the bargain, took over the castle. That was another link broken. At once all the suppressed angers of the West broke out. The best men in the country around Sligo flew to arms and within a month Bingham had to report that four-fifths of the Province was out of control.

Clontibret had the opposite effect on the colonists. They began to bicker among themselves and in this disunion they made some bad mistakes. From the start the Lord Deputy Russell had wanted Bingham as his commander: with the worst of grace he had accepted Sir John Norreys, a querulous though gallant man. He acted accordingly now. He decided on the gesture of venturing over the road to Fort Monaghan himself, and this time he brought artillery with the idea of going on to attack Tyrone's castle at Dungannon. He left Norreys behind him at Newry to protect Dublin and the Pale. He did not attack Dungannon for the reason that when he came to its site it was gone: Tyrone had destroyed it. The one positive thing he did was in Armagh. There he found the cathedral 'city' on its hill sending red flame and smoke to the clouds; he also found that Tyrone had been sentimental enough to spare the cathedral itself and he decided to turn it into a fortress—an excellent exchange for the wooden fort destroyed on the Blackwater. But the final lines of his otherwise disingenuous report, and the whole tenour of the much more honest report of Secretary Fenton, measured the futility of the journey. He admitted himself that his forces were, as a result, greatly diminished in numbers and decayed in health. The comments of Fenton and Sir John Wallop were undisguisedly gloomy, the one saying that it would be a lingering war and that the Irish were more likely to get the advantage of it, and the other warning the Council that this war was going to be much longer and more costly than Elizabeth seemed to think.

Fenton, indeed, was highly sarcastic about it all, and here we get another glimpse of the personal animosities that drove the already worried colonists to scratch angrily at one another. He mocked at the Lord Deputy for pretending that Tyrone had an army of 14,000 men—'I think they made his cow-keepers and horseboys parcel of that number.' He declared that there was nothing that they could do but wait for the harvest and try to take it from the clans so that they might eat themselves out in a winter war. And he concluded pointedly by enclosing a bill for 'the monthly entertainment due to Her Majesty's garrison, being £6,184 7s. 3d.'; which must be multiplied by about eight to get modern values, making a disastrous total of over half a million for a war not yet begun. By the same packet Wallop was complaining to Burghley about Norreys's greed in the matter of Munster rents; even as Norreys was complaining to Cecil about Russell's jealousy, and crying that he was 'desperate of any reward for his service but disgrace and beggary'—and he, too, was sardonic about the exaggerations of the 'victuallers of Monaghan.' At that stage Russell grew weary of trying to get his own way, threw the prosecution of the war into Norreys's hands, and returned to sulk in Dublin.

3

It is now August (1595) and Tyrone, without a roof on Dungannon, was content to bask in the fern and watch the harvest being gathered while his enemies quarrelled among themselves. He saw the winter drawing on with its long nights and short days, excellent weather for guerillas. From his friends and spies in Dublin he no doubt received full reports of what the Council was doing. It was one of the constant complaints of the colonists that his secret service gave him information about every decision immediately it was taken.

In effect the Council was taking stock of the situation for the first time. (It consisted now of Norreys as Commander-in-chief, Bingham from Connaught, Wallop from Munster and the Deputy and Secretary Fenton from Dublin and the Pale.) They knew well what should be done but, as usual, they found that they had not the means to do it. The traditional strategy of all Ulster campaigns dictated that Bingham should attack from the west in order to throw the western Irish back into the lap of Norreys who should at the same time attack from the east; from there, so much nearer Dublin and supplied by much better communications they would be able to press back the Irish into the hinterland; newly garrisoned fortresses, so the theory ran, would finally oblige Tyrone to eat his substance in the hills all through the winter while the attackers fattened on the harvest in the lowland.

When he came to count his numbers, however, Norreys found the Lord Deputy demanding at least 800 men for the defence of Dublin and its immediate frontier; Bingham demanding 1,800 men for the attack from the west; that he himself needed garrisons for the eastern outposts; and when all this was done that he still required an army to face Tyrone, for which, so the Lord Deputy maintained, at least 2,000 men were essential.

When he turned to the muster-roll he found that he could not scrape up the one half of what he needed. Bingham had a poor 600 of his own and could be given not an extra 1,200 but a bare 200. All he could gather for his own northern march was about 1,600 foot and horse, and at that the Dublin palisades would have to defend themselves. He was as badly supplied as Bagenal and Russell before him and wrote that 'our journey can take no great effect.' Tyrone could therefore well afford to concentrate on his harvest and, in practice, beyond making some tentative peace-offers, he did not bother his head about the English army at all. He permitted Norreys to revictual Armagh, and was, indeed, so careless as to let him get away with 2,000 cows in a surprise raid. That stung him and when Norreys marched a second time to supply Armagh with fifteen garron loads of biscuit he 'boggered' the food-train and there was one sharp skirmish in which neither side gained or lost anything.

It measures the depression of the colonists that in the first flush of satisfaction at having twice revictualled Armagh without hindrance Sir Henry Duke wrote in elation that this last skirmish was 'a great overthrow of the traitors . . . they lost so many men that two such meetings will nearly end the war.' All too soon it became plain that, in fact, nothing at all worth recording had happened. On the contrary Fenton, who was always the saner and more reasoned observer, was depressed enough to write, 'The borders are greatly wasted, and the heart and inward parts weary of their heavy burdens, men's minds are stirred, and the whole state of the realm disquieted.' By the end of September supplies began to run out. Both Fenton and the Deputy were so reduced in spirit that the first recommended 'underhand means' against Tyrone, and the second broke out savagely against the clansmen that he 'will not surcease to use all the Florentine's practices to make them cut the throats of one another.' That was a sharp decline since the previous May when Thomas Flemying, Lord of Slane, offered to assassinate Tyrone in his own house, and Burghley passed on the offer to Dublin, and Dublin did not avail of it. Later they were less squeamish. It was all summed up in Wallop's lengthy report—in answer to Elizabeth's bitter complaints—that 'it will prove the longest, most chargeable, and most dangerous war that in man's memory hath happened in Ireland, the success of it hitherto showing no less.' While Norreys points out that the army is now all but starving; he has not more than five days food on hands; the most he can hope for from Dublin is 'some biscuit'; and, he cries, 'Can an army fight on bread and water?'

The fact is that they have only just begun to discover the full meaning of Tyrone's strategy. They have to convoy every food-train. The more men they get the worse it becomes since the army eats its head off while conveying food to the garrisons who promptly begin to eat the tail it leaves behind. The most food they can carry, through shortage of horses, is a week's supply and nothing can be done in a week's march. And how the devil will they ever be able to carry any more as long as Tyrone keeps raiding to the borders of Dublin for every horse and hackney of which he can deprive them? Could England possibly send them 500 horses? That is the tune on which the 1595 campaign concludes. Food! Food! Food! It crops up every day. As for economising, it is out of the question. The entire army, to give an example, only drank twenty tuns of beer in the four thirsty months from June to September—which, for 7,000 men, Wallop's figure on September 27th, 1595, works out at less than half a pint of beer per man each day; a great saving to Her Majesty, admits Wallop, if it had not resulted in widespread dysentery through drinking bad dyke-water.

So, at his ease, Tyrone draws in the harvest, and down in Dublin the generals are quarrelling, and Wallop is beseeching Burghley for food and money, and Burghley cries that he cannot get money and he peers like a miser at every account sent in, and Norreys begs to be withdrawn, and Fenton secretly asks that Bingham should be withdrawn (there revealing yet another personal rivalry), and Bingham asks for a fair trial and says that he does not know who is bringing charges against him, and that he has spent sixty years of his life for his Queen; but the only answer he gets is that his accounts are unsatisfactory and—basest ingratitude of all—that it is *he* who provoked this rebellion![14]

By contrast, Tyrone, on old Turlough's death, had himself proclaimed at the crowning-stone at Tullyhogue as The O'Neill, according to the full ancient Gaelic rite. The golden slipper was thrown over his head; the white staff was placed in his hand; the clansmen cheered. There Tyrone made his first concession to the Gaelic symbol. It is, however, significant that he made the gesture only after he had burned his feudal boats, and was later prepared, in dealing with the English, to promise to abandon the title.

That September (1595) Tyrone must have known that if he held out through the winter he stood a fair chance of reducing the whole English army to terrible straits. For when Norreys, after again victualling Armagh—hungry himself but knowing that they were more hungry—had hastened back on an empty belly into Newry to find that a long-expected cargo had not arrived, he all but gave up the ghost. Nothing but a little meal, he groaned, and no wood to bake it. 'We are at our wits' end,' he wrote down to Russell and he cursed him because it was eight days since he had told him of their condition. He was desperate. Starving himself and with Fort Monaghan now clamouring for food, and rumour rife that the sheriff was being lured to surrender to Tyrone—what was he to do? It was just then, in the autumn of 1595, in that utter extremity of the colonists, that Tyrone seriously sued for peace and pardon.

4

Why did he sue for peace and pardon? To begin with, this was not the Earl's first effort to bring matters to a temporary halt. There had been talk of it in June, and again in July; and in August Elizabeth had coyly indicated that she would not be averse to a proposal; and later in the month he had definitely asked for pardon and gave pledges, including one of his natural sons. Norreys had resisted his efforts hitherto—partly because, as a soldier, his job was of a different order, and partly because he was afraid of what Elizabeth might say if he had done otherwise. (As a matter of history when Tyrone's proposals came before the Council in Dublin the Council retired in dismay from them, and refused to discuss them at all. Your Dublin officers lived, then, in a healthy dread of their Prince; as if, like another Queen, she might at any moment cry 'Off with his head!') Norreys now agreed to listen to Tyrone only because the alternative looked like a military disaster. Tyrone's motive in courting peace was, one might say plausibly, that the alternative for him looked like a military victory, and that, taken all in all, a military victory was not his present aim. His tactic was that of a leader of armies which fought in comparatively small groups as guerillas wasting the enemy. He wasted their energy, their money, their time. A military victory in the sense of a vast overthrow of numbers by numbers was always out of the question.

Tyrone was the first to grasp this fact: an able politician and an able general, and the only big man in all Irish history from beginning to end of that dual order. One must believe that he had the foresight to consider the time when this war must come to an end, and consider what that end was likely to be. Therein he differed completely from his allies who were by comparison simple-minded men, even more simple-minded than old Turlough had been. Red Hugh O'Donnell, for example, seems to have foreseen no end but the fantasy of a Spanish fleet (he had not seen the wreckage of the last one strewing the sands of Donegal), hosting up from the Pillars of Hercules with a great Spanish army to the gates of Dublin, and Elizabeth on her knees and, thereafter, all that had been re-established once more, as accustomed, as solid and as permanent as childhood, completely, unassailably, and for ever as it had been before the Saxon came. To Tyrone the best end that could possibly present itself must have been some compromise whereby he and his friends might live behind an attenuated frontier in a state of permanent tension as Gaelic or semi-Gaelic kinglets—the grudgingly accepted rebuttals of the complete imperialist claim. (In 1597 when he was three times as strong as now he asked that Tyrone be made a County Palatinate, and had he got it he might well have been content.) He must have known, then, that no satisfactory result could be won by a snap-victory. A satisfactory 'result' could only emerge from a gigantic, long-drawn agony, and that could not happen until he had turned the wild rabble of land-vikings about him into a solid army.

He knew that he was surrounded by border-raiders, a people mentally conditioned by the foray—here to-day, vanished to-night, a disparate and disunited series of individualistic clans, the undisciplined lone wolves of the border. They would have to be beaten into something more keen, more sharp, more enduring than that. Even as it was, this winter of his first campaign, they were beginning to gird at his stiff control and were looking for the accustomed pardon when they could go home and enjoy in a fool's paradise the fruit of their raids. In spite of him some were already beginning to trickle from his grasp. He had to guard Maguire like a jealous mistress, just as he had had to lock up in some of his island prisons the sons of Sean whom he could not persuade.

He knew that he could possibly, though not certainly, crush

Norreys. He knew that Norreys knew it. He knew that he could get such temporary terms as no rebel ever got before. He was subsequently able to drag on the war by that method for year after year, wasting his enemy, strengthening his own power, and always waiting for Spain. Hence this 'peace' and many more like it later.

This is no ingenious supposition. The English generals themselves and their advisers saw the thing in that way and said so. They regarded the idea of a truce with dismay: they did not trust Tyrone; and they knew that a truce would be a serious blow to their influence. Here are their own words. 'Tyrone,' said the Deputy, 'has no meaning of sincere dealing. He will not be content with less than absolute demand like a Prince of Ulster. Fenton said the same: 'Tyrone's word is no assurance.' Norreys: 'I am every day more in despair of the rebels' intent to submit themselves in that sort which shall be to Her Majesty's liking': which comes to the same thing whether he means that he is afraid that they will make a peace that will satisfy Elizabeth, or afraid that they will not. They knew, above all, that to forgive now so powerful a rebel, who had dishonoured and damaged their prestige, was a fatal blow to their authority. The Queen's Marshal puts this very well that July in one of the most significant remarks ever passed on the political aspect of these wars, 'Tyrone,' he said, would always profit 'by persuading his followers that he may have peace when he will: which, by the passage of time, has made such an impression on them that I fear it is not easily removed—especially if they see no speedy and resolute means of proceeding in his persecution.' In the light of these remarks it must be evident that the moral and political value of a truce was immense.

Naturally there were reasons for the coldly practical nature to recommend the peace. These practical reasons were chiefly three. Tyrone's allies were unreliable. He had no Scots mercenaries. He had reason to believe that Philip of Spain was sending help.

As for the first—his allies were held only by his personal domination and he could never rely absolutely on any one of them except O'Donnell. They had at first seemed solid enough. When he was publicly proclaimed traitor in Newry on June 23rd not a man budged. Several Irish, however, refused to join the infant confederacy. Several like Hugo O'Hanlon fell fighting against it. Others like O'Connor Sligo were apparently ready to be bought. ('Such Irish as come in depend on Her Majesty's purse and must be maintained.') Others, already persuaded, like Hugh Magennis, had to be brought to heel by Tyrone's raiders. On July 13th an O'Reilly came in to Kildare down at Kells in County Meath. On August 13th the Tanist of O'Donnell's country and an O'Dogherty were reported by Norreys as willing to do Her Majesty good service. Three days later Neill M'Hugh M'Phelim O'Neill was parleying and offering to bring in Art, Tyrone's brother. He asked as his reward the estate and pension of Sean M'Brian O'Neill. And he did come in, though unfortunately for his greedy hopes Sean M'Brian also came in and so saved his beeves. In effect Tyrone could never trust even his strongest allies, even such fine fighters as Maguire; and actually, at one time, (1598) he so mistrusted Maguire as to put him in chains. Turlough M'Henry and his son Conn M'Coll abandoned him for a time in '97 at the first sign of active attack by the English. He could never trust any of the line of old dead Turlough. Magennis was never secure in spite of his marriage to Tyrone's daughter. O'Reilly never forgave him for not supporting a claim to succession. The examples are endless. M'Mahon was another of those who Tyrone had to put under restraint in times of crisis. The sons of Sean were all imprisoned, but their fosterers the O'Donnellys were old haters of Tyrone and he was constantly obliged to suppress them. And so on. The English knew all this, and carefully docketed the internal fractures of the Irish system and were keen to bribe the septs to 'revolt'—a significant shift in the use of that word since it indicates that the effective king of the North is already Tyrone. Red Hugh O'Donnell was in exactly the same position with his people. It is the old Celtic tribalism at its worst, akin to the old feudalism of England, which would never make a nation until it was first prepared to make a king; never win liberty until it was willing to be ruled; never win power until it was ready to obey.

As for the Scots, the Lord Deputy swore that in September 1595 there were not one hundred in Ulster and Connaught. Here we hark back to the murder of Hugh Gaveloch O'Neill by Tyrone. For Hugh was the son of that MacLean woman who became Countess of Argyle and later the mistress of Sean O'Neill. The MacLeans never forgave this execution and were still itching for revenge: a serious matter for Tyrone since Argyle was the Lord

Lieutenant of all the Islands and Out Islands of Scotland, and nobody could gather forces there without his permission. The Scots went so far as to offer 3,000 men to fight against the Irish, but Elizabeth was too cautious to let these fierce fighters cross over from Cantyre even on her own behalf. (It had always been a rule of policy with the Irish government to keep out the 'needy and beggarly' Scots, 'a people that have wild pretences to Ulster and have long footed in some parts thereof and yet the Crown of England cannot expel them.') James MacDonnell, the son of the famous Sorley Bwee MacDonnell, was likewise ready to cross Tyrone's path and actually held up consignments of powder which Tyrone had kept for safety in Glasgow and the Islands. So bitter was Tyrone's need of Scots mercenaries that he tried to lure them over by offering every bachelor Scot a well-born wife and a dowry. Besides the British Navy was watching the Straits. In August an army of Scots from Skye, said to number 4,000, was bottled up in the Isles east of Belfast Lough by the Queen's ships the *Popinjay* and *Charles* which sank or took five galleys attempting to land.

As for Spain, although the reports of intended invasion were endless and hectic, like that of the Mayor of Waterford which spoke of 50,000 men being raised there for Ireland in June, the facts were much less fearsome. Great stores of gold and treasure had indeed been sent by Philip—how much nobody knew and the Mayor of Waterford probably exaggerated when he spoke of 'one Portugal million'; communication, too, which had been erratic for several years, now became frequent, with importunate appeals on the one side and ambiguous assurances on the other.

No direct promise, however, came until the following year from 'by the Grace of God, King of Castile, Leon, Aragon, both Sicilies, Jerusalem, Portugal, Navarre and the Indies': and for that, also, Tyrone was prepared to wait, impatient, possibly a little sceptical, but doggedly hopeful.

He waited on one other ally. There occurs in one of these letters of his to Spain at this time a fine image (one must realize that he is thinking of the fire of Faith)—'Within a year the heretics shall fail like smoke in the presence of fire'—a metaphor struck out by the impact of the new religious enthusiasm on a hitherto almost wholly worldly-minded man. As yet that fervour had barely flickered through the forests like the torch of a rare traveller. Its potentialities were enormous. We saw that when its light played about James Fitzmaurice and the Earl of Desmond. We saw how it fell when they fell. We saw it crackle again in the North when Red Hugh came home, as if rebellion would always make the air inflammable and the spark flame at every secular detonation. The only trouble was that after Desmond died the idea lacked personification. There was no Fitzmaurice as long as Tyrone stood aside in the shadows. He was not, indeed, a natural zealot. His mind was set in a more secular mould than James Fitzmaurice and was much more complex. Zealots see things in a blazing light that flattens out every contour and destroys every shadow; their optimism is notorious and their good cheer and benevolence a rule; *in sua voluntade e nostra pace*; God's will be done—whether in victory or defeat. When the idea of a war for (among other things) religious liberty struck Tyrone's imagination it must have struck the man's consideration even more forcibly. His secular bent would have humanized it. It would, that is, have fitted into its place in a complex scheme of life—been just one more symbol of the whole Gaelic mode. He would not have hesitated to use it and abuse it in a bargain. One may say that only because, in fact, he did so. For in those peace-talks of that winter when he was ultimately told that he must drop 'liberty of conscience,' he dropped it complacently. James Fitzmaurice would have bared his breast to the sword rather than make the apostate gesture. But Tyrone was like eighteenth-century Daniel O'Connell—both Renaissance figures, calculating, whorled with reservations, a humming conch of *arrière-pensées*. It does not affect the point. The Earl of Desmond had been a weakling; in leadership his association with a national cause had dilated him. The same was to happen with Tyrone. He may have thought to use the cry of a religious war as a pennant. It blew out into a banner. The idea ended by taking possession of him as all germinating ideas do, by happy contagion.

This work of the Jesuits and seminary priests in stirring up war will never be recorded fully. The breathing of simple men on old emotions do not ruffle the pages of State Records although they may often fan the slightest seed of fire into a great blaze, and it often happens that a gentle nostalgia is more powerful to bring people to a desperate gesture than direct agitation. The report that Tyrone, by the end of '94, is wholly governed by the priests does not make a complete picture of the new evangelism unless we see it through the same sort of small human detail by which the people saw it; put the general statement, for example, beside the little complaint of the Protestant Bishop of Cork that after meals, in Munster, men bowed their heads and murmured a prayer for the return of their good Lord James, meaning Desmond's son. Again which was it—we shall never know—the Jesuits like Master Montford, always now at Tyrone's elbow, or the power of those childhood affections, that enlarged that little complaint from Cork in September into the great complaint of November that the Mayors will not come to church, that four refused to become mayors on religious grounds, that the priests have become so influential now that they even persuade doctors to refuse to attend apostate clergy? How can we say which it is that has worked its way so powerfully about the Shannon shore that the Bishop of Limerick in the November of '95 must cry, 'If Tyrone's directions and authority be sent from Rome, as the great number of Popish bishops and seminaries in this land assure the people, then "Actum Est" and Tyrone is the hope of all Irishry?'

We know, too, that heated arguments were going on all over the country in those first years in which the more scrupulous, who had accepted the Queen's rule, began to worry themselves about such theological points as 'rebellion,' and 'treason' and so forth—the sort of argument with which in modern revolutionary times we Irish have been equally familiar: the old protesting and the young contemptuous, and every farm and bothy and castle and cabin in the country re-knitting the religion of Europe and the patriotism of Ireland into a new web. There also the wandering priests would argue, and quote the Spanish books, and against the Patristic teaching about submission to the temporal power (even where it was unjust) the young priests would cite the superior authority of the Pope and the excommunication and, therefore, deposition of Elizabeth, or the teachings of Aquinas and the schoolmen who followed him; as twenty years later they would quote the new books of Suarez or Mariana on the lawfulness of tyrannicide. In all this, Ireland was thus coming slowly into a great European stream of thought. Men's minds, for centuries completely at sleep, content with a patriarchal, indeed primitive convention in which force and physical fear and lust for power had been the sole criterion, were beginning to move towards a definite philosophy of life and a hitherto unheard of objectivity in relation to themselves and the world about them. No doubt Tyrone did not see all this clearly, but he must have seen at least that religion was a coagulant, and that he would do well to wait while it worked its inspiration on his people.

So he allowed the 1595–6 campaign to close uneventfully in the cold of the wet, wintry weather that was his one reliable ally. He would patch up a truce, prolong it, bind his people, lure the Scots, fish in Spain, encourage the zealots, blow up the fire higher and higher, be, as Sir John Dowdall said, a firebrand to his country. The truce was declared as from October 1st, for three months, later prolonged to February 1st, later prolonged for a further two months to May while he dragged out a cynically hypocritical discussion of peace-terms.

That same bitter weather killed poor Mabel Bagenal. In the spring he concluded a new courtship, and was at his remaining castle, Castleroe, up on the lovely wooded Bann, fishing for salmon and enjoying at the age of forty-five his fourth honeymoon. His new wife was Catherine Magennis.

5

The whole of that truce period of '95–6 was shameful in the extreme for the English and affected the Irish exactly as everybody had foreseen. The English knew generally that Tyrone was quite disingenuous about the peace. With intercepted letters from Tyrone to Philip in their hands, asking for aid and offering the throne of Ireland, the Dublin authorities had nevertheless received their instructions from Elizabeth as to the possible conditions of a peace and a pardon for the 'arch-traitor'—as everyone now called him. Yet when Norreys proposed sending positive proof of the man's 'treachery' to London Cecil wrote in his own hand that he must not do so as the Queen would not wish to seem to know anything about such great treason. All Tyrone's protestations, therefore, about his dear wish to 'obtain Her Majesty's gracious favour' no more deceived the enemy than their pretended trust deceived him. He knew that they would declare war when they could declare war, and as Fenton's letters to Burghley show they had that intention: his most outspoken scheming was in July 1596—'If Her Majesty will not, for the excessive charges, take the way of force, but will close up the sore with a mild plaster, their (the rebels') reasonable complaints may be admitted for the time, which in after times may be easily cancelled and forgotten.' The Lord Deputy himself raided Connaught in March '96. Tyrone had constant cause to complain about Bagenal. The English themselves furthermore knew that Tyrone knew what they intended. 'The rebels have sure intelligence that Her Majesty mindeth to prosecute the war.' All their complaints therefore—Tyrone's or Norreys'—about breaches of the truce ring hollow. Bingham frothed at the state of the West: 'The rebels perform no articles of the truce but daily commit murder': Norreys 'the rebels lose no day but they take some castle, murder some subject, or burn some town in the Pale': Fenton: 'Tyrone sets on the MacMahons and the O'Reillys.'

In short the people realized that English stock was at bottom, and their sauciness showed that they knew the English could do nothing forcible against them. The most striking example of that was the sudden loss of Fort Monaghan which was almost certainly part-bribed, part-bullied into surrender. The MacMahons were the agents but everybody recognized the handiwork of the man in the shadows. The English had to swallow the loss; as they had to do when Tyrone resolutely refused to allow Armagh to be revictualled and demanded that the garrison should be withdrawn.

In spite of all this double-dealing on every side it is, nevertheless, just barely possible that the colonists—and conceivably Tyrone himself—nourished at the back of their minds the idea that a real settlement might not be altogether out of the question. It is a considerable tribute to Tyrone's personality that he could make that slight chance effective for his ends—presuming that, of the two, he was the less sincere. Almost every man who ever came in contact with him fell for a time under that spell and only bitter experience taught them all, from the elder Essex to the younger Essex, that his charm was a mask. Indeed this deceptiveness of his is one of the great pitfalls, as one of the great attractions which his life offers to every biographer, so that whether we accept or resist his outward-seeming we find ourselves, as everybody who had anything to do with the actual man found themselves, in a bog of indecision. The English colonists never trusted him: yet they were never *quite* certain; and between this indecision and their actual military weakness they were all the more easily deceived even when they felt that he probably was playing some new deception on them. And we must remember that their weakness in man-power was not the dominating factor in that gullibility since Essex, who met him at the head of a powerful army, was as effectively deluded to his destruction by Tyrone's charms as the weakest general before him.

The final 'peace' terms were debated in the most unseemly manner in a storm of wind in a field outside Dundalk in January (1596). When she heard of the details Elizabeth raged at the indignity: the words 'war' and 'peace' had been used instead of 'rebellion' and 'pardon'; and the commissioners had actually addressed the traitors as 'your loving friends' and 'our very good lord.' She was so furious that when Gardiner came to the Palace at Richmond to explain she would not have him in her sight. The Commissioners had themselves realized how insolent the Irish demands were: but what option had they? The parleys had been more like the preliminaries to a battle than a peace, with Tyrone and O'Donnell on horseback and armed men fidgeting on the hills, and the talk going on for three hours; and although Tyrone had, as always, been courteous and diplomatic, O'Donnell had been resolute and haughty. It was an excellent Codlin-Short partnership for this sort of negotiation. ('Of course, if it were not for this wild man O'Donnell. . . . Well, then, you had better ask O'Neill . . .') Their demands again began significantly with 'That all persons have free liberty of conscience.' And it is interesting as a light on the weak condition of the Reformation party that the Lord Deputy deliberately suppressed this demand when putting the various clauses before his Council in Dublin—'lest it procure too great a following, being plausible generally to these countrymen.' It had been hard, too, to swallow such a clause as 'that no garrison, sheriff, or other officer shall remain in Tyrone or Tyrconnell, or any of the inhabitants' countries afore-named, except Newry and Carrickfergus'—that is the coastal region of the extreme east. But the rebels refused to budge, and the talks dragged on and the spring came, and nothing was done on the government side to start a new summer campaign.

The upshot of it all was that Tyrone, at his ease, was maturing his plans for the next assault while Elizabeth was trying to make up her mind as to the terms on which she would pardon him for the last one.

6

In the first week of May (1596), while Tyrone was enjoying his new happiness with his new Countess at Castleroe, one Captain Alonso Cobos sailed into Lough Foyle, bearing despatches from King Philip. The Earl, immediately his runner brought the news, galloped across country to meet him. It was a remarkable dinner to which Cobos sat down that evening in May. There was Red Hugh, full of pride and eagerness, Tyrone gracious but alert, his brother, his fosterers, old O'Kane, The O'Hagan, his mother, O'Rourke, Maguire, MacWilliam Burke, and Harry Hoveden, and (strangest figure of all) Salomon, Turlough's former secretary—Cornish or a Jew—in attendance on his new master who had overthrown his old. After the meal Tyrone and Red Hugh conferred privately with Cobos. They swore to him that they were the vassals of Spain, begged him for 6,000 men with money and arms to support another 10,000, and gave him every assurance of their certainty of victory. That trio talking eagerly over the wine into the night give us the pattern of the alliance: the suave, deliberate, aristocratic Spaniard; the angry, impetuous young O'Donnell; the ruthless, dissembling, arrogant Tyrone. Cobos retired to sleep, but the other two continued their own discussions. As a result of them they wrote at once to the Lord Deputy, informing him that Cobos had arrived and how they had told him they could have nothing whatever to do with Spain because they had been received back into the favour of Her Majesty, and to prove their sincerity they surrendered King Philip's own private letter. (This was a folly, and another one of those details of behaviour which make one doubt the completeness of Tyrone's diplomacy, seeing that Elizabeth was certain to use the letter against both him and Philip in some future piece of international blackmail.) From that on there was a still more frequent coming and going with Spain; officers arriving to collect tactical information, patashos coming with arms and muskets, more officers to train the Irish kernes landing in the rocky coves, and one spy turns the story into Legend with the report that the Earl O'Neill is about to become King of Ireland and that there is a golden crown at this very moment a-hammering for him in a goldsmith's shop in Madrid.

Tyrone generally informed Dublin about these arrivals from Spain, knowing that Dublin would in any case be informed by somebody else if not by him. One does not know whether to call the game he played a cunning game, or to say that it was at times a rather childish game and that he attributed more simplicity to the government than he would have allowed anybody to attribute to himself. For example, he did not mind allowing

MacWilliam Burke to receive ammunition from two Spanish ships but he refused a landing to 100 Spaniards who came into Lough Foyle at the same time; and who was deceived when some Scots made a great show of swearing that the Irish would have to receive them whether they liked it or not? Is this part of 'the cunning of simple men,' or was the English government really as ingenuous as all that? But it is curious how ingenuous otherwise intelligent men can be. Thus, Tyrone now used a dual title—The O'Neill with the Irish, and Earl of Tyrone with the English, and some disputants considered this a serious problem, seeing that as 'Tyrone' he was indubitably a traitor and could not be supported by the orthodox, but as 'O'Neill' he was no traitor and not only could be supported but should according to every moral law. Perhaps, after all, Tyrone had taken a sound measure of his age. (He had not, of course, assumed the title of The O'Neill from any regard for logic-chopping theologians, but to please the clansmen who attached so much value to the symbolism of the native title.)

England was now on tenterhooks. She had gambled on a peace. She knew that Ulster was now far stronger, better armed, and in better fettle. Spies were bringing hair-raising stories of the amount of powder that Tyrone had freighted from Danzig; the lead, muskets, culivers, morions, swords, and daggers that the Manchester merchants were freely selling to him; the powder, culivers, and muskets sailing in from Glasgow and Liverpool, and Chester. It was known that merchants travelled to England to the great fairs like Bartholomew Fair and brought back arms for the Irish under the pretence that they were buying for loyal subjects. Once three expert Scots workmen came across to start a factory for muskets, culivers, and pistols in Ulster. One Alexander Stuart of Glasgow sold Tyrone as much as £2,000 worth (in Elizabethan money) of gun-powder. The English soldiers themselves were known to sell their arms for food and passage-money to England. In vain the colonists held up Irish merchants along the coasts, searched the barques on the Chester and Liverpool waterfronts, raided the houses of agents who fled before the detectives arrived. Exactly as if Tyrone were Michael Collins and this was not 1596 but 1920 the guns and ammunition still stole into the country in innocent-looking hogsheads and dry-vats under the noses of his watchers.

The colonists made up their mind that they were about to

be badly deceived. Sir Edward Moore had been waiting patiently at Dundalk from June 9th to June 22nd with the Queen's pardon in his hand, and Tyrone would not come to receive it. Neither had any rebels 'come in' from Connaught. In fact by July it became plain that Ulster was just as solidly in revolt as if there never had been a truce and that Tyrone was far more powerful than ever before. Norreys prepared for war. Tyrone's spies informed him at once, and at once he offered to take his pardon, and with a shameful weakness the government agreed. Tyrone accepted it with delight; he said that it was more precious to him than his original patent; in his joy at being pardoned he had a volley fired to honour the event; and then with long, doubtful looks at his smiling bearded countenance the commissioners who had brought the Pardon drew away to await events.

CHAPTER TWO

THE CAMPAIGN OF 1596–1597

I

Now well into the summer of 1596 Tyrone knew that he was safe against serious attack for a good many months to come. He used his time with energy. Here at last he begins to emerge from his own secrecy and as he steps from the shadows his great bulk is like something that has been long gestating, larger and more terrifying than an ordinary mortal. Something of the Cyclops sits on his stocky body; an abnormal patience, pitilessness, cunning, imaginative force glitters from under his red eyebrows and is reflected in Lord Brough's uncontrolled language about him, as when he calls him 'This Base Beast,' or 'The Great Divill,' and cries in his fury 'May God confound him!' While his figure throws this horrid light on Dublin Castle he glows over Ulster, where his domination is growing more and more absolute, as The Great O'Neill, and over Connaught where he is The Lord O'Neill. The legend swells. One says that as King of Ireland he will be crowned in Spain. A waiting woman on his Countess, Ann Wilmar, reported that he is not only expected to win the Irish war but carry war into England where he will become a leader of the people and reform religion. He is obviously firing the imagination of the whole country. Nothing, perhaps, shows this so strikingly (while at the same time annotating his tremendous difficulties) as his entry into the tribalistic maze of calm rivalries and family intricacies in the West. It is neither easy nor necessary for us to hold the complexities of these families in our minds, but we must get at least the dazzle of the picture if we are to form any idea of the enormity of his task.

Take as a typical example the sept of the MacWilliam Burkes of Mayo. The two great lines of Connaught, ever since the Norman settlement, had been the Burkes of Mayo and the Burkes of Clanrickard. These adventurers had become mightily prolific and had so intermarried and interbred that their line was to be found all over the province. Bingham's constant execrations against them show what a curse they had become to the colonists. They were more of a danger to them than all the wild O'Flaherties ('From the fury of the O'Flaherties O Lord deliver us'), O'Malleys, O'Haras, and O'Rourkes put together. Had they not become disintegrated by time they should have produced the Tyrone of the West.

Of the Mayo Burkes the chief had been William the Blind Abbot, Edmund M'Riccaird of the Iron, and Richard the Devil's Reaping Hook, all three a little before this period. They had been Bingham's great enemies, the object of his outrageous fury, contempt, and brutality. They had been listed long ago by Burghley as 'bad men.' A few lesser septs had been somewhat less active, though never wholly quiet, such as the Burkes who lived about Kilmayne, or Shroole, and (from the English point of view) the most hopeful of them all had been Oliver Burke of Tirawley. But their political story is hopelessly complicated by inter-breedings and internecine wars with scores of other septs whom we may now comfortably permit to escape the memory. An example or two will suffice. Grace O'Malley, the piratess, had by Richard of the Iron a son called Theobald of the Ships: yet, though thereby a Burke herself, she opposed all the other Burkes because she felt angrily that he should have been made the head of the clan. Nevertheless her son, by an O'Flaherty, married a Galway Burke and sided with his step-brother's enemies. In a time of crisis nobody could tell what twist these fantastically confused family stories might take. So, in the Armada crisis the O'Flaherty son of Grace O'Malley decently assisted the Spaniards, whereas the Sea O'Flahertys and the Island O'Malleys slaughtered them wholesale. Every family in the West repeated that confusion. A stranger walking among them went barefoot in a field of basilisks.

It was into this welter that Tyrone thrust himself to choose some one man who would become The MacWilliam Burke. The colonists had picked one David Burke. They had educated him at Oxford, sent him to study at the Inns of Court, and made him a Justice of the Peace. The rival was Theobald, or Tibbot, the son of Walter the Lefthanded. Red Hugh and Tyrone established this Tibbot. The English threatened him. Tyrone hurried west to induce him to 'come in'—in other words he started to play the same game he had earlier played with Maguire and Red Hugh: that is, a long weaving of deceptive promises of peace, raids that break them, counter-raids to revenge these raids, appeals to Tyrone from Dublin, assurances from Tyrone to Dublin, conspiracies hatched by Tyrone in Connaught, in short (or rather in long) a protracted heart-scalding experience for the colonists and their officials, with nothing to ease it but the Lord Deputy crying, 'The Earl is corrupted with the dregs of treason.' What it amounted to was that Tyrone was laying his hands on more and more liege-men. A whole new Province was coming under his sway.

The example may be multiplied a dozen times over as his terrific energy, and his irresistible personality sweeps the septs under his control. He set up his own O'Connor and his own O'Reilly; won over the MacDermotts and the O'Flaherties, Magennis and the O'Hanlons, M'Connell and O'Kelly; lured in the Butlers, stiffened the O'Byrnes and the Kavanaghs, the O'Moores and the O'Connors, until—the figures were given to Dublin by Sir Conyers Clifford—there must have been between three and four hundred septs in arms. The sum of it all is that Dublin had to report to London that out of the Four Provinces of Ireland not one was clear of treason and 'three of them universally corrupted with rebellion.' This year Tyrone's raiders burned to within twelve miles of Dublin city. The colonists did nothing against him until January (1597) when Norreys was driven to do something definite and marched out from Dundalk. Tyrone at once protested his loyalty. Norreys was delighted to hear it and made yet another truce!

Only in the west did the colonists do anything to cover their general shame, and that was not until the spring and autumn of 1597. Twice Conyers Clifford blotted Tyrone's ledger of triumphant success by driving his nominee Tibbot Burke out of the province—though, perhaps, the fact that he did it twice has a less satisfactory innuendo than if he had only done it once. Twice he pushed farther north than any English force except Fitzwilliam's and Perrot's, piercing even into Donegal itself, Red Hugh's stronghold. These raids by Clifford, the destruction of the countryside by his men, the shadow of Famine that followed, and the wavering of lesser clans who 'came in' by the score—Clanjordans, Barretts, Clandonnells, O'Malleys, others—correct any idea that Tyrone was going to win this war without fighting it or that he was building in a season a monarchy that the centuries had resisted.

The mere hunger of the country alone mocks at that idea. The summer of '96 had been wet and cold. The crops had been poor and grain scarce. The English troops had suffered so much that in the autumn of '96 not fifty out of a hundred men stood up in each company. By October London had so drained the west of England and Wales, which were Ireland's granary, that Dublin was trying to buy corn in Denmark. By March '97 prices had become iniquitous. By May the country was so wasted that many villages were empty, the ground untilled, no harvest expected, the English troops in the Lord Deputy's words 'living on air,' most of them sick, the remainder feeble. By June '97 Clifford reported 5,000 deaths from famine in Connaught alone, and the new Deputy Lord Brough was crying in anguish from Dublin—'No bread, no beef, no fish, no flesh. . . . We hear of great quantity of rye come into England. The very report of it makes our hungry jaws gape.' By August prices were trebled. All that naturally weighed more on the English than on the Irish. Some of their bands, like Sir Thomas North's, were now simply a miserable, unfurnished, naked, starving rabble, dying at random or struggling through the briars and the bogs with their very feet 'rotted' for want of shoes. But the Irish suffered too, though they were better accustomed to hardship and had the wild hinterland behind them with crops stored on the thicket islands or pitted in the earth, and their multitudes of cows to feed them with milk and curds and cheese. Yet, in winter, how indescribably, how squalidly they must have lived in the dripping woods! And even in the summer when milk became scarce, for in the field they hardly ever ate flesh meat, they must have been lean and tough and brown as the Cherokees or the Iriquois.

Tyrone's triumph then was of such a sort that when the drums of war began to beat in Dublin where the new Deputy, Lord Brough was preparing for an attack—the Earl's spies would have passed on the date—the Lord of all Ulster and Prince of Three Provinces found it advisable to write instantly (May: June) a palavering letter offering 'submission.' He received back a brusque reply which must have come as a surprise to him. For Brough was one of those laconic, no-damn-nonsense soldiers whom the hardy Elizabethans produced as a model for all future English martinets —humourless as Dogberry, bold as Achilles, impenetrably contemptuous of all natives, savage in his blood-lust, without policy and a trial to all politicians, never put out by anything but the 'cowardly' tactics of a guerilla enemy who would not face him man for man. This may seem to describe another Bingham: and he was a Bingham but on the grand scale. An Elizabethan dramatist could have put him right into one of his plays and his style had enough of a rude classic flavour to make him fit there perfectly: forceful, condensed, epigrammatic, and it would have been blunt if it were not also what the age called 'curious.' Thus a letter of his to Cecil, that July, might have been written in a rude form of blank-verse. (I change nothing of what he wrote):

'The traitor holds our idleness in contempt . . .
Therefore be her Majesty's ensigns advanced.
Our hopes many. If he will fight we have the cause,
And to that end be we paid t'execute
The due of our profession: if he fly
Pursuit must needs bring him into disdain . . .
And the waverers in this intermission and suspense
Will now, when th'ensigns be displayed
Bethink them of a prince's strength.'

(Which shows, in passing, how near Shakespeare's verse was to actual speech.) And many a ranting poetaster would have been glad to steal—'I will, God willing, stick to him, and if need be lie on the ground and drink water ten weeks, unless sooner blessings fall upon my labours.'

His friend Cecil sighed a little and smiled a little at these missives, and wrote back a long letter highly illuminative of the chasm between soldiers and courtiers in that reign, as in every reign. His comment, *ex abundanti*, was not that the style was too flowery but that it seemed somewhat quaint to the ears of the

Privy Council, for 'you do too much imitate the succinctness of Tacitus which for a man to write to a Councel is not held to be proper.' Brough was obviously enough the heroic type cast in the usual simple mould. More sophisticated men could easily underestimate his type, and that is what Tyrone did when he received Brough's reply to his offer of still another truce.

> 'You must alter,' wrote Brough, 'your manners, knowing against whom you have offended, and seek remission, which when you so crave it may find passage. In the meantime take of me of this caution. As hitherto you have had experience how much rather your Majesty would forgive than use her sword, so if your perseverance in these ill-demeanours cause her to draw it, you shall find the ever-living God hath not committed it to her in vain. And doubt not but Her Majesty, who hath broken the neck of the Spanish boasts and threats against Her Realm, and relieved her distressed neighbours in France and the Low Country, from his violence, and in his own bosom destroyed his magazines and burnt his shipping . . . is able if so she be provoked to chastise and take vengeance of all seditious and tumultuary persons in her proper kingdoms. Therefore presume not on your numbers, nor your paces, nor bushes, nor bogs . . . but retire yourself into the trial of your conscience where you may truly be told that your destruction must needs ensue if you by penitence make no meditation against so just a wrath. . . . It is high time you have remorse in your soul, and prostrate yourself for mercy lest the heavy stroke of your sacred Queen inflict that which no guilty mind can resist nor obdurate avoid.'

To this the Earl simply wrote another palaverer. Brough snubbed him brutally. A preliminary raid on his camp gave him a more painful warning; nothing but the merest chance saved Tyrone, and his Countess from capture. The two had even to leave their horses and tear through the woods on foot, and the Lord of all Ulster suffered the indignity of losing his hat as well as the expense of losing his horse. He drew his forces behind the Blackwater to await Brough.

Brough marched prompt to the hour with 3,500 men. According to the usual strategy Clifford drove north-west. This time they left no army to defend the Pale for the very good reason that Tyrone's commandos had burned the Pale to the ground and it could support no army. So that if Tyrone should dodge behind Brough, then Brough would simply have to wheel about. By July 12th (1597) the English were at Newry, and true to their promise at the Blackwater on the 14th, facing the Fort. The river had been spiked and the passage was under heavy fire from the defence beyond. That was the Fort, an earthwork or sconce in the Dutch fashion with a thick hedge, a high rampart, and a deep ditch. Brough had a thousand men here. In the Fort were only forty men. Nevertheless, in the first attack on the fort Brough's men broke and the skirmish was in grave doubt when Brough himself rallied them, wading to his waist in the middle of the river. He complained sharply, later, that they were an ill-trained lot with hardly enough wit to obey or even understand his commands so that he, although their general, had to lead them as if he were a mere company captain. 'It is the rawest army that ever Prince so long paid.' The forty men in the fort resisted the whole day, but they could not hope and can hardly have been expected to hold the position. Most of them escaped before the English finally took the sconce. Tyrone took no part in the skirmish but held his forces in the woods hard by to await the graver outcome.

The real test now remained—the entry into the fastnesses of Ulster. Here Brough drew back, for as he faced into that darkness he realized, for the first time, what these Irish wars entailed. All the passages had been plashed and counterplashed: that is, the woods had been woven together, branch on branch, in the most thorough fashion. His soldiers began to desert: 'English raw and of the last levy.' He found that he could not trust his own captains, since some of them partly sympathized with Tyrone, and some were cowardly. 'I came a stranger to them and could not imagine so bad and false a people.' It was only now that he saw his danger if Tyrone should wheel behind him, and the Council in Dublin saw it too—perhaps with better reason—and advised him not to advance into hunger and disease. So Brough stayed where he was, cursing this cowardly rebel who never faced him but kept sniping him with his shot and flying from bush to bush before him. Bagenal, however, got his chance to take revenge for Clontibret. He raided into Dungannon itself, burned the town, and destroyed Tyrone's mills—an insult that must have stung. But taken by and large the expedition had accomplished little. It was now August and another winter on its way to waste an enemy who, by then, would have spent three years on the war with nothing to show for it.

The government realized this gradually. Brough had to withdraw his garrison from Armagh. He held the Blackwater Fort, but by November (1597) the Lord Justice declared that the revictualling of it had 'ruined the army,' and in the year after Ormonde cried that the 'scurvy fort' was always falling, never victualled once without an army, and had better never have been built. News from Clifford in the west emphasized their feelings of dismay.

To begin with, Clifford had failed to reach Ballyshannon on the 14th of July, that is simultaneously with Brough's arrival on the Blackwater: the ravaged state of Connaught and the shortage of food had delayed him and the delay proved disastrous. It was the 29th before he was sitting on the ford of the Erne opposite O'Donnell's castle. The ford was high and he could not cross it, but he cleverly acted as if he intended to and pitched his camp. Red Hugh was thereby lured into drawing his men away from every other ford up and down the river. Of these there was a good ford, about five miles down-river, at Belleek, and there Clifford sent Sir Callisthenes Brooke in the dark about an hour before dawn. He then followed himself in a forced march at day break. The Irish followed as swiftly on the opposite, or northern bank but the convex course of the river (to speak by the map) gave them the longer journey. Clifford cut across the arc. Brooke held the ford, and thus, by a brilliant piece of strategy, the army passed across safe, though not scatheless. Clifford now sat three miles from Ballyshannon, at Abbey Assaroe, and most happily for him a ship which he had ordered up from Galway arrived next day with field-pieces. He set his guns at the castle and shot away a flanker. He then set seven hundred men to lock up the garrison, and waited until morning to attack more sharply. With courage and blood his men won a cellar that morning. Maguire and O'Rourke now brought up their men to attack the besiegers, but Clifford gallantly held his ground, despite heavy fighting.

He was now five days and nights under arms, and with victory in his grasp his food was running out. To his horror he found that Maguire and O'Rourke did not attack him next morning but were passing southward over the river to his rear, cheering madly. News had come of Brough's failure to pass beyond the Blackwater, and Tyrone was on his way to join forces with O'Donnell and decimate the common enemy. To his credit, Clifford held on like a terrier until he got full confirmation of this report. Then he turned back. His retreat was a gallant one. He refused to march by night. 'God forbid,' he exclaimed, 'that any such cause of pride should be given to them.' He lost a field-piece in shipping it. He had but one barrel of powder and little lead. Half his companies were Irish. He had two Connaught earls with him, Clanricard and Thomond, but he swore that for all the good they were to him he had but their persons. It was sixty miles to his nearest place of relief, and in that sort of country twenty miles a day would be a tremendous march. He addressed his men, and at daybreak he set off, with drums playing and ensigns flying. There he took his punishment. O'Donnell attacked savagely and ceaselessly. Clifford closed his ranks and marched on. O'Donnell followed, attacking murderously for hour after hour. Then the day broke suddenly into torrents of rain and no man could fire a musket and the fighting closed in with blood on every knife and javelin. In six hours Clifford marched eight miles, and then he had no powder left, and his army was a straggle. O'Donnell's foot then drew off, but his horse kept up the attack for another seven miles. It was a great tribute to Clifford that he was not decimated, and it is hard to see why the Irish did not destroy his forces to a man. When he was back inside walls again, and could look about him Clifford could only admit that the general expedition had failed: more, that Tibbot Burke, whom he had twice driven over the Erne, was coming back again into Connaught. To fight these guerillas was the labours of Sisyphus indeed. One final bit of bad news marked that July in deep black in the calendar of the colonists: that was a successful attack by one of Tyrone's best commandos in the south, Captain Tyrrell, who cut the forces of Lord Trimleston to pieces at a place known as Tyrrell's Pass.

Brough kept his bitter courage intact in the face of these disasters, and though his men were half-starving, girded his old loins for another march on October 5th. Meantime he offered a spy who came to him £1,000 to assassinate Tyrone. He was himself dead by October 13th. He had not been well, one night, and asked for a drink, and somebody had mentioned Sir Garret Moore's liquor and said that it was good drinking. Brough went into Moore's tent and received a drink and fell, almost at once, into a see-saw between cold shivering and burning fever. They knew he was cold by feeling his face, and hands, and feet, but he kept calling for white wine, or claret, diluted with water or beer, and kept tearing at his clothes in his paroxysms until his whole waist was naked. Then he would throw out his arms. Then he would creep into bed and order big fires to be lit about him. Whether it was poison or the common Irish ague he was dead within a week. As he died he moaned for his dear Queen's sake, commending his body to her to be buried how and where she willed, his Garter and George to her hands, his hopes to his wife, and what goods he had for the rearing of his children that they might be brought up in the true fear of the Almighty.

Left without a general, without a plan, and virtually without an army, there was nothing for Elizabeth to do but make one more peace with the man now so often christened that she had choice of a dozen names for him—The Running Beast, the Great Divill, the Great Bear, the Northern Lucifer, or, crowning all, Beelzebub.

2

It would, from one point of view at least, be a satisfaction to know that Brough actually was poisoned. It would mark this as one of the very rare occasions when the Irish came anywhere near the perfect finish of European practitioners. All through the century they had had many excellent examples of the art of political assassination. They appear to have been obtuse students and continued to murder in the old, unenlightened fashion. Whenever they wished to remove a private individual they simply killed him, often in public; or if they employed assassins they tried to cover the thing up with some botched-up story that nobody could possibly believe. Tyrone, at the removal of Sean's son, Hugh Gaveloch, actually stood by, and was inevitably charged with holding the rope himself. And then those histrionic explanations and emotional scenes afterwards before the Council at Dublin. Compare the smooth removal of Red Hugh, years later, by poison in Spain—so smooth that it can still be argued if he really was poisoned by the English. But the Irish seem never to have learned even the rudiments of poisoning, not even in modern days, when people are despatched unimaginatively either with the obvious strychnine or arsenic, or, actually, with rat-killer. Against that there is only one example of a badly botched

English effort on Tyrone, that of a man named Walker in the summer of 1601. Yet, even there, the decencies were preserved. This Walker, with the approval and connivance of the Lord Deputy, Sir Harry Davers, and Cecil, got so near Tyrone that he could see his white breast through his black frieze jerkin inviting the knife. He actually drew his sword under pretence of defending Tyrone in a dispute, but he 'gave way to effeminate thoughts,' as he confessed, and did not do it. When he got back to Dublin his employers very properly threw him into jail and Lord Mountjoy declared that he thought the fellow 'little better than frantic.' It is gratifying to note with what discretion the editor of the State Papers containing the account lists it. 'Thomas Walker, the fanatic, his designs on Tyrone.' No Irishman could ever have been talented enough to handle this indelicate affair so nicely. Under these circumstances we can have but little reason for believing that Brough was poisoned. Had he been found with his throat cut one might feel a little more secure. It is true that the autopsy, performed on Christmas Eve, in the dim candle-lit cellars of Dublin Castle by Edmund Cullen, Barber-Surgeon, did not show that his 'head gave in abundance' which was considered a sure sign of poison since the venom always 'works out through the organical parts of the head.' But this is the less strange seeing that poor Brough, by that date, had been over two months a corpse. What a post-mortem it must have been; a typically Elizabethan conclusion to any horrid, blood-stained melodrama by Kyd or Marlowe.

3

Tyrone dragged out the pause following the disasters of July (1597) in parley after parley into the summer of 1598, although every man must have known well by now that in this dicing for time he was gambling on but one word—Spain.

Ormonde was now the Lord General of the Queen's army, but he led nothing more than a ragged rabble, and when he came north to confer with Tyrone he hid the bulk of his forces, for very shame, in the back streets of Dundalk. Once again the conference took place in the open, with the Irish troops insolently dotting the hills. Tyrone spoke across a brook. In '96 he had been modest. Now he spoke like a man who had fixed his star to the Celtic Hesper. Thus, Ormonde was accompanied by the Bishop of Meath, that same Jones who had married Tyrone to Mabel

Bagenal, and when the two asked him to send in pledges he refused absolutely and when, with the typical colonial contempt for all native traditions, they explained complacently that every gentleman in Ireland always sent his sons 'out of this barbarous country' to be trained in civility, his reply was contemptuous.

'You are much mistaken. You do not know the North as I know it. If my sons were out of this country their people would despise them. And if they were not here in Ulster how would *you* treat them? They would be treated as I was treated by Sir Henry Sidney when my father died. The people made Turlough the O'Neill—my father's enemy! And Sir Henry supported him against me! And he was supported by every Deputy ever till the day he died.'

This was a revelation. Tyrone had never before let out one murmur of this, all through the quarter of a century and more since he came back to Ireland as a youth from the English Court. Nobody had ever suspected before that he had resented the delay in giving him his title. How silent he had been! How darkly he had hidden his grievance! Ormonde was aghast and begged him to remember Her Majesty's goodness, how she had lifted him from the dust, given him a pension, 'preserved thee by her motherly care,' advanced him to the great honour of an earldom. Tyrone mocked him.

'Her Majesty never gave me anything but what belonged to me. And as for what I have gotten I got it by my own scratching of the world, and not from her goodness. Have I not spent my blood for her? Have I not kept quiet for thirty years? Bounden to serve? To offer her my sons? You shall get none of my sons, but my word and oath for keeping the peace. I am resolved never to deliver any of my sons. And do you think that I esteem my sons so much? Between me and God if they were both,' turning to his sons who stood by him, 'in your hands all this while I would have done just the same that I have done.'

They begged him to consider the matter to the next day but he waved the idea aside.

'Nay, no more considering. I will never do it. And, further, if it were not the time it is, with the Queen's word given, they would not be here at all. I am sworn to my people to bring them home with me—my people who now respect them but would not respect them if they were not in the country scratching for themselves.'

One can feel in that outspoken rush of angry feeling the relief that it must have given Tyrone to speak out at last. The dammed-up arrogance of the man is free—and it is surely that rather than a suppressed sense of injustice that pours from him? For, in those early days with Sidney, what he felt on seeing Turlough tolerated must have been chiefly disappointment, and that emotion would not have become bilious until, in his pride and in his security, he still suffered prick after prick from the Bagenals and the Fitzwilliams, and their petty spies and agents. By then, returned to the ways of his fathers, more an O'Neill than a Tyrone, conscious of the loyalty and admiration of his people and of the suspicion and indifference of the colonists, he must suddenly have asked himself, in his fury at some new snub, 'Why do I tolerate these insults? Why have I ever tolerated them? Who are they, and who am I? And to think that for all these years...' And then his mind would race back furiously over the long list of injustices that he had suffered at the hands of these people, and he would forget the time when he was a 'little rascal horseboy,' as well as the time when he willingly took their help, even to the point of fighting against his own people to retain it and exploit it.

Now his pride had its day-out. He told Ormonde and Jones that he spoke for the men of Leinster and the men of Connaught, and that they must be given back their ancestral lands on whatever peace was made. Ormonde cried that these men had nothing whatever to do with the Earl, and as for their lands, that was finished with because they had been granted away to English settlers. Thereupon Harry Hoveden burst out that these patents could very easily be reversed. But Tyrone had cooled now and explained that he desired only an equity of land for his people.

'But, I pray you, said Ormonde, 'do you mean that if my two traitorous nephews were alive that you would want to have *them* considered in this peace?'

'I would indeed,' cried Tyrone.

'And I would as soon be hanged,' cried Ormonde, and swore on it, and that day's talk ended angrily with all the horsemen galloping away from the brook. To sting Ormonde's temper the more Tyrone sent his Gaelic secretary riding after him with a letter that had just come in from Red Hugh. The secretary read the letter which, as it was being read, was translated into English by Miler Magrath, Archbishop of Cashel, for the scowling Ormonde. Red Hugh was protesting against a peace of any kind now that Leinster was on their side, and Connaught in their hands, and Ulster untouched. He swore that he would break the peace if he had left with him but one horseboy to ride at his side.

On the next morning Tyrone asked what they proposed to do about religious liberty. Ormonde broke into a fury and asked,

'My Lord, what have you and I to do to meddle with matters of religion?'

And drawing away from the fire of that controversial subject he set Jones to discuss it with him. It was as well; for Tyrone again let his pride have full rein. He was speaking for all the Catholics of Ireland who would fall on the English if they were interfered with. He was speaking for the Pale and Dublin. In dismay Jones warned him that he would undo himself with this kind of talk. Tyrone merely wheeled his horse about and spurred back to Ormonde and pressed the entire sheaf of papers containing these conditions, or petitions, into his hands. Ormonde dared not accept such a paper and thrust them back in terror. Tyrone forced them on him, into his breast, and short of throwing them to the winds Ormonde had to take them although he swore that he would throw them into the fire when he got back to Dundalk. For all that Ormonde sent a copy to London though carefully marking it 'Suppressed.'

Tyrone's demands, petitions, and requests were for Liberty of Conscience, full Pardon, complete restoration of all his Titles and Patents, the return of his pledges, the restoration to his followers of all their ancient lands, the withdrawal of every garrison, and that Tyrone itself be made a County Palatine. In short, everything must be as it had been before the colonists pierced into the west and north, and he would be in his *Palatium*, or Palace of Dungannon—petty emperor, far greater than Earl, equal to such stuff of kingship as, say, Henry of Lancaster, who had been a like ducal power before he took the throne of England. Is it any wonder that Ormonde, that cautious riveter of his own satisfying local power under the Crown, swore that he would throw the mad document into the first fire he met? He excusably felt that its title seemed satirical—'The Most Humble and penitent Submission of me, Hugh, Earl of Tyrone.'

That was just before Christmas (1597). By his usual methods Tyrone prorogued further meetings from March to April and April to June. With each delay he became more and more arrogant and less and less accommodating. Jones observed ominously that all his oaths were now reduced to one oath, 'By this cross on my sword.' And in all his long day-by-day debates he still insisted on speaking not for himself but for all his people—as Fenton said, 'A confluence of discontented people drawn from all parts of the realm to seek refuge from him in their grievances, some for title of land, some for goods, as though they were to be relieved upon a parley hill in Ulster by the censure of a traitor.' It was on that point that they broke finally after arguing for four days out there on the showery hillocks. He argued the claims of each captain after another, O'Reilly's, Kavanagh's, Burke's. Red Hugh had come in now to take part in the discussions, though only after a great display of unwillingness, and he declared that he would break on the claims of that Tibbot Burke whom Clifford had twice pushed out of Connaught. In a word the two stood for the rights of something that began to look like an emergent Irish nation. And that was a thing that had not been seen in Ireland since the ancient days of the High Kings at Tara. Bishop Jones could not understand this new spirit.

'My Lord and O'Donnell,' he besought them, 'are you to forsake your prince for Tibbot Burke? Is Tibbot Burke so precious a jewel in your eyes that you will hazard your estates for him? Will you offend God, provoke your Prince, and undo yourselves for Tibbot Burke? I pray you, My Lord of Tyrone, deal plainly with me. Suppose we devise some way of satisfying Tibbot Burke? Will that make an end of all this? Or is there something else in the matter?'

At that Tyrone took Red Hugh's arm and said,

'Stay, My Lord, I conceive your meaning well enough. Come O'Donnell and by God's hand let us deal plainly with the Bishop. And with Jones and Sir Harry Brounker they went aside. 'I will not deny,' said Tyrone, 'that we have written into Spain for Spaniards. And I confess that there is a day agreed between us. I will not tell you whether that day is past or to come. It may be they will deceive us. It may be they have already broken with us.–'

'Nay,' said the Bishop, butting in, 'but I know. They *have* deceived you. And are good warrants always to deceive anybody who trusts them.'

Red Hugh chucked him by the sleeve there and interrupted him, and said,

'If everything that is in debate here were ready and cleared up perhaps we *would* forsake them?'

'But isn't everything cleared except Tibbot·Burke?'—from Jones.

'No,' said Tyrone. 'There is O'Reilly. And others—to all of whom we have given our oaths.'

'So you make your demands infinite?' wailed the Bishop.

To which Tyrone answered that he had given his oath and must keep it, and O'Donnell said that he would never be at peace unless Burke had his seignory, and Tyrone added again O'Reilly, and Onie O'Moore, and all the others, and O'Donnell summed it up with '*all* the men who have taken part with me!' And when the Bishop cried out that that could only be done by banishing the English inhabitants, Tyrone said:

'It must be done!'

That finished the parleys. The old Bishop went back sadly to Dublin and wrote that 'a traitor will be a traitor.' The Gaelic captains had hated all this talk and were constantly raging at Tyrone's fondness for it.

'Wilt thou never be wise?' they protested. 'Can no counsel take place with thee? Hast thou nobody to treat with but the Earl of Ormonde who clipped the wings of Desmond and overthrew him, his house, and all his posterity?'

Tyrone knew what he was doing. His crops were sown. He had saved himself six months heavy outlay, more indeed than he could continuously afford, for his army and mercenaries were now costing him, in our money, up to £4,000 a day. He was spreading his influence wider and deeper every day. And that he needed it all he knew better than any man about him. He knew that the barometer of war would soon be soaring.

CHAPTER THREE

THE CAMPAIGN OF 1598: MARSHAL BAGENAL

I

The campaign of 1598, though tardily begun, was swiftly over. Since Ormonde became Lieutenant-General, and Sir Henry Bagenal was given practical command of the army, and the local Council in Dublin planned and decided the campaign, it was, in effect, a test of the Anglo-Irish colony's capacity to manage its own affairs. Tyrone exposed them as knaves and cowards, and Elizabeth did not spare them the scorpions of her tongue.

For months and months the local advisers had been recommending to London the setting up a garrison on the extreme tip of Ulster, Lough Foyle. This was the great new plan which would take Tyrone in the rear, divide his army, and 'impeach him on his outer limb.' It was a sound scheme provided that it was effectively seconded from the south, but it would cost an enormous amount of money and Elizabeth had to endure the shame of a few more disasters—which cost her far more in the end—before she would agree to budget for it. Nevertheless the plan was so strongly recommended that 2,000 men were levied, to be sent as soon as possible to Lough Foyle.

Tyrone countermoved by beating the drums in Leinster and besieging the Fort of the Blackwater, whose garrison was soon reduced to eating horse and wild greens growing on the sides of the sconce. Dublin took fright and decided to protect the frontier. Under the subsequent blast of Elizabeth's contempt they all so bickered and lied, and tried to throw the blame on one another for their decisions that it is hard to know now what they did decide. One thing is clear—that Bagenal's personal hatred of Tyrone had a good deal to do with what followed. On June 17th the Council decided to send him to lie on the frontier with the troops available, Ormonde remaining behind to tackle and defend Leinster. On the 26th Bagenal took up his command. On July 18th 1600 of the first 2,000 men promised from England arrived in Dublin. Ormonde, the Commander-in-Chief, was away in Kilkenny—men said protecting his own estates as usual—and until he returned to the city the Council did not well know what to do with the new levies. But as the men were, as usual, turning into rowdies and terrifying the citizens of Dublin, selling their arms, and deserting daily, 1,000 of them were sent to Bagenal on the frontier. Bagenal was chafing to get at his ancient enemy's throat and welcomed them eagerly, although they arrived greatly reduced and with a serious loss of arms. Tyrone was just as willing to sting Bagenal. His guerillas ranged over Leinster ravaging without pity, and he let Bagenal know that every road and river northward was so plashed, spiked, or trenched that nobody would ever dare to venture as far as Blackwater Fort.

The Dublin Council, without the spur of personal hatred that was eating at the heart of Bagenal, having no insults to wipe out and no dead sister to bewail, had meanwhile kept on postponing an attack on Tyrone. At one stage they advised Bagenal to come to terms with Tyrone for the surrender of the Fort, but Bagenal, wild with fury, tore up the letter and raced down to Dublin to protest against their dishonourable advice, and for six weeks after importuned the Council to let him attack. Worn down, the Council finally begged Ormonde to command the attack if an attack must take place; but Ormonde, although he was the Commander-in-Chief, shirked the job—either because he wanted to protect his own vast property in Leinster or because he was too shrewd to take the responsibility of leading any attack on so powerful an enemy. In the end the man who desperately wanted his own way got it. Had he succeeded everybody would have admitted a share in this common decision: he lost and everybody tried to dodge responsibility.

Bagenal moved north against his enemy about August 7th. At eight o'clock on the morning of August 14th he left Armagh. About two miles from Armagh he fell into a full battle with Tyrone. It is the most famous battle of all these campaigns and became known as the Battle of the Yellow Ford. That night out of Bagenal's army of 4,350 men, his remnants of about 1,500 men lay cooped up in the Cathedral of Armagh with the Irish fires winking on the hills around. Bagenal lay among them a corpse. They had lost all their colours, their cannon, about twenty captains, all their ammunition and food. They had lost Blackwater Fort, and the year's fighting. They had almost destroyed the reputation of England among the clansmen. Tyrone's fame was almost at its peak.

2

What had happened is of the first interest as a picture of war in the sixteenth century.

Bagenal led an army on the march—a long, straggling, cavalcade of footmen and horses, with all their colours, carts, ordnance, and vivandiers, an impressive line weaving its way among those little hills of Armagh, so many little islands among the boggy meadows that are, even to-day, moist in midsummer. Then, before three-and-a-half centuries of drainage, every step must have clogged the heavy cart-wheels. That cavalcade of 4,000 men must have measured very little under a mile from the 'Forlorn Hope' to the last straggling camp-follower in the Rear. As they were making for Blackwater Fort they had very little choice as to their road because they had to cross first a little river called the Callan, and the regular place of crossing was at a ford known as the Yellow Ford because, for some reason, the water ran discoloured at that place. To-day a few little boreens, little more than cow-tracks rutted with cart-wheels, wind into these unemphatic hills and stop suddenly at a farm or a ruin. The squat tower of the Cathedral in Armagh rises to the south. The hills of Benburb are like shadows on the horizon towards the west. One is aware of the presence of water on all sides, in dykes and drains and little streams and sedgy meadows, and low scrub invokes the woods that once further confused a generally featureless terrain.

Bagenal's cavalcade approached the ford in a wide sweep from the east and when he was about half a mile from it he realized that the sniping that had been going on almost since he left Armagh, and which he would have taken for granted as a regular feature of any such march, was this time a prelude to a serious engagement. Holes dug in the ground, and spiked, edged in his outlying horse. Heavier firing forced him into what he must have begun to foresee was an ambush. In the scrub of juniper, hawthorn, and pine he could see Tyrone's young men dodging in and out, picking off the men on his flanks like so many wasps. Tyrone kept these younger men for the lighter sharpshooting warfare: his veterans were for the savage in-fighting. That opening technique was to waste the enemy's powder, demoralize, and diminish him. Still he plodded on and when he was partly over the ford, beyond which is a sharp hill, and then an open boggy space, his van was at least in sight of the look-out on the top of the Fort. Midway along the open boggy space, however, Tyrone had dug out an elaborate trench, a mile long, five feet deep, and four feet wide. In addition there were more of those 'elephant traps,' that is holes covered with wicker and grass to catch the horses as they chased the decoy kernes to the right and left.

The van crossed ford, hill, and bog until they were within gunshot of the trench and there the battle broke. But the rear was still well out of sight at the ford and behind it, and they neither knew what was going on in the front nor could assist even if they knew. Tyrone took the van and O'Donnell simultaneously fell on the rear so that the battle was now general. (Bagenal had divided his army into three divisions of two regiments each, and made the fatal mistake of leaving about one hundred and fifty paces between each regiment.) Regiment number One, raked from the trench, spread out and charged it, and crossed it. Beyond, it discovered a slope surmounted by a sconce and down this slope came the onrush of Tyrone's horse to break the line that had already been frayed in taking the trench. By this charge they were thrown back towards and across the ditch before Regiment number Two, under Bagenal's personal command, could come up to their assistance. While this second regiment was fighting its way forward to the front Bagenal lifted his vizor to see more clearly what was happening, and in that second he was shot dead through the forehead.

Meanwhile back along the extending line the Centre was in difficulties in the bog where the cannon had stuck fast. There they were being attacked on their flanks. Kernes, with their five-foot javelins held over the head, would rush forward, hurl their pieces and race back. The gallowglasses, corsleted and battle-axed, would take over for in-fighting. The usual musketeers covered the retreat of both until the next wave was ready to charge. Regiments number Five and Six in the rear, were also getting it hot and heavy from Red Hugh, Maguire, and James MacSorley, both horse and foot, and in one-and-a-half hours solid fighting were not allowed to know what was going on in the front and centre and did not, in fact, move a quarter of a mile from where they stood when first attacked. In the middle of the melee a fresh disaster befell the Centre, under Captain Cosby, when two firkins of powder blew up. One report says that at least one regiment of the Centre, regiment number Three of the whole army, did get across the ditch to help the Vanguard. If so, it was in vain. The Vanguard was, for all practical purposes, already lost.

At Bagenal's death Wingfield, originally with the Fourth regiment, took the command and ordered the two regiments behind to retire. Unfortunately Captain Cosby who received this order found, when he was milling about with the Fourth in the effort to contact Five and Six and draw off in good order, or thought he found a chance to attack with some hope of success, and at once he got into fresh difficulties. Wingfield had no option but to call back Five to assist the insubordinate Cosby, and at that all hope of an orderly retreat was lost. Two more barrels of gun powder now exploded among the demoralized

English and completely shattered what spirit was left in them. Tyrone saw his chance and hurled fresh multitudes of his men at Wingfield—the van being now a shambles.

Wingfield was wildly trying to cover his men who were pulling at the bogged cannon. The oxen heaved and strained. The defence circled about them. The lightfooted Irish cut through with enough men to hamstring the unfortunate beasts, and there was nothing left for the English but to hack their way, every man for himself, back and back out of the slaughter, and under the protection of their horse at the rear, fly for the protection of that cathedral tower rising so invitingly over the hills to the south. To their credit Bagenal's regiment guarded his body as well as their own lives, and managed to get it back through the struggling welter of men out of the battle-zone. To their credit the English horse held the ford open for their foot, and protected them all the way back to the city. There the weary remnants of the morning's mile-long cavalcade clambered in the sweltering heat up the hillside into the old cathedral, barred the gates and doors, and flung themselves down in their exhaustion and their wounds. They had left nearly three-fourths of their comrades strewn behind them in the bogs and scrub and soggy fields. Everywhere they looked, when dark fell, were those besieging fires.

In summary, the immediate cause of Bagenal's defeat was the isolation, at the crucial moment, of the Vanguard from the Centre, and of the Centre from the rearguard: and the further isolation of the respective regiments of the first and second formations of the army—all this at a time when the whole army was being attacked on the front, rear, and flanks. This state of affairs arose because Bagenal, in view of the difficulties of the terrain, was unable to deploy his army laterally and had to take the risk of going into battle in column of route.

In their terror the Dublin Council completely lost their heads. They wrote to Tyrone a letter that marks the scummy low-water mark of their oozing courage. They said that his enemy the Marshal was now dead so that he could no longer feel the same enmity towards the colony, and they begged him to let the remnants of the army go free from Armagh. Always ready to make a good bargain Tyrone agreed, on condition that the Blackwater Fort and Armagh were again given up. He had nothing to gain by the slaughter of more men, once again proving that he fully understood that he would never defeat the English by a military victory, but rather by a long and protracted series of costly campaigns. Besides, O'Donnell and the rest were eager to return home and gather the harvest and drive off the inevitable local vultures who were always ready to profit by the absence of rival septs.

3

The news of this new victory of Tyrone's had an astonishing effect on the country. A wave of feeling that was like one vast geyser of long suppressed discontent gushed up and smothered the colonists until, within a few months, Tyrone was virtual master of Ireland and could see the outline of a rapidly-forming Confederate Army. Everywhere men were claiming old titles and the colonists abandoning them. Desmond's nephew, James Fitzthomas Fitzgerald, claimed his uncle's title and set out to fight for it. The people jocosely called him the Sugaun Earl, or the Hayrope Earl, but Tyrone supported him and sent down his best commandos Lacy and Tyrrell to join Ownie O'Moore and the other southern guerillas and ravage the terrified colonists along the southern Shannon. Viscount Mountgarret claimed the title which Ormonde hitherto held and boastfully invited Tyrone to dine with him that Christmas in Ormonde's castle at Kilkenny. And Mountgarret's influence was wide. His son married one of Tyrone's many daughters. One of his sisters was married to the Baron of Cahir, another to the Lord of Upper Ossory, a third to the Devereuxs of Wexford. The Earl of Thomond's brother, Theigue O'Brien, was in arms. The Kavanaghs of Leinster found a leader in Donal Spainneach (the Spaniard). Piers Lacy, John the brother of Lord Barry, and the two sons of Lord Roche went over to the Irish. The Baron of Cahir threw off his allegiance. Even the Earl of Kildare became suspect. By the December of that year (1598) Norreys could only list four principal men not in revolt; of these two were in arms for the colony and the Queen, and the other two could not command ten men for her service. The country was 'impassable for any faithful subject, especially all who wear hose and breeches.'

How quickly the fire spread we may see from the fact that the least promising province, Munster, cowed since the Desmond wars, was now also up in arms. The Yellow Ford took place in August. By September Tyrone's commandos were down on the borders of Munster, and Norreys writing frantically to Dublin that he could make no resistance. By October Ownie O'Moore was ravaging at will and the province could not muster one hundred horse to face him. Norreys was in despair, and everybody complaining that while they were being butchered Tyrone was fooling Ormonde, still Commander-in-Chief of the colonists, in the North. When Ormonde finally came south he found that the settlers were flying on all sides from their estates, and even from the towns, into the walled cities like Cork and Limerick. It is a sharp light on the state of the country that when Norreys was at Mallow Ormonde bade him come to meet him at Kilmallock, which is about twenty miles away, and the Lord President refused to come without a special convoy. When Ormonde reached Mallow he found it deserted. It was the same story everywhere, settlers flying and leaving their spoils, arms and ammunition to Tyrone's men. The city of Cork was jammed with refugees 'rifled and spoiled, man woman and child, yea of the very clothes from their backs.' Ormonde could do nothing. Behind his back in Ossory, Tyrone's lieutenants were burning and destroying his own country unchecked. The South, in imitation of Tyrone's tactics in the North, flitted through the great woods on his flank and tail, and when he turned back to defend his own ravaged estates closed in behind him and took possession again.

The list of wealthy castles and dwelling-houses abandoned in that year, with their furniture and stock, seemed well-nigh endless. Maine and Pallas abandoned by Sir Henry Ughtred whe fled to Limerick with his wife; Edward Fitton, the county sheriff, fled to England; Sir George Bourchier put in Ulick Browne who gave all to the Irish; Newcastle, abandoned by Sir William Courtney; Foynes and Shanid; Tarbert left by Justice Goold; Kilfinnane left by Aylmer; Adare and Bruff by Thornton; 'Generally all the English in Kerry ran away'; in Cork, the President Norreys 'ran away first' from Mallow and discouraged all the Englishry about him; Tracton, Castlemahon, Mallow; all the English of the seignory of Sir Walter Raleigh and Sir Warham St. Leger; Mogeely and Rosscarbery; the Bishop of Cork fled into the city; Saxey the Chief Justice of Munster fled bag and baggage to London; Stovel lost Carrigrohane two miles from Cork city. . . . That was in county Cork and county Limerick. Waterford and Tipperary repeated the same tale until the walled towns were full of homeless people who slept huddled in churches and public buildings in the greatest misery of mind and body. The words of the poet Spenser, driven out of his own castle at Kilcolman, convey that misery impressively: 'Out of the ashes of desolation and wasteness of this your wretched Realm of Ireland vouchsafe, most mighty Empress our dread Sovereign, to receive the voices of a few most unhappy ghosts of whom is nothing but the ghost now left buried in the bottom of oblivion. . .' And seeing to-day the ruins of Spenser's castle at Kilcolman, in County Cork, on that remote hillside under the Ballyhouras, one can readily imagine the terror of the dark night when the dispossessed Irish rose out of their own naked misery and sent up his house in flames. (We have only Ben Jonson's word for it that a new-born infant was burned in this sack of Kilcolman.) But horror was all over Ireland in the winter of '98, people flying into the bogs and hills, houses burning, suppressed rage taking a bitter unmeasured revenge for those sixteen years of slavery since Desmond rose and fell. It gives a measure of Elizabethan dismay that Bingham was dragged out of his obscurity and put beside Ormonde, an old bull-dog gone beyond service both for age and illness. He lay in Dublin inert, and presently died there leaving the army once more without a head.

Men now commonly spoke of Tyrone as Prince of Ireland, or King of Ireland, and he was regarded as such abroad where his messengers were treated as ambassadors. That winter his hand was not merely heavy on the English in Ireland; he became a threat to England itself, recalling the prophecy of Ann Wilmar that he would become a leader of peoples there and a reformer of religion. He sent O'Hagan, whose hereditary office it was to inaugurate the O'Neills, across to James of Scotland to offer him the crown of Ireland—which seems to suggest that he was envisaging a Catholic monarchy and an Ireland content under it. James ignored the offer but it was wildly believed that he had some sort of understanding with Tyrone. A spy reported to the English around this time that James had given him a personal gift as one of Tyrone's messengers; and he swore that there was some sort of secret collusion between the two. That contact marks the beginning of the Irish Jacobite allegiance. Philip of Spain wrote a warm letter of congratulation on the success of the Yellow Ford. It was common rumour that the Pope was sending him a Bull to excommunicate all heretics, and some said that the Holy Father was having a crown made for his coronation. His reputation abroad as a soldier, as witness books like *La Spada D'Orione* (Rome, 1680) with its praise of Ugo Conte di Tirone Generale Ibernese, probably dates from this year in which he just became an important European figure, known and admired by every general on the Continent.

4

It was an extraordinary transformation. What was happening to Tyrone was what happened to Desmond. He had started a war for reasons more or less personal. Ambition had been his spur, wounded pride had stung him, the deep-rooted, atavistic thing which is in all Irishmen had salted those wounds. As he drove deeper and deeper into the war he found more and more justification for it. The enlargement of the impulse had meant an enlargement of the war, and so an enlargement of the man until, as always happens in the history of men and peoples like him and his, he became a symbol or personification of all the forces latent in him and them. The conflict thereby became more than an Irish conflict. It was now watched from abroad as a phase of the whole European conflict of which the wars of the Low Countries, the Armada, Bartholomew's Day, the internal conflicts of France, the Scottish scene, the conspiracies of the Papacy were all a part.

The priests had long been trying to force this wider issue but for lack of a leader, a human mould to hold their ideas, all their efforts had hitherto evaporated in the secrecy of casual inspiration that lasted little longer than the breath of a conspirator on a frosty day. Now they have the man and the movement. They are no longer a secret or casual influence but an open power. They control and direct. They are not only preachers, but messengers, spies, propagandists, secretaries to the fighting-men, smugglers of arms, interpreters in small affairs and large. Tyrone's language, Mountgarret's letters, reflect their zeal and the breadth of their ideas.

In a very little while Tyrone will be sending out documents like this: it is addressed to Lord Barry, Viscount Buttevant:—

> 'Your impiety to God, cruelty to your soul and body, tyranny and ingratitude both to your followers and country, are inexcusable and intolerable. You separated yourself from the unity of Christ, His mystical body, the Catholic Church. You know the sword of extirpation hangeth over your head as well

as ours, if things fall out otherwise than well. You are the cause why all the nobility of the south from the east part to the west, you being linked unto each one of them either in affinity or consanguinity, are not linked together to shake off the cruel yoke of heresy and tyranny, with which our souls and bodies are oppressed, all those aforesaid depending on your resolution, and relying unto your judgement in this common cause of our religion and country. You might, forsooth, with their help and the rest that are combined in this holy action, not only defend yourself from the incursion and invasion of the English, but also, by God's assistance (who, miraculously, and above all expectation, gave good success to the cause principally undertaken for his glory, exaltation of religion, next for the restoration of the ruins and preservation of the country) expel them, and deliver them, and us from the most miserable tyranny and cruel exaction and subjection, enjoy your religion, safety of wife and children, life, lands, and goods, which all are in hazard through your folly and want of due consideration. Enter, I beseech you, into the close of your conscience, and like a wise man weigh seriously the end of your actions, and take advice of those who can instruct you and inform you better than your own private judgement can lead you unto.'

It is possible that Tyrone did not dictate this letter. It may have been written by the Jesuit, Father Archer, who was constantly at his service in those years. Nevertheless it is signed 'O'Neill.'

Knowing that Spain and Rome could here banish all suspicions that these Irish wars were mere tribal feuds Tyrone sent his most trusted lieutenant, Hugh Boy MacDevitt, to the Continent to force the issue to the limit. Other Irish were busy at the Spanish court, or at the Port of Ferrol. By the beginning of 1599 it seemed as if these ambassadors were producing results. Three fleets were being made ready. The Adelantado was preparing one at Cadiz; the Duke of Medina a second at San Lucas, and a third was rigging in Lisbon. MacDevitt had high hopes of obtaining his suit for six thousand men, and there were enough rumours of large masses of men being held or made ready in various parts of Spain to suggest that six thousand for Ireland would be but a small number from all that were available. Then when Tyrone's hopes were high, and at a time—the end of 1598—when he needed all the assistance that Spain and Rome could give him, his hopes suddenly dwindled. Philip II was dead and there was a general feeling that Philip III was inclined for peace, and if England were relieved of the Spanish threat she would be free to give her full attention to Ireland. Elizabeth was rising in her wrath. 'We disdain to bear affronts from a rabble of base kerne.' It was no longer a question of sending an army of two thousand men, or four thousand men, or six thousand men. She opened her purse. Sixteen thousand foot and all but fifteen hundred horse were got ready in England to clear the arch-traitor out of her path. Two thousand additional men, over and above these, were to arrive every month. In addition there would be many volunteers eager to take service under the new English general. Robert Devereux, Earl of Essex, at the head of the largest army ever sent across the Irish sea.

CHAPTER FOUR

THE CAMPAIGN OF 1599: ESSEX

> 'His greatness was such he was called the Earl of Excess . . . or if the wealth of England and Spain had been put into his hands he would have consumed it winning towns and towers in the air, promising much and performing nothing.'
>
> Sir William Warren: May 28th, 1601.

I

THE AFFAIRS OF the Earl of Essex, though merely incidental to the story of Tyrone, go far to explain the Irish success in the 1599 campaign. Essex came to Ireland against his better judgement and was already dispirited before he sailed. He had barely patched up that bitter quarrel with Elizabeth, of the year before, when she had banged him on the ear and he had clapped his hand to his sword. The occasion had been a quarrel at the council table as to who should be sent to Ireland; she favouring Knollys, he Carew. For two months they had not spoken, and the court had been like a barnyard when the chief cockerel is being henpecked. The reconciliation had seemed complete; but monarchs do not forget such gestures as the flight of a hand to a hilt, certainly no English monarch mindful of times when feudal lords could make or mar a kingdom. Once back at the council board Essex so violently opposed the proposal to replace the dead Bingham by Mountjoy that when his own name was slyly suggested by his enemies, and no alternative forthcoming, he was unable to wriggle out of it. The wisest head in all England, Bacon, who had earlier favoured the idea now advised him against it, pointing out acutely that Elizabeth would become sultry and sullen in his absence, that nothing he did would please her, and that nothing she did would content him. Essex himself knew full well what these Irish wars meant: he had not won a reputation as one of the best soldiers in England on nothing. He knew of the disease that would consume his armies, the famine and misery that would make them lose heart, 'And yet all these were better endured,' he wrote to his friend Willoughby, with reference to court intrigues behind his back, 'than to have a Hanno at Carthage, or a Cato at Rome, barking at him who is everyday venturing his life for his country abroad. All these things which I am like to see, I do now foresee.' It was no spirit in which to undertake a serious war.

So, while the kernes ranged the island in their thousands, soaked by the heavy rains of late winter, and the English garrisons held themselves shivering behind their walls, and every storm blew the cloaks of the travelling priests between their legs, and the besieged townsfolk listened to the rain battering their casements, Essex and his gallants were listening as gloomily to their ships tugging at their Welsh moorings, unable to stir from the quays. Although he was but thirty-two Essex, waiting at Hillbree, shook with the ague, and hearing the rain pouring on the roads outside before the westerly wind, cursed the 'moist, rotten country' to which he was bound, and occupied himself by writing melancholy letters to the council at Richmond. He complained of everything. Elizabeth had refused to make his stepfather Sir Christopher Blount a member of the Irish Council. ('I am sent out maimed beforehand. . . .') Sir Callisthenes Brooke was sending him in discouraging reports of the army. ('If the body of the army prove unwieldy of joints I must desire to be freed from all imputation. . . .') He heard stories that he was being blackened already at the court. ('Your Lordships might rather pity me than expect extraordinary successes of me . . . for if I have not inward comfort and outward demonstration of Her Majesty's favour I am defeated in England.') Still held by the foggy weather and the ceaseless wind from Ireland he grew so gloomy that he rode west across the mountains, bidding the ships to follow, as if he could break the spell of the weather by getting even that little nearer to Ireland. When he arrived at Beaumaris in the dead of night and wet to the skin, his mood was even more gloomy. 'How miserable cold the army is, how uncertain the winds are, how hard it will be to keep the army in strength in that wretched country.' Or: 'I had a natural antipathy against this service . . . but *jacta est alea*. I go in the best cause.'

The exacerbation of that foreboding gradually developed the chilly atmosphere in which he carried out the whole expedition. Day by day he froze the blood of the adventure, dampened his friends, and encouraged his enemies. He saw in everything not his own hand, nor the hand of Fate or Misfortune, but the hand of Injustice and Intrigue. London watched with a patience which became mulish, and Elizabeth found herself moving from one cold fury to another at his immeasurable folly in mingling personal discontent with affairs of State, and at their common impotence to deflect the enormous humiliation to which he and she must subject one another, to England's cost. The man, therefore, who made his state entry into Dublin as Lord Lieutenant, with all his magnificos about him, in their short cloaks, great ruffs, and rich swords, hid not only a rheumatic body but a gloomy mind beneath his trappings and his noble airs.

He had reason for complaint; but what general had not? And as Elizabeth afterwards reproached him he had 'had his asking.' It was useless for him to point out to Richmond all the leaks in the vessel of his power. The only comfort he got from Richmond was that they knew only too well how their sendings to Ireland drained away, but that it was a great comfort to them to know that the Queen at last had a commander whose worth and power would rectify these great enormities. He found the enormities soon enough. For example, this was April, and food had been furnished to last until June—so the Council, now moved to Greenwich, told him. Ten days later he was writing back that there was not food enough in Ulster, either for horses or men, and no grass until the summer came, and the cattle too lean either 'to be driven or eaten,' so that it was impossible to face Tyrone. It was the old Irish policy of 'scorched earth' that faced him at the very first step of his adventure. Where ultimately all that three months' supply of food went only the victuallers and the store-masters could tell: some rotted, some stolen, some stored away in northern magazines for a campaign that never took place, some eaten on futile minor expeditions or his fatal journey through Munster. The great army was likewise suffering from the usual sickness and desertions so that, as Essex put it, large though the army was 'the plaster barely covered the wound.' The Dublin Council strongly advised him against an attack on Tyrone—possibly for the selfish reason that they wished their own hearth to be first swept clean. Essex agreed to clean up Leinster and Munster now and to face north in July when the grass was up, the cattle fattening, and Tyrone's harvest ready to be taken and spoiled.

2

This decision was his ruin. It left Tyrone in the position of the watcher. By stripping the country south and west of the Blackwater, by his raids around the Pale, destroying food and stealing away the horses without which Essex could not transport food northwards, and lastly by rousing the south and west, he had forced Essex away from him. That southern expedition would be the first test of the new spirit in the country, and since ultimate success depended, not so much on him, as on the strength of the confederacy that he was creating he followed the march of Essex southward with intense interest. We may follow Essex with the same interest. The journey was devoid of military value but for that very reason it illustrates perfectly how great armies seemed to vanish into the air in Ireland without accomplishing anything.

Essex sent forward about 3,500 of his army, on May 8th (1599) as far as Naas in the County Kildare, some twenty miles from Dublin. He left the remainder in Dublin where, presently, sickness put about half of them out of action. He could not accompany his army until the next day because transport was so indequate that supplies had to go and come, and go again. That made progress extremely slow. He left 200 men at Naas and moved on five or six miles to Kilcullen. The next day he moved on about five more miles to Kilrush. He was following the old Norman road that sweeps like an arrow from Dublin down to Kilkenny and thence along the valley of the Nore to Strongbow's Ross and Waterford. He had the great champaign of Kildare and Leix stretching away in rolling waves of wooded horizons into the infinity of distance southward and eastward of his line of march, a rich and enviable country over which the clouds came floating in an endless succession up from the Shannon shore. He moved on another three miles until, outside Athy, he met Ormonde and got his first glimpse of the Irish 'rebels.' These were no other than Lord Cahir and Lord Mountgarret, in Ormonde's custody, suing humbly for pardon.

This was the same Mountgarret who had only recently written to Philip of Spain that he had done more than any of his predecessors for the cause of Christ and Ireland, and who had boasted to Tyrone that they would sup together in Ormonde's castle at Kilkenny. This, therefore, must seem to us a swift and humiliating debacle for Tyrone's most prominent lieutenant in Leinster, a cowardly balloon-pricked surrender, and a poor augury for the Confederacy. We must not be certain that Tyrone, in his castle at Dungannon, took it too much to heart. For whatever else we do in trying to be then-minded one thing we have to do is to suppress the romantic or chivalric conception of warfare in dealing with the sixteenth century in Ireland. The kind of war that Tyrone and his allies had to fight had its own fierce code, and we must not fall into the stupid error, which was the ruin of so many generals who opposed him, of complaining that he did not fight according to some other set of rules. Thus, it was men like Lord Brough who called him The Running Beast, and his men 'naked kerne . . . cowardly rabble . . . rogues . . . offal.' If that contempt arose from conventional ideas as to how this war should be conducted, then they paid dearly for their conventionality and there is no reason why we should imitate them; and, indeed, the very fact that Essex lightly dismissed Mountgarret as a 'unwieldy coward' is almost enough to give us pause. A sharp reorientation of the mind is, in any case, made necessary by the discovery that all Mountgarret's followers remained actively in the field. His son Richard was a rebel in the middle of the following century during which he was on the supreme Council of the Confederation of 1642.

Tyrone probably took a fairly sympathetic view of Mountgarret's behaviour, being in this as in everything entirely free of the curious romanticism, if we may so call it, which was so persistent in the English mind. He never despised his opponents and there is not a single record, as far as this biographer knows, of a complaint from him about any tactics however ruthless that his enemies cared to employ. To take a parallel from a later war he would never, for example, have been so conventional as to despise the ragged rabble of Valley Forge in the American War of Independence, as the English generals of the time did—again to their cost. It was that realism that won him such a reputation abroad where, on his retirement, he was greeted in city after city as one of the great soldiers of his day—where it was sufficient that he had defeated half a dozen of Elizabeth's best generals, as many armies, protracted a war against England for seven years, and cost it millions of pounds. It is interesting, and a salutary warning to Irish readers in particular—who have all been brought up to accept the patriotic myth about Tyrone—that this 'romanticism' is not confined to English generals: the most famous and patriotic of all Irish writers on the wars of Tyrone, John Mitchel, cannot stomach these suings for pardon and simply refuses to believe that any Irishman could be so lacking in nobility as to kneel to an English Deputy. In fact, Tyrone did it himself as often as it suited him.

Essex moved on into Athy, and left one hundred men there. He went on to Carlow and left three hundred and fifty men there. He sent 750 men into Offaly. He revictualled Maryboro and left 500 men there. He left 100 men at Ballyragget. His original force was then reduced by two thirds. He had accomplished nothing. The guerilla wave would always close in behind him once he moved on. The town or castle would always return to the woodsmen once he ceased to victual it. Thus a reporter told Cecil, speaking of these garrisons at Maryboro and the Offaly Fort, that the enemy was so strong that the garrisons did not 'dare look out.' That brief march, about fifty miles, gives us an exact picture of a large army dwindling away, without achieving anything.

There is one other informative incident in this march. That is the victory of the Pass of the Plumes. Whose victory this was nobody can tell. Essex claimed it and the Irish claimed it. As far as one can see it was a savage skirmish in a wooded pass, between Stradbally and Abbeyleix, in which the English gallants left behind them many of the gay feathers from their hats, so that to this day the place is called The Pass of the Plumes. Essex reported that in the skirmish he lost five or six men. The Catholic-Gaelic-Latin chronicler O'Sullivan Beare says 'several men.' The nineteenth-century patriotic biographer Mitchel says 'many of his men.' Professor Curtis, the most modern historian, says 'a detachment was cut off.' A standard Irish history by Hayden and Moonan says 'his rearguard was shattered,' and counts it as one of a 'series of disasters' that 'marked his way.' It is not surprising that the modern guide-book, (Muirhead's, of London) should speak of this place as 'the marshy level where Essex was defeated.' All of which goes to show that the native tradition sometimes does prevail against the propaganda of State Papers. It also shows once again how a slight victory would always be magnified by the people, and how damaging it would be to that prestige by which, chiefly, the colonists dominated the people.

The rest of Essex's march was of the same order. He had one or two successes, as when he took Cahir Castle with his cannon and by assault. But Elizabeth wanted only to know what he was achieving against Tyrone and thanked him little for it—thereby fulfilling Bacon's warning; in fact she said bluntly that cannon had always been able to blast a way in Ireland and what was this new 'victory' anyway but the taking of 'an Irish hold from a rabble of rogues': an unfair comment, since Cahir Castle was one of the most powerful keeps in Ireland. Conversely, every Irish success was wafted through the country at once, and reached the Continent magnified ten-fold thanks to the priests who relayed them, as through loud-speakers, in Brussels, Madrid, Paris, Rome. That, as much as the positive failure of Essex to do anything against the main enemy, stung Elizabeth to fury. Essex returned her anger in querulous despatches which kept on mingling his private affairs with purely military matters. That was not without precedent. English generals condemned to the Irish wars were always at the mercy of disloyal colleagues whispering against them in London and were always pleading for a greater sympathy and understanding. But no commander ever expressed himself so tactlessly and so near the hem of the royal robe as Essex. There is hardly a letter of his which does not reveal that this man was fundamentally lacking in balance, and that his birth, charm, good looks, and favouritism had raised him to offices for which, in spite of all his natural gifts, he was unfitted. The harsh realities of the sixteenth century Ireland exploded the Essex myth as they did so often with similar gentlemanly disputes before and after him.

Elizabeth's patience was finished that July. She very properly reprimanded him for the impertinence of his letters which so often had the air of a sulky youth rather than a resolute general. One letter of her's is worth quoting.

'Your two months journey hath never brought in a capital rebel against whom it hath been worthy to have adventured a thousand men. For of their two comings-in two were brought to you by Ormonde (namely, Mountgarret and Cahir). Whereupon ensued the taking of Cahir Castle. Full well do we know that you would have long since scorned to have allowed it for any great matter in others, to have taken an Irish hold from a rabble of rogues, with such force as you had, and with the help of the cannon, which was always able in Ireland to make its passage where it pleased. And therefore, more than that, you have now learned, upon our expenses, by knowledge of the country, that these things are true which we have heretofore told you, if you would have believed us, how far different things would prove there from your expectation. There is little public benefit made to us of any things happened in this action, which the President, with any convenient addition to his numbers by you, might not have effected, now or hereafter, in a time more seasonable, when it should less have hindered the other enterprise, on which depends our greatest expectation. Whereunto we will add one thing that doth more displease us than any charge or expense that happens, which is, that it must be the Queen of England's fortune (who hath held down the greatest enemy she had) to make a base bush-kerne be accounted so famous a rebel as to be a person against whom so many thousands of foot and horse, besides the force of all the nobility of that kingdom must be thought too little to be employed.'

Then, with absolute pertinence, she points out to him that the sum of it all is that Tyrone may now be merry to 'see such a portion of our fair army, and led by the person of our general, harassed out in encountering those base rogues, who were no way strengthened by foreign armies but only by such of his offal as he was content to spare and let slip from himself, whiles he hath lived at his pleasure, hath spoiled all where our army should come, and preserved for himself what he thought necessary. . . . Little do you know how he hath blazed in foreign parts the defeats of regiments, the death of Captains, and loss of men of quality in every corner. . . . It is therefore apparent that drafts and surprises would have found better successes than public and notorious marches.'

As if that were not enough to bring any man to his senses she raps him sharply for his arrogance in knighting young men in his service. He was so notorious for this that he had actually made with his own sword one fourth of all the knights in England, for which if he lived in our day he would undoubtedly have earned the gratitude of every cartoonist in the country. Even in his day men mocked him that his sword never left its sheath except to create knights. 'Our honour,' fumed Elizabeth, 'hath dwelt too long with us to leave that point now uncleared that whosoever it be that you do clad with any honours or places wherein the world may read the least suspicion of contempt or neglect of our commandments, we will never make dainty to set on such shadows as shall quickly eclipse any of those lustres.' Finally she orders him to march at once to the north that the axe may be put to the root of the tree.

Essex could have made but one riposte—that she had, as in fact she had, sanctioned the excursion into the south. To which she placed on record the uncomfortable counter-riposte that no man 'shall ever win honour by obedience where our country shall receive harm by our commandments.' She repeated her order, peremptorily, to march against Tyrone, and she added her express commandment that he must not venture to return to England without her permission.

3

Still Essex hesitated. And still Tyrone waited for the attack. So far he had been extremely fortunate, but to say that his good fortune and his immunity were due simply to the folly of Essex is unfair to both of them. His immunity was due to his own strength which he had built up doggedly over a number of years, and to his influence which he had deserved to win; and if Essex was wrong to have gone into Munster neither was there any certainty that a frontal attack on Tyrone's guerillas would have been any more successful than similar frontal attacks previously attempted. What Essex should have done—and his real weakness lay in his contempt for his enemy which prevented him from doing it—was to have planned a long-term campaign against Tyrone, a two or a three year campaign. He had not that kind of mind. He was a buccaneer, a cut-and-thrust raider, and all his military training had been of that type. Besides, even Elizabeth was not yet educated into a proper respect for Tyrone's strength and ability and it was not until the collapse of Essex that she realized fully what she was up against and girded herself for what we would nowadays call total war.

As the weeks passed and no news came of a grand attack by

Essex she passed from fury to bewilderment and back again. The fact was that everyone in Dublin, apparently without exception, was agreed that it would be most unwise to attack Tyrone now with depleted and discouraged troops. Essex asked for another 2,000 men. He got them, and he still demurred. It can never be said of Elizabeth that she was speechless but it is plain that she did not now know what to think. She and the Privy Council went over the whole ground again and yet again and could make no sense of it. 'What would you have us believe,' she cried, 'if we did not think you loyal but that either some of you cannot forget your old goodwills to that Traitor, or else are insensible of all things save your own particulars?' That Ireland and Tyrone were ungovernable she could not believe, and yet, in that summer of 1599, the fact seemed inescapable. As if to prove it O'Donnell, that August 5th, fell on Conyers Clifford in the Curlew Mountains where he was moving against him with a large force and routed him completely, killing Clifford, his Colonel, Sir Alexander Ratcliffe, his lieutenant, sergeant, and hundreds of his men. With that battle to cheer him and with the knowledge that in the north he must be prepared to meet the combined forces of O'Donnell and Tyrone, Essex can hardly be blamed for his hesitations.

The end of the Essex adventure is one of the mysteries of history and another emphasis on the enigma of Tyrone's personality. Here is the sequence of events. On August 21st, five weeks after Elizabeth's first command to move north, the Captains and Lords and Colonels of the Army, at a Council of War, wrote and signed to the number of eighteen, a letter declaring that the expedition was unwise and against their judgement. On the 28th Essex wrote to the Privy Council that he was even then putting his foot in the stirrup to march against Tyrone. Within a few hours Tyrone had the information. On September 2nd he made contact with Tyrone and from that to the 5th his men followed him through the woods, but only slight brushes took place. That day when Essex was on his way to Louth Castle near Dundalk Tyrone's messenger O'Hagan came to offer a parley. He was dismissed haughtily. On the next day there was another skirmish. Once again O'Hagan came to declare that Tyrone desired Her Majesty's mercy and a parley. Essex agreed, and they met, alone. It was a curious meeting, for Tyrone was on horseback, in a river, with the water to his horse's belly, and Essex stood on the bank. What they said to one another will never be known. A further meeting was arranged. They agreed to a truce. Tyrone withdrew into the heart of his country, and Essex dispersed his army.

When Essex arrived back in Dublin he was greeted by two stinging letters from London, written *before* this last amazing decision of his, the burden of which was that he was either an incompetent or a braggart. The Queen's sarcasm was cutting. His army is sick? Then why did he not act when it was well? The winter is coming? Then why did he not move in July? If the spring is too soon, if the summer has been spent or misspent, if the harvest has been neglected, then Her Majesty must conclude that no one of the four quarters of the year is satisfactory for the Earl of Essex. Did he propose to end this war at all? In Heaven's name would he and the Council put their heads together and try to tell her what they proposed to do—and when they had decided she would then tell them what they ought to do. As he read these letters, knowing that he had already decided to do worse than nothing, Essex was torn between chagrin, wounded vanity, dismay, and rage, and lost his head completely. He appointed two Lords Justice to take his place and, in the face of Elizabeth's express command not to stir from Ireland, he crossed to England. The rest of the story is his own: the irruption into the Queen's bed-chamber at Nonsuch in the early morning, the dyed red hair hanging down about her astonished face, the leap of heart as her eyes wandered up from the muddy riding boots and travel-stained apparel to the closing door; then a gracious welcome—and then, under the influence of the common light and the common sense of day and the advice of Cecil and her Council, the cold rebuff; imprisonment; deferred pardon; disgrace, despair, meditated revolt, death.

4

What then had happened at that river-side of Athclynth? What magic did Tyrone play on the son of his old friend, the first Earl of Essex, to draw him from a resolution hammered home so often by his Queen and Council? Two days before he had dismissed O'Hagan. The very day before he had been full of eagerness to fight, and then, in one short half-hour it all vanished. It is true that he was already, even before he set out, toying with the idea of hurrying back to England: that he undertook the expedition against his wish: that he was already decided not to face any of Tyrone's cunning trenches, although ready and willing to meet him in open field, and that his captains were in low spirits. Yet, something was thrown into the scale at the riverside. Shall we ever know what it was?

Remember, these were desperate men. Underneath the polish, the breeding, the courtly manner, the real nobility, were the hearts and spirits of desperadoes. Take a man like Sir Christopher St. Lawrence, one of Devereux's troop. He was, literally, fit for anything. When they were in London on September 28th, and had crossed the Thames at Lambeth, riding hell-for-leather for Nonsuch to get there before any enemy should bring word to spoil that surprise entry on which so much was gambled, they saw Lord Grey on the road before them. St. Lawrence calmly suggested to Essex that they kill him there and then, and afterwards assassinate Cecil in the Queen's Court. Again, Mountjoy, when all their lives seemed in danger, proposed that they negotiate with James VI, get him to muster his army on the borders, and then bring across the Irish army themselves and march on London. Remember, too, that Tyrone had swaggered in the streets of London as a youth, caught the wild spirit of the times, and was familiar with the type—he had been directly associated with Essex's father in a characteristic buccaneering adventure in the north—and would, at least, have known how to talk in that gambler's language to Essex. The question is, Did he? Certainly, when Sir William Warren was in talk with Tyrone at the end of month, at Dungannon, Tyrone did say to him that 'within these two months, he would see the greatest alteration and the strangest that he could imagine, or ever saw in his life.' Warren did not understand and asked Tyrone to explain. But Tyrone merely shook his head, and said Ha-ha, and repeated what he had said two or three times, and even said that he hoped before long 'to have a good share in England.'

All we know for certain is that the rumours were flying. Here is a typical one, a third or fourth hand piece of gossip suggestive of the general atmosphere of speculation and puzzlement in Ireland. One David Hetherington riding to the edge of Kildare heard from a horseman of the Provost Marshal that he had heard from a kerne of Ownie MacRory's the extraordinary story that 'Essex is in trouble for us and for that he would do no service upon us which he never meant to do for he is ours and we are his.' A still stranger story from the north was saying that 'Essex will be King of Ireland.' The most impressive piece of evidence that Tyrone had been trying to work up a first class international conspiracy with Essex (which is not at all out of the question, Essex's eyes being fixed on the throne of England either for himself or for James of Scotland) comes from Matthew de Oviedo, a Spanish Franciscan, who later became Papal Archbishop-elect of Dublin and first Rector of the Irish College at Salamanca. Writing to Philip III on April 24th, 1600, he said: 'That your Majesty may understand what you possess in these Catholics, I may say that O'Neill had almost prevailed upon the Earl of Essex to desert the Queen's cause and join that of your Majesty, and surrender all the Realm to you. O'Neill in the course of the negotiations promised Essex, on behalf of your Majesty, that you would show him signal favour, and as Essex was distrustful in consequence of certain injuries he had inflicted on Spain, O'Neill gave him his son as a hostage. What more could the most loyal Spaniard have done?' Oviedo, however, is writing without first-hand experience, and after the event, and the reference to the hostage—obviously a fabrication by Tyrone—tends to deflate the whole story: and Tyrone was naturally ready to tell Oviedo any tall story that would bring help quickly from Spain.

If we may believe Essex we do know that Tyrone flattered him to the top of his bent. He told him that he would not have spoken as freely to any other man, not spoken at all in fact to any other man because he could not have trusted any other man as he trusted Essex. And we may be sure that he used the fullest voltage of his charm and persuasiveness to instil that same 'trust' into Essex. We can see him, with tears in his eyes, telling this man seventeen years his junior and, by comparison, a babe in the arts of chicanery, that he knew that he was talking to a friend, the son of his first friend, and that he would never wish to deceive the son of Walter Devereux who had given him his first step-up in life. And for the moment it is possible that Tyrone really felt the tragedy of the thing, that he should be opposed to Walter Devereux's son, and deliberately let his affectible Irish imagination warm his heart and transform his manner; and so enveloped them both in a genial, sanguine, excited mood of optimism—created the feeling that this was the grand, critical meeting, between two men who really understood the whole situation and would solve it at last. The only record of the actual talk, if it is a record, is in the Trevelyan Papers which purport to give Tyrone's actual words:

'My honourable good Lord, since it is not unknown to your Lordship how I married the sister of Sir Henry Bagenal and living together, because I did affect two other gentlewomen she grew in dislike with me, forsooke me, and went unto her brother to complain upon me to the Council of Ireland and did exhibit articles against me. Upon this they sent for me and because I came not on their first sending they proclaimed me traitor before I meant to go out, and then I had no other remedy but go out to save my head. And so ever since I have been in this rebellion. And never since hath there been, until the coming of your Lordship, any Deputy that I did dare put my life into your hands: but, my honourable good Lord, my love to my dread, the Queen's Majesty, and the love I did bear unto your honourable father deceased, which was such as shall never be put out of my heart, next to the love I bear to your most honourable name and fame in all the world, for your prowess and marshal discipline, holding your honour's word and promise, make me at this time to yield myself to your Lordship, desiring this, to vouchsafe to speak unto the Queen for mercy for me. And by my hand I swear what your Lordship shall think fit for me to do or undergo I will, and for ever after will be a most true and loyal subject, and during my life I nor none of my followers shall hold up hands against your Lordship except it be to save my head, Etc.'

(What may be covered by the *Etc.* we do not know.)

He caught Essex at his lowest ebb, desperate, ready to catch at any straw, and whether he dropped treason in his ears or merely gave him a chance to strike a truce and get back to England, he won his bloodless victory. Immediately she heard of it Elizabeth summed it up in one outraged sentence. 'To trust this traitor on his oath is to trust a devil upon his religion.' It was, for the rest, left to her to swallow the astonishing fact that an army of 16,000 men had gone across the Irish Sea to smash their Golden Calf, her new name for Tyrone, and that it was now scattered to the four winds without striking even one solitary blow against him.

5

Tyrone prolonged the truce as usual through month after month. Ormonde was again the negotiator. He found the graph of Tyrone's ambition soaring off the page. In '96 Tyrone had been content to ask for liberty of conscience, the removal of garrisons, and a form of county administration for the North. Now he demanded, in effect, what later centuries called Home Rule. When Cecil saw the full list of his demands he scrawled across the page 'Ewtopia.' He said, and truly, 'He means to be head and monarch of Ireland.' These Articles are the first document that speak out the full pride and dignity of an emergent nation—a new nation, coherent, self-aware, forward-looking, intelligent and intelligible, where there had been before an incoherent dynasticism. Here are some of his chief demands.

> That the Catholic, Apostolic and Roman religion be openly preached and taught throughout all Ireland as well in cities and borough towns, by bishops, seminary priests, Jesuits, and all other religious men.
>
> That all cathedrals and parish churches, abbeys, and all other religious houses, with all tithes and church lands, now in the hands of the English, be presently restored to the Catholic churchmen. . . .
>
> That there be erected an university upon the Crown rents of Ireland, wherein all sciences shall be taught according the manner of the Catholic Roman Church.
>
> That the Lord Chancellor, Lord Treasurer, Lord Admiral, the Council of State, the Justices of the Laws, the Queen's Attorney, Queen's Sergeant, and all other officers appertaining to the Council and the law of Ireland, be Irish men.
>
> That all statutes made against the preferment of Irishmen, as well in their own country as abroad, be presently recalled.
>
> That the Queen nor her successors may in no sort press an Irishman to serve them against his will.
>
> That O'Neill, O'Donnell, the Earl of Desmond, with all their partakers, may peaceably enjoy all lands and privileges that did appertain to their predecessors 200 years past.
>
> That all Irishmen may freely travel and traffic all merchandises in England as Englishmen, paying the same rights and tributes as the English do.
>
> That all Irishmen may freely build ships of what burden they will, furnishing the same with artillery and all munition at their pleasure. . . .

That Elizabeth would agree to such demands was out of the question. For over three hundred years English monarchs and the English Parliament were to refuse far less. Yet she would, at this stage, have granted him terms that he would not have dared to ask four years before. Which means that, as for himself, and his ambitions, he had won his war, and could as for himself enjoy the victory. Cecil said so explicitly to Ormonde in the November of 1599. 'If Tyrone had ever any purpose to become a subject, Her Majesty is likest to receive him with tolerable conditions, for she cares not for anything he holds in comparison with his obedience.' That is the true English angle on the Irish question of that century—the monarch against the feudal knight. Had Tyrone now been able to direct his affairs into that court he could have ended as the greatest Earl in Christendom.

He could not. In his own heart, in the order of his alliances, in the nature of the whole structure that he had built up throughout the country, he had so far outstepped personal ambition and personal pride as to have transformed utterly the original situation. He was, for the hour, powerful beyond his dreams. There was no lord in England or on the Continent as powerful. He had instilled his own vision into others. He was a leader of men. He was now locked into that vision, its creature as well as its creator. That winter of 1599 his instruments, his allies, were so strong with the momentary strength of his vision that they would have rounded on him had he thought of compromise. Within a year he was to find that he had offered to his people a destiny beyond them, and they were abandoning him one by one because he would not or could not waver. That was not true of all of them. In sheer resolve O'Donnell was fully his equal, perhaps even his superior, and many others followed him without faltering. Taken one by one the remainder were often men of as great courage. What they lacked was something inherent in their system of life, a lack which made the English call them uncivilised; to wit—Government.

CHAPTER FIVE

THE CAMPAIGN OF 1600–1601: MOUNTJOY, DOWCKRA, CAREW

'We hold it a very good piece of policy to make them cut one another's throats, without which this kingdom will never be quiet.'

—Lord Mountjoy: July 19th, 1601.

I

Tyrone reached the summit of his career between January and March 1600. The only part of Ireland then in government control was a tiny tract twenty miles by eight miles between Dublin and Drogheda. There were still nominally 14,000 men in the Queen's pay but the Irish were free to go and do what they would. The soldiers were little short of a rabble. The citizen-colonists were so reduced that they became sick of sheltering behind bolted doors and town-walls, and so hard pressed for food that they must abandon everything and go back to England, or turn marauders themselves. The Earl of Thomond's picture of Limerick (January 14th 1600) is a picture of anarchy: the Mayor pulling the hats off lieutenants and gentlemen and stamping them into the mud, soldiers being flung into prison, the towns-folk threatening to make an end of the whole garrison in a day. That was typical of the Ireland which Lord Mountjoy, the new Lord Deputy and Commander-in-Chief, inherited from Essex and all his predecessors.

Tyrone made full use of the situation. He left his most trustworthy lieutenants to guard the north and set out, against the terrified appeals of his people, to make a Grand Tour of the south. He took with him about 2,000 men, possibly less—which is the measure of his contempt for the 14,000 English soldiers eating their heads off in scattered garrisons. He drove down through Longford and Westmeath, sending his messengers ahead to Munster captains like Lord Barry and Lord Roche, urging them to join him in the fight for faith and fatherland, or else suffer the consequences. To show what he meant he devastated on his way the lands of Sir Theobald Dillon who had rejected his messages with spirit. ('Do you think that I would forsake so royal a mistress and my natural Prince for your sudden coming to Dillon's country, assuring myself that I shall never see you there again?') By February he was in Munster and had joined the Sugaun Earl of Desmond. He skirted Ormonde, who from his tower in Kilkenny saw his own Irishtown blazing down to the Nore beneath him. Indeed Ormonde was so shaken that he thought of following the Gaelic example and razing his castle. Having ravaged O'Carroll's country, Tyrone pushed on to Cork, receiving submissions and preaching everywhere the Holy War. That triumphant progress, in mid-winter, from north to south was his great hour of Kingship. He turned back in late February. Ormonde and the new Deputy hastened out from Dublin to cut him off. In a masterly retreat which, as his enemies freely acknowledged, sent his reputation still higher, he evaded them both by forced marches across the vast central bog-lands and was back in the north early in March to prepare for Mountjoy.

This man, who was to turn the scales against Tyrone, was of a very different character to all the other generals who had preceded him in these wars. We know a good deal about Charles Blount. Lord Mountjoy, because his is the central figure of a book which was published in 1617 and must have seemed like red-hot journalism to the Elizabethans. *The Itinerary of Fynes Morison* was the sort of book which American war correspondents have frequently published in our day after they have spent, as Morison did, ten years or so travelling about Europe in the van of great events. Through the admiring but wholly uncritical eyes of Morison we see Blount as a quiet, fastidious, retiring, studious man; the younger son of a decayed house, whose father had ruined himself as a kind of inventor—his invention was to have been the Philosopher's Stone. The son early took for his motto, *Ad Readifacandum Antiquam Domum*, and in pursuit of this object his fortunes had run a not unusual up-hill course before he became Lord Deputy of Ireland. He had angled for a good marriage. He had been for many years a bosom friend of Essex and had nearly succeeded in this when he became betrothed to his friend's beautiful sister Penelope Devereux, the inspiration of Sidney's *Astrophel and Stella*; but the beauty, having first broken the hearts of half the Court, married somebody else. He had fought in the Low Countries. He had been with Essex at Cadiz and been knighted there. He had become his friend's rival at court, if at a far remove, from the day when Elizabeth noted and admired his trim, straight figure, his long white fingers as of a student, and he had blushed when she permitted him to kiss her royal hand. But though he held his own the competition was too keen and he was not built for a courtier's life; he never won such useful favours as Essex's sweet-wine monopoly, never discovered how to live on the Queen's largesse. He had carried himself well in the wars of the Continent, but they had not so far given him his chance, and when somebody proposed him, back in 1598, as Lord Deputy for Ireland Essex had scornfully turned him down as too inexperienced and bookish. With the fall of Essex Elizabeth remembered the blushing young courtier of years before, evidently with affection, for when he wrote from Ireland that he was being neglected, in fact 'treated like a scullion' she answered him jauntily as 'My kitchenmaid,' assuring him of her tender gratitude. Whether it was she or her councillors who recognised his quality he was a well-chosen successor to his doomed friend.

He was indeed, as Essex had said, a bookish man: he was also serious and determined, and after making every allowance for the fact that he profited by the costly experience of his forerunners his conduct of the war revealed him as one of the most resolute and clever soldiers that Elizabeth ever had. When the offer came to him he had tried to turn it aside. A command in Ireland was no sinecure. But there was one strong argument for accepting it, and having accepted it for making the most of it, namely that the disgrace of his friend had involved him. (Essex compromised him seriously in his final confession.) Ireland was his last chance to recoup what had gone down the drain of his father's laboratory and he made it good.

Tyrone, who knew the dainty life that this modest courtier had led in London, is said to have laughed when he heard of his choice. He said that Mountjoy would lose every chance of beginning a fight by the length of time he took over his breakfast. He was mistaken. Once in the field Mountjoy laid aside his elaborate menus, the panadoes and the delicate broths, the rich foods and varied wines, and was content with a crust of bread sometimes flavoured with butter and a pick of sage, and a cup of stale beer. His one luxury was smoking, which he never ceased. So with dress. At court he used to wear white and black satin and taffeta, quilted waist-coats, three pairs of silk stockings, wide ruffles, beaver hats. In the Irish bogs he was very sensibly concerned only with keeping warm, and wore heavy jerkins, three or four wool and worsted stockings, as many as three waist-coats, and a cocoon of scarves. By nature he was laconic, a man whom the corrupt officials could neither persuade nor pump; cold, stern, and silent; often throwing out false scents to deceive, averse to hot language, never swearing, controlling an unruly Board with a glance of his black eye. In fact there was a good deal of Tyrone in this man in whom Tyrone at last met his match. The days of hard-swearing Bingham and blustering Brough were over. Mountjoy was the one thing that the Irish nature dislikes intensely in an enemy and admires intensely in a leader—a calm, patient man, slow to promise, firm in his word, not without evasion, relentless in his pursuit of any object, and most obstinate.

Morison said that Mountjoy died of an obstinate pursuit of unrequited love.

2

With dismay Tyrone heard that Mountjoy proposed to do what Essex had failed to insist on. He found that, at last, the long-threatened fortress was to be built in his rear, up on Lough Foyle, with another garrison at Ballyshannon in the rear of O'Donnell, and lesser garrisons wherever possible. That policy, as we know, had been advised over and over again, and shirked as often on the ground of expense. Now, with 14,000 men in Ireland, and the whole weight of support from the Privy Council behind it, the policy became feasible for the first time. So thoroughly did Mountjoy carry out that policy that within about a year and a half Tyrone found a ring of forts closing in on him—Carrickfergus, Derry, Culmore, Dunalong, Newry, Fort Norris, Carlingford, Lifford, Elagh, Burt, Coleraine, Strabane, Masserene, Edenduffcarrick, the Moyrie, Lecale, Armagh, the Blackwater, Newtown, Castlederg, Castlereagh. Three or four more and he would be utterly hemmed in. There was one other method of warfare which Mountjoy employed, and that was Famine—'the chief instrument of reducing this Kingdom.' He was to employ it pitilessly.

Having made his sortie from Dublin to cut off Tyrone on his return march from the south, and failed (chiefly through bad intelligence-work) he now returned to Dublin, set his army in order, and sat down to that patient and thorough staff-work which he knew to be necessary for his northern campaign. Meanwhile the Lough Foyle expedition was under way. As to why Tyrone permitted a score of forts to be built around him, in a country where there had never been more than half a dozen, that expedition explains everything.

It was under the charge of Sir Henry Dowcra. While Mountjoy was preparing in Dublin, Dowcra was collecting his army in Chester. He was to sail for Carrickfergus on the east coast, there pick up fresh men, and sail on around the northern coast. Dowcra arrived at Carrickfergus on April 27th (1600) and finding a favourable N.N.E. wind on the 12th May set sail for Lough Foyle. On May 11th Mountjoy marched to the southern border of Ulster with 1,700 men, was joined by Bagenal with a further 600, and later strengthened by extra horse under Southampton, another of Essex's desperate friends for whom, as for Mountjoy,

Ireland was now the only place in which to recover the Queen's graces. Tyrone left O'Donnell and a force of his own men under his brother Cormac and the chieftain O'Kane, whose territory bordered on Lough Foyle, to attend to the landing in the north. He faced, himself, to meet Mountjoy. The event proved that Mountjoy did not so much wish to fight Tyrone as to draw him off from Dowcra.

The timing was perfect. Tyrone who had been at Strabane, at the southern end of the Lough, was down at the Blackwater on the 14th of May. Precisely on that same day Dowcra sailed down the Lough with some sixty-nine sail in three squadrons. He ran aground, floated on the tide, stuck again, floated again, and so did not touch land until the 16th. O'Donnell thus had ample information of his arrival. Inexplicably, the only opposition Dowcra met on disembarking was a few shots from a hundred men on the shore who then retired to a hill-top to join their horse and watch. Dowcra immediately landed some horse and foot and faced up the hill against these horsemen. He was promptly bogged. He withdrew, and no more fighting took place there. He had by now landed all his men, about 3,500 of them, and began at once to set up an earthen fort to hold about 200 men, a task which took him six days. All that time the Irish made no assault worth mentioning. He reconditioned a half ruined castle called Ellogh or Aileach, and all he suffered was sniping. On the sixth day, leaving 600 men at his first fort, Culmore, he marched his entire army, now under 3,000 men to his main position, the present city of Londonderry, then the abandoned site of an ancient monastic settlement known as Doire Choluim Cille or the Oakwood of Columcille. That site was a virtual island with the Foyle on one side and a sodden bog on the other. From the hill the noble river could be seen winding away to the north through the vast terrain of Inishowen which vanishes into the dim horizons towards the North Atlantic. To Dowcra the sight must have been as if he had landed on a peak in Darien, with his squadron's masts comfortably visible up-river, his army squatted among the antique ruins, and the great woods across the river silent and threatening. He unloaded his cargoes of timber, his '100 flock beds,' his one piece of cannon, his two iron culverins, all his tools and food and utensils, and then his two master-masons and his two master-carpenters set the new colonists to work. His pinnaces daily took his men across to the birch woods in O'Kane's country for more materials, 'and there was not a sticke of it brought home but was first well fought for.'

Now, apart from that slight forest fighting the Irish had done nothing. Why? The main reason is, evidently, that they were not inventive; they were excellent at one kind of fighting but they could not adapt themselves to any other kind. The explanation given by the native chroniclers is somewhat feeble. 'When O'Donnell perceived that they were not in the habit of going outside their encampments through fear and dread, he made no account of them, and assembled his forces to proceed into the south of Connaught to plunder.' Though if that means that he was leaving them to the hands of Time, Famine and Disease, he was justified up to a point. By the beginning of the winter out of his original 3,500 men Dowcra had only about 800 men fit to bear arms. But if the chroniclers' explanation means that the settlement could otherwise, and therefore, be ignored, then O'Donnell miscalculated badly. He underestimated both the moral and the military influence of this rear attack. Tyrone appears to have been more shrewd for when he drove south against Mountjoy he took with him the son of his old enemy Turlough Luineach—Sir Arthur O'Neill, foreseeing, as O'Donnell did not foresee that the arrival of Dowcra would cause weak men to waver. And if one man wavered the danger was that other sheep would follow him through the gap. Tyrone was right. Arthur O'Neill escaped from him and offered his services to Mountjoy. He said that he would 'pursue Tyrone from place to place with fire and sword and have spies in his camp whereby to draw upon him Her Majesty's forces both by day and by night.' Then he made his way to Dowcra offering him men, food, and information, and promising to bring in also O'Dogherty the chief of Inishowen (the great peninsula to the west of Lough Foyle) and, best offer of all, Niall Garv O'Donnell, Red Hugh's rival. Dowcra was naturally delighted and made him the largest and most unscrupulous promises, even promising in the Queen's name to establish him as the real Earl of Tyrone. But what he was really angling for was Niall Garv, who was more than powerful enough to be able to split the clan. From June to October (1600) Dowcra kept on luring him in and at last he got him. He promised him the whole of Tyrconnell and for the moment gave him 500 men to take Lifford Castle—which he did.

This behaviour of Niall Garv was wholly of a piece with that decrepit and diseased antiquity which Tyrone had tried to reform. His whole character reflects the system. He was valiant beyond criticism, and he was proud with the pride of his ancient race. That was the sum of his virtues. Otherwise the impression which he made on Dowcra who had no reason to dislike him was borne out by every detail of his career. 'An unbridled nature,' commented Dowcra, 'which is apparently prone to tyranny where he may command, to proud and importunate beggary where he is subject, to extreme covetousness whether he be rich or poor, and unseasoned of any discipline, knowledge, or fear of God.' And the one thing which Dowcra could not stomach was the see-saw of his continual grating, now by beggarly, now by the most unmeasurable demands. That opinion did not prevent him from saying to Mountjoy that Niall Garv's revolt—there again we see the word 'rebel' properly used in relation to the kingship of Tyrone—was a sign of 'how God doth work for Her Majesty,' and that it was God who 'hath turned the hearts of two principal men to join with Her Majesty.'

These defections, which were to be followed by others, are the first proof that O'Donnell miscalculated. The second proof is that Mountjoy had no intention of allowing Famine to defeat Dowcra. Here again Tyrone was better informed and before the provisions arrived he made an effort to attack Derry with O'Donnell. By then Dowcra was too well entrenched and the thing failed lamentably. That was about five months since Dowcra had set out from Wales.

A glance at the map will show how much the expedition had achieved within those few months. Dowcra had taken or built Culmore, Ellogh, and Derry. Niall Garv made him a present of Lifford and ultimately Castle Derg, and took Donegal Abbey for him in O'Donnell's absence. Arthur O'Neill's defection gave him Dunalong, and through his son guaranteed Strabane. He had two native allies who prevented O'Donnell from giving Tyrone his full assistance, and guaranteed him from starvation. He summed it up himself when he said that everything he did was done by 'the help and advice of Niall Garv and his followers and the other Irish who came in with Sir Arthur O'Neill, without whose intelligence and guidance little or nothing could have been done of ourselves. Although it is true withall that they had their own ends in its—which were always for Revenge. . . .'

3

The great argument for the Lough Foyle settlement had always been that it would hook Tyrone like some great fish by the nose. That is exactly what it did. Tyrone found himself distracted by Mountjoy when he wished to face Dowcra; by Dowcra when he wished to face Mountjoy; and he had to keep his eye on both if he wished to face a third enemy, Chichester, who had strengthened the old east-coast position of Carrickfergus, then called Knockfergus, on Belfast Lough. It was then that his allies should have assisted him. We have seen that O'Donnell failed him against Dowcra. What of the South? There his commandos Tyrrell and Ownie O'Moore, two guerillas of the first order, straightway overran the province, raiding everywhere, taking herds within two miles of Dublin; and with the Kavanaghs they even made an attempt to burn the outskirts of the city. The Dublin Council complained bitterly, and had the Deputy been any other man but Mountjoy they would probably have forced him to come to their assistance. But Mountjoy had taken the measure of the Anglo-Irish as well as of the general military problem and he abandoned them cynically and ruthlessly. 'The baseness and dishonesty of the English-Irish inhabitants hath been the chief cause of the hazard of this kingdom,' were his actual words for these whiners of the Pale, and when the Lord Chancellor began to wail of his great losses from an attack on his house at Rathfarnham, now a suburb of Dublin, he wrote dryly to Cecil that it would be wiser to take the account historically rather than canonically. His attitude was that if he had 20,000 men in the province of Leinster alone he could not check the guerillas. In fact he had left as many men in Leinster as he took to Ulster, but they were 'drowned in petty wards and in the guards of towns.' So, although the commandos worked like demons to tear Leinster apart they could not distract Mountjoy. He was evidently content to let them ravage and burn if the Anglo-Irish were such poltroons as not to stop them. His task was to lop off their leader and inspiration.

Munster was even less successful. There Tyrone had taken up Florence MacCarthy and made him the MacCarthy More. It had been a mistaken choice since MacCarthy was a rogue, fond of his ease, and generally sleepy with sack. Moreover Mountjoy had a first class second-in-command in Munster, the new Lord President, Sir George Carew, a wily diplomat and a ruthless soldier in whose hands MacCarthy melted like a lump of grease. On the arrival of Carew, MacCarthy, instead of rousing such fighting men as O'Sullivan Beare or James Fitzthomas of Desmond, wasted month after month in trying to keep in with both sides. As he was chief of all the Carbery and Desmond forces, his dishonesty hamstrung Tyrone's friends, and it did not in the least deceive his enemies. 'That idiot Florence' is the summary of Carew's opinion of him, who was able, thanks to that idiocy, to confine his attentions to harassing the Sugaun Earl of Desmond in Limerick and Kerry. One example of Carew's cunning is enough. The Connaught mercenary captain, Dermot O'Connor, had treacherously taken the Earl prisoner and was about to hand him over to Carew when the people protested violently. O'Connor produced a letter written by Carew to Fitzthomas thanking him for his offer to deliver O'Connor alive or dead. That quietened the gullible people who did not know that Carew had specially written that letter in order that it should be intercepted; nothing but the intervention of a priest, a little wiser in the ways of sin, saved Fitzthomas in the nick of time. A little earlier Carew had hired one Nugent to assassinate John Fitzthomas, the Earl's brother, and when the plot went awry and the people hanged the spy Carew commented, 'No great loss.' Which sufficiently indicates his ruthless nature. Tyrone's subsequent furious contempt for Florence MacCarthy was unbounded. 'A damned counterfeited Englishman,' he called him, 'whose only study and practise was to deceive and betray all the Irishmen in Ireland.' And when MacCarthy was in the Tower he lived down to that description, spoke about his great services as the 'chiefest causer of cutting off the Earl of Desmond' and begged for another chance that he might 'now be chiefly instrumental in cutting off Tyrone.'

All of which, however interesting, was hardly of much assistance to the Confederacy. It did not help that Connaught, like Leinster, had its own way all through 1600. Mountjoy abandoned that province also. He had his hook in the nose of the great fish and he would not let him go. In one sentence Tyrone was suffering the set-backs of every man who has to fight on more than one front at a time. Distractions began to pile up against him as, one by one, month after month, his lesser allies began to turn away from him.

Here one can no longer evade a judgement on the Tyroneian

technique. The trouble about dissimulation, mock obeisances, constant truces, frequent pardons is that they threaten to sap the character. A big man may do that sort of thing, though never with impunity, and only where he is surrounded by a number of men as big as himself. With small men the will can very quickly become infected by even a pretence at surrender, since the comforts which follow on dissimulation—so readily purchased, so flattering to one's sense of one's own cleverness—corrupt by the very ease with which they have been attained. Only if a man's private purpose is as firm as steel, and as clear as day, and as urgent as a passion can he manage his mind through the winding and shallow channels of conspiracy. The great danger is the effect of such a technique on the little men who are his instruments, his lieutenants, and sub-lieutenants, and sub-sub-lieutenants, and ordinary rank and file. They do not argue out what they do or see done. They are not led by a personal vision so much as by the example of their leader. He may ask them, therefore, to retreat once . . . twice . . . three times. At his peril he makes a habit of it, since the time must inevitably come when they do not wait to be told. If these unintelligent men without vision begin to play the game of dissimulation how swiftly may not corruption follow? They, too, will deceive when hard pressed, and withdraw, and then (so they say) they will recant. But if to recant now means a return to a danger greater than before, what more natural than to prolong the pretence a little further, and prolong it yet further, and so prolong it that the hour for action is gone, and the will is rotted, and their very souls no longer their own?

The English colonists were clever at this game of corruption. Their corresponding technique of negotiation, pardon, and reward was as powerful to disintegrate those Gaelic captains as fire-water among the Indians or opium among the Chinese. And the devilishness of it was that it was perfectly fair, and quite moral, and that it was suggested to them by the Gaelic way of life itself, with its hand-to-mouth and quite amoral code of the border raider. May one not pity a man like Florence MacCarthy as much as one blames him? How could Tyrone blame Turlough's son for doing what he had so successfully done against son's father? Could O'Donnell blame Niall Garv when he himself had stood bareheaded in the church of Dundalk and craved pardon of the Queen? Nor can one argue that O'Donnell had been chosen by his clan and Niall had not, since Turlough had been chosen by his clan and Tyrone had not. All we can say in defence of the technique is that Tyrone had no option. It is one of the dogmatic rules of life, and particularly of politics, that one works with what one can work with, and Tyrone *did* try to reform his material even while he worked with it.

That year of 1600–1601 the list of his allies 'coming in' to Mountjoy or to Dowcra grew and grew. Let us first glance at the list and then analyse it. Sir Arthur O'Neill, old Turlough's son, with his brother Cormac O'Neill; Turlough MacHenry of the Fews, Tyrone's half-brother; MacMahon of Monaghan, whose final treachery at Kinsale crowns all; Niall Garv O'Donnell of Tyrconnell; Conor Roe Maguire of Fermanagh; a faction of the MacDevitts of Inishowen; Ever MacCooley MacMahon of Farney; O'Cahan, or O'Kane, who was one of Tyrone's oldest associates and was married to his daughter Rose; dozens of little men from Upper Clandeboye and Lower Clandeboye. . . . They fell away from their Golden Calf, their Prince, their Uncrowned King, one after another. . . . O'Reilly factionists in Cavan, Henry Oge O'Neill another son-in-law of Tyrone; Arthur Magennis of Lecale, both son-in-law and brother-in-law of Tyrone. . . . The collapse was staggering.

When we search for the reasons for these various defections we find that although the motivations are vulnerability, crude factionism, and sheer treachery, the basic thing is always the crazily chaotic Irish system rather than personal weakness of character. These men failed Tyrone not from any natural bent towards treachery but because they had been made incapable by centuries of anarchy, of bringing this incipient unity (forced on them by Tyrone) to any effective, continuous, well-timed action; and, so, their atavistic lust for dynasticism issued as insubordination, individualism, and incapacity for centralised leadership, and treachery was the accompaniment of these things rather than the germ. One might say that they were not so much anarchs by nature as by second-nature, i.e. they were victims of a tradition and a system that had by the sixteenth century become quite unworkable and corrupted all who attempted to live by it.

Examine those deserters. How many of them had ever been really 'allies' of Tyrone? Sir Arthur O'Neill had always been a rival of Tyrone; a typical dynast incapable of rising above his tribalistic concept of society. Turlough MacHenry of the Fews was a man whom Tyrone had never trusted completely. Indeed Tyrone had actually imprisoned him with his wife in a crannog castle in 1598. Yet he was affected mainly by his own vulnerability and he returned to Tyrone when the Spanish invasion occurred. At the worst he was by nature a 'waverer' rather than a traitor. MacMahon, however, was a traitor, pure and simple—mainly simple, one imagines. Niall Garv also was a born pirate; Tyrone never had him on his side—the most he had was his inanition—a man certain to break out as soon as he saw a chance of loot. Maguire of Fermanagh was not, of course, the famous Hugh who stood firmly by Tyrone until his death in the field; that Maguire was succeeded by Cuchonnaght Maguire who also stood by Tyrone to the last; this man was the usual dynastic rival who rose against Tyrone and Cuchonnaght simultaneously, indifferent to everything but his own personal advancement. I have listed the MacDevitts of Inishowen rather than the local chief Sir John O'Dougherty, who can at most be charged with pushing the Tyroneian technique to the limit with Dowcra, without ever actually submitting. On his death in February, 1601, the usual succession dispute arose: then Red Hugh O'Donnell set up Sir John's brother, Felim Oge, and these MacDevitts set up young Cahir O'Dougherty, a lad of thirteen, and it was in that way that the factions turned on O'Donnell and Tyrone. But Ever MacCooley can only be classed as a traitor, another of those dynasts of whose loyalty no leader could ever be sure. O'Cahan's treachery, likewise, was flagrant. Not only was he married to Tyrone's daughter, but his wife had been Red Hugh's wife, divorced by him in 1595. (The Gaelic matrimonial standard was rather a low one.) Henry Oge O'Neill, Tyrone's son-in-law, was one of the most treacherous of all; he personally undertook to betray Tyrone in 1601. Magennis, likewise, may be counted simply as an unreliable. Clearly, treachery only accounts therefore for a section of these fallings-away.

Of them all Niall Garv O'Donnell offers the most striking example of the craziness of the system and the corruption it bred. Niall Garv was out for loot, and nothing else but loot, even though he may well have told himself that what he wanted was to be, simply, the king of his own castle, and may even have had somewhere at the back of his head a lunatic notion that he could drive out Dowcra when he had exploited him. His behaviour that winter is a terrifying illustration of the anarchy which had kept the island so weak and defenceless for centuries. Dowcra, who was by no means a squeamish man, was genuinely amazed by the spectacle and the incident is, indeed, primitive.

What happened was this. Niall, having allied himself to Dowcra, cessed his men on O'Dougherty and O'Dougherty objected. Now, had Tyrone been as powerful that winter as he had been in the spring he would have had to decide between the two. As it was, Dowcra became the authority. Dowcra did not decide in favour of the stronger man. He asked Niall Garv on what basis had he thus claimed power over another man's land. Niall must have thought the question simple-minded, but his answer was just as simple-minded, for he replied that the land was his ever since the Queen had given him all Tyrconnell. Dowcra replied that even if she had there were many other men in Tyrconnell besides the O'Donnells and that he had never conceived that their interest was to be given up completely. To that Niall replied with all the arrogance of his new ambition that he not only counted Tyrconnell as his property but that his power stretched into Tyrone, and into Fermanagh, and even into Connaught, and in fact wherever the power of the O'Donnells had reached before him. He declared that he acknowledged no man's right or interest but his own; that he claimed the very persons of the people as his own; and that he would consider himself wronged if one foot of all that vast terrain, one human being, were exempted from his rule.

Now, Dowcra was in what we would call 'a jam,' and we must remember that at this moment O'Dougherty was still his enemy, and it would not have been held harshly against him if he had yielded to Niall Garv for the moment. He temporized so far as to say that Niall would receive no wrong from him and passed on his problem to Mountjoy. Again, nobody would hold it hard against Mountjoy if he had blatantly deceived Niall Garv, and Mountjoy was, in fact, quite prepared to betray men like Niall Garv. The times were never dainty in that sort of thing and he himself has left it in writing: 'There be some few of these rebels,' he told Cecil that July (1600), 'of the most stirring sort that would make good rods to scourge these traitors and after be thrown into the fire themselves.' Nevertheless whatever his motives, and the uppermost can hardly have been opportunism, he advised Dowcra that the most that Niall could extract from the O'Dougherties was the rent which they sometimes paid to the O'Neills on their east and sometimes to the O'Donnells on their west, according to whichever was the stronger. But, he went on, it was in any case now an extinct arrangement since Niall would hold his land directly from the Crown. If he thought otherwise they could have it all pleaded, in due course, before the courts, and for the rest he would refuse to Niall no part of what had been promised to him. For all that, he concluded O'Dougherty (and again mark that this O'Dougherty was then in arms against Mountjoy) 'must and should be' exempted meanwhile. Niall Garv was furious and indignant, much more so than one might expect of a man who was trying to raise his fortune only at the expense of another.

To complete the picture two comments are necessary. The first is that it was Mountjoy and Dowcra who had encouraged Niall Garv to claim Tyrconnell over the head of the existing chieftain, Red Hugh; though it was not their fault if Niall at once translated English law and custom into terms of Gaelic law and custom. The second comment is to ask what would a native *Rí*, or king, or chieftain, such as Tyrone, have done with this problem. He also would have defended O'Dougherty. His motives would have been diverse. Apart from the vindication of Gaelic custom Niall was the enemy of his ally, Red Hugh. For another, he was a freebooter. But over and above that Tyrone was a civilised man who had brought his knowledge of the world to bear on the Gaelic system, saw what a rickety thing it had become, and knew coldly that there must be some kind of permanent and established order other than the power of an endless series of local pretenders—whose pretensions made them nothing more or less than robber-barons. That emerges clearly from the long parley he held at Dundalk in 1597 with Bishop Jones when, as we remember, the O'Moores and O'Reillys were claiming to be restored to all their ancient lands that had been made over to English colonists. Tyrone made it clear that he would have been content at that stage with the restoration of an equitable moiety of those lands; which means that he would have gone so far, in the interests of stability, as to recognize the English colonization; only demanding that room be made, now, for everybody to live side by side in some sort of security and equality. For it is clear that the whole tenour of the man's mind was that of a man of order—the one Irishman of his time with any such conception of society in his head. His settlement of the general problem would have been both more humane and more likely to last because he would have balanced native tradition against the New System. But had he, by some magic, actually become King of Ireland the first task he would have had to face was to establish an entire *Code Tyrone*. Otherwise the country would have fallen back into its ancient anarchy once his personal influence was removed.

There is no need to analyse other defections north and south. The death of Hugh Maguire, the third most powerful man in the north, produced a repetition of the Niall Garv—Red Hugh situation. What had happened between the two O'Dougherty rivals on the death of the ruling chieftain happened again with the MacMahons of Monaghan, and there we see Mountjoy 'blowing the fire,' as he said himself, between the two factions, telling each MacMahon that came to him that he would not hear him until he brought in the other's head. The O'Rourke's went the same road. Others left Tyrone through personal fear. Others like Donal Kavanagh had no option since he could not defend them.

As Mountjoy and Dowcra prospered, Tyrone became so discouraged that he declared to his confederates in a meeting at Strabane, that very summer of 1600, 'I will for one quarter of a year bear up the war and by that time if things fall not out well I will exhibit conditions of peace as I know the English will not reject.' Possibly it was merely an effort to induce his allies to stick it out, for he remained in the field the whole year, hacking away at Mountjoy, though unable to stop him from pressing up mile by mile to the very borders of his deepest fastnesses. And Mountjoy took his thorough time. When he found it dangerous to press on to Armagh he halted midway and built a new fort at Mount Norris. When he found the passage of the Moyrie to Mount Norris threatened by Tyrone he fortified the pass. Time and again Tyrone circled and wheeled about him and there were repeated and severe clashes. In spite of everything the moral fight was going against Tyrone. Then winter came when he should normally have gained a rest, and Mountjoy stuck in the field and it became evident that once his line of forts was complete nothing could dislodge him. He infected his subordinates with his own spirit. Chichester pushed across from Knockfergus on the coast to the edge of the Great Lake, established a fort there at Masserene, and actually crossed the Great Lake by boat, time and again, with raiding parties who burned to within four miles of Tyrone's capital of Dungannon. By the summer of 1601 the chain around Tyrone was almost complete. That August O'Donnell suffered a dreadful blow when Niall Garv took Donegal and Assaroe for Dowcra.

The credit for all this must go back directly to Mountjoy. The perusal of his letters to the Council and to the Queen reveals, at the very first lines, the clear-headed, intent activity of the man. Day after day he is active. 'Every day we did work and almost every day fight.' He knows that the only answer to guerilla war is to keep the enemy on the run, to break him up, to discourage him. He never exaggerates small encounters into great victories as his predecessors did—he dismisses them as trifles—but he knows the value of accumulated and persistent attack. Thus, the killing of Ownie O'Moore, one of the finest of the southern guerillas, which gave the government Leix County, was followed by the coming in of another fine guerilla Donal Spainneach Kavenagh which gave the government County Carlow and County Wexford. He did things that no general had done before him. He kept in the field through the worst weather, wasting Tyrone's money and dispiriting his men by forcing them to leave their homes and shiver in the bogs and woods. Above all, day in and day out he laid the tribute of Hunger on the altar of Victory. He destroyed the harvest of 1600 and he prevented the sowing of crops in the spring of 1601. His eye was always on the winter of 1601 when Famine would walk beside him against Tyrone. Gradually the old Desmond terror began to creep back over the land, that destruction whose effects Spenser had so terrifyingly described. And when we remember what hunger meant to those days—no palliatives, no charitable organizations, no alternatives for the rock-bottom food of bread and milk, not even the potato—it is a horrible image to see Tyrone's former ally, his own half-brother Turlough MacHenry, keenly assisting the work of destruction. Mountjoy himself was amazed to watch his knife flashing in the corn and the sweat shining on his body, and wrote to the Queen that he was 'the most eager in Her service, and quarrelled with all that would do no more than he.'

We can imagine the sob of rage and misery with which Tyrone heard that piece of news—his contempt, or if he was superhuman enough to feel it, his pity. For this Turlough had fought beside him in the past, and was indeed to fight beside him again and to the end. Like Essex he well may have groaned that he wore a plastron but no curate, that is, his front armed but his back bare. He would have spoken the truth. The English had always said that the branches could not live without the trunk. It was the well-nigh limbless body that stood, to the end, like a ravaged oak, blasted but immovable. Though hard-driven that spring and summer of 1601 he was still what he had been when he first stood at bay on the borders of Tyrone. The English government well knew the truth of that. They were to know it for several years more.

CHAPTER SIX

THE SIEGE OF KINSALE: 1601. MOUNTJOY, DON JUAN DEL AQUILA, TYRONE, AND RED HUGH O'DONNELL

I

In historical records one of the most misleading things is the over-simplification that comes from the historian's foreknowledge of events. Because he knows the result beforehand he is inclined to pass quickly over preliminary struggles where they were in vain, but where they succeeded to describe them with an assurance that nobody at the time can have felt. The story thereby becomes more intelligible but less complete: it loses most of the tension and all the unpredictability of the time. So it was in this struggle between Tyrone and Mountjoy. They saw no clear event. The conclusion was always in the balance. Any skirmish might enlarge itself unexpectedly into a decisive battle. There were many things outside their control which persistently exasperated them, so that although self-confidence might prophesy success it could never guarantee it.

Tyrone had suffered an accumulation of disaster all through 1600 and into 1601. They were dark shadows; they were not the shadows of Fate. He was too powerful for that—it would give the wrong nuance were we to say even that he was 'still' too powerful. Always he had in mind the great trump-thought of Spanish help. Let but a fleet come sailing round the northern coast and, he well knew, on the breath of its sails—on the breath of its merest rumour, all his difficulties would be undone. Those who had defected from him would defect now from his enemies. Dowcra would be starved out. Chichester would be kept indoors.

Mountjoy would march to Lough Foyle at his peril. Every dissension would be smothered. His authority would become supreme again. The Phoenix Feather would transform everything.

On his side, Mountjoy felt no absolute certainty of success. He had planned a slow demise for Tyrone and no matter how impatient London became he refused to promise anything spectacular. He wrote in August (1601) to Cecil to remind him of that. 'Whatsoever others have undertaken, I beseech you sir to remember, that in all my dispatches, I have declared that the uttermost you could looke from us in this summer should be to plant such garrisons as must take effect next winter, and that we should proceed slowly, and come short of our purpose, if we were not continually supplied with meanes, and in time of victuals and all kinds of munitions.' He constantly enlarged on the fact that Tyrone was a powerful enemy and had more fighting men, and declared it 'as busie a warre as any is in the world,' and confessed himself so harassed by the guerillas swooping down from the mountains and out of the forests that 'these rogues keep us waking all night.'

Behind these generalizations we have to see the countless day-by-day incidents which in every such war discourage optimism by their constant sequence of fresh demands, new worries, grave doubts, hurried calls to arms, personal quarrels, a tension which emerges only in some brief mention of an advance or a retreat and is never crowned by anything more satisfying than a partial success—which the very next day might as easily reverse. Thus, it is nothing to us now that Mountjoy was quarrelling bitterly that summer with his Lord President in Munster, Carew. But how exasperating and worrying it was then! It is merely a line in a forgotten dispatch that Tyrone once 'poured three thousand shot into our camp' that August, and was barely held back from forcing the position. Then it was neck-and-neck, and every nerve taut, and no man knew but that the next attack might win him the day. Not merely Time but the Result has made such events as these seem slight, and for both reasons few people are troubled to follow them to-day and the whole story thereby becomes fore-shortened, over-simplified, loses the human touch, indeed loses everything until some novelist like a Scott or a Balzac arises to recapture the immediacy of the times. Take, for another example, an incident like the recapture by O'Donnell of Newton Fort.

Dowcra had held Newton and his men trusted a clansman named Turlough MacNeilson who, like so many others had at first helped the English against their own people but hated them at heart. Through the connivance of MacNeilson the guerilla forces took Newton by surprise and killed every man in it. For that Dowcra swore to get the 'traitor,' and paid some other wretched Gaelic churls to dog him and kill him. MacNeilson was possibly one of a band of what we should now call saboteurs —men hanging loosely about the country to do what damage they could. He never slept in the place that he first visited at night. He would go to a rough bothy in the hills, light a fire, and creep away to some other hiding-hole where he might light another fire, and so to a third place or even to a fourth before lying down to sleep. Dowcra's cut-throats hunted him for weeks and though they got several of his men and killed them he always eluded them. They brought several of his men alive to Dowcra who, as he says calmly, 'caused the soldiers to hew them in pieces with their swords.' Still they could not get their man. Finally they set a boy to watch him. MacNeilson eluded even this spy, time and again, until one night when the boy clung to his trail pertinaceously and did not leave him until, through the bushes, he saw his man lie down and pull off his trews. Then he crept away and raced back to his band who stole stealthily after him, surrounded the lone guerilla, killed him and hacked off his head which Dowcra thereafter exhibited to all and sundry as a 'ludibrious' sight.

We have to multiply that incident ten-thousand fold to realize with what intensity this savage war was kept boiling day after day through the woods and bogs of Ireland. And we have to keep on reminding ourselves that this is the sort of bitter human drama that lies behind every word in the State Papers, the dispatches of the generals, the text-book brevities. Dowcra's own narrative is full of such incidents, and we visualize a bloody procession of them when, for example, he gives one or two instances of dispirited guerillas coming over to his side, and then recanting as their spirit came back to them; for he would at once take out their pledges—their friends or relatives, perhaps their own sons—and hang them straightway from the nearest tree. And yet those guerillas would, perhaps, come in again and give more pledges, and be reviled by Dowcra 'with the most profound execrations that the tongue of man could express,' and they would work for him until . . . 'they flew out again.' Once we get a grip of that struggling, writhing tangle of intense hate, and fear, and resolve, we must see that up to the very end there was no certainty about this savage war.

As late as July 1601, Elizabeth herself was so dissatisfied with the progress Mountjoy had made that she held him in grave suspicion of being partial to Tyrone, and declared that he was too puffed up with pride at being in command of a great army. His corresponding complaints are, like those of every Deputy before him, frequent and bitter. These dissensions, similar dissensions within Ireland among the settlers, the weakness of the magistrates, the corruption of the army authorities, of the purveyors and sutlers—Dowcra, for example, once received food so rotten that he traced it to an order for corn given and collected two years before for Bagenal—all these torment and hamper the campaign of 1600–1601 as they had done every campaign since the war began. To such examples there is no end. It is not too much to say, after watching its hazardous and indecisive course year after year, that the truth about this war is not so much that Mountjoy won it as that Tyrone lost it.

When, therefore, that August of 1601 Mountjoy received news from London that the most recent messages from Spain reported that a fleet was ready there either for the Low Countries or for Ireland, and that the Low Countries fleet had been further strengthened from Italy, he knew exactly what that portended. (He knew that the 'Low Countries' had been earlier agreed between the Irish and the Spanish as a code-word for Ireland, and that he might expect a Spanish landing very soon.) The Irish also had the news and the one thing that made Mountjoy believe the report implicitly was the sudden rise of arrogance among them. What Tyrone had counted on happening was happening. When he heard the news he must have shouted that the war was on the turn. The one question that now held the two antagonists taut was—Where would the landing occur?

Tyrone could measure Mountjoy's quandary precisely because he could measure his own. A fair medium guess at the time was that the invasion would be on the western coast by way of Sligo, as happened long afterwards when the French landed in 1798 at Killala. If Mountjoy drew off to this coast to meet them the Northern clansmen would promptly rise again. If he stayed where he was the Spaniards would rouse the country and at the head of an enormous jacquerie drive up to the north through O'Donnell's country, wipe out Dowcra, and face him on the Blackwater. But if the Spanish did not land at Sligo, if they landed at Limerick, or even Galway, what was either of them to do? There it seemed, at first glance, that if the Spanish were so incredibly unwise as to land at Galway, or anywhere south of it, Mountjoy need only stay where he was to deprive Tyrone of the full value of his trump-card. For the moment, however, everything pointed to the west or north, the two most disaffected regions in the country, as the obvious site for a landing, and Mountjoy had actually ordered supports to be sent from Munster into Connaught, and was on his way to the west in September when news came that the Spanish fleet had landed on the *extreme south* of Ireland at Kinsale. O'Neill's spirits sank to the bottom of his boots. Mountjoy whooped with joy. Then he did something totally unexpected. He was at Kilkenny when the news came in conference with Carew. He sent Carew back to Cork. He dispatched the captains of the Pale to their posts. He himself, though totally unfitted for such a march, made hot-foot for the south with all the men he could lay his hands on, relying on the speed of his decision to cover the defects of his troops, and so impress the people as to stop, at least for the present, the current of a wholesale uprising. It was one of the boldest moves he ever made and it must have taken the wind out of Tyrone's sails, and he must have wondered, in his dismay, what else lay behind it. Nothing lay behind it except, to mirror his own bitter mood of that moment, what lay evident in front of him—that ring of forts.

Mountjoy was otherwise counting on three things: the foul weather coming on, the distance (from tip to toe of the island) that the Northern Irish would have to march in that bad weather if they wished to contact the Spanish in Kinsale, and the value of the work he had done against the North over the last year and a half. In spite of himself Tyrone must have admired the man's self-confidence. For the general information was that the Spaniards numbered between three and four thousand men, and these some of the best soldiers in Europe, Italians, Portuguese, men from the Azores and Northern Africa. And they had brought with them sixteen hundred saddles, which meant that they expected to get horse in Ireland and take the field at once. Their strength in sail was between twenty-five and twenty-seven, of which seventeen were men of war, six galleons, and the rest small boats of a hundred to a hundred-and-fifty tons. Tyrone knew that the most that Mountjoy could command was 4,300 fit men. For the rest, all he knew for certain was that Mountjoy intended to bottle up the Spaniards before they could get loose in the country, and that, from his great distance, he had no hope of forestalling him.

If we look over Mountjoy's shoulder we find him stating the problem exactly so. 'If the Spaniards should prevail at first all Ireland will follow. I am trying to protect Munster at first. If we be royally seconded out of England we may go on this winter in the north and continue our war here, which I am confident will ruin all our enemies in this country. If not, the King of Spain will make good what he has begun and put this Kingdom in a great hazard. If the forces from England arrive in any time I will again strengthen the Northern garrison. If they thrash the North, Spain cannot uphold the Irish, or make their army to live in this country.'

Mountjoy further maintained that the reason for the choice of Kinsale was two-fold, and if he was right Tyrone had been doubly deceived. The first reason was that Florence MacCarthy and the Sugaun Earl of Desmond had managed to persuade Spain to land in Munster. Tyrone was never to know the truth of that since both MacCarthy and Desmond had fallen, some months before, into Carew's hands and were at that moment cursing their fates, and cursing Tyrone, in the Tower of London. It was Carew who developed this theory, which he gave as part of the confession extracted from Desmond himself: it was supported by other confessions taken at the time, specially that of Don Dermuchio, i.e. Dermot MacCarthy, 'the principal agent used by Florence MacCarthy to bring the Spaniards hither.' Mountjoy's second reason for this landing was that Philip III had in mind not merely, and not even primarily, an invasion of Ireland but also an invasion of England. For an English invasion no port in north or west would have been so useful a jumping-off ground as Kinsale, or Cork, or Waterford. (Mountjoy had spoken of Waterford in his own forecasts though he finally favoured the West.) Whatever the reasons for this calamitous choice they were fast becoming for Tyrone as academic a matter as they remain for us to-day. His concern was what to do now that the dreadful mistake had been made.

The medieval town of Kinsale waited meanwhile for the

decisions of the three protagonists; wondered tremblingly what fate it had inherited. On September 21st the Spanish ships had come over the horizon and into the curving river-harbour. Two days later their general, Don Juan del Aquila, had stepped ashore on the little quay, with his dark-faced captains in their edged helmets and their great breeches, and the darker-faced sailors from Africa and the Azores, with their barbarous ear-rings and coloured turbans lifting their long oars in salute. The small English garrison had fled, and the more timid or the wiser inhabitants now took refuge in the autumn fields. At night the taverns were packed with these foreign soldiers, and the men were gay after the long voyage. But the foreign muskets grounded forebodingly on the walls and the old town-hall bell rang like an omen, and the great woods on the surrounding hills seemed unusually dark.

As the days passed and the Spaniards did not fan out into the country, and no news came from Tyrone, Kinsale and Munster and all Ireland began to look towards Mountjoy. He was in Cork city at the end of September. But a week of October passed and yet he had not moved. Tyrone guessed what he was doing—simultaneously equipping his men and bombarding London with appeals to reinforce the North. The guess was right. Another week passed and yet the help did not come, and the Munster Irish were beginning to waver. Mountjoy, likewise, could guess that the North, especially Red Hugh, was in a frenzy between resolution and indecision about coming south. He had taken the initiative. If he lost it the event might prove him a rash fool instead of a determined general. Accordingly, dreading inaction, although he was without artillery, adequate munitions, or victuals, and the weather so pitilessly foul that, even after he gave the order to move, no troops could stir out of rain-battered Cork for two whole days, he took the field on October 16th. By that show of confidence he concealed his utter weakness from the Munster Irish, led his army safely over the great brow of the city, and down over the rolling uplands to the sea. Then he sat helplessly on the hills above the town of Kinsale. Through the mist blowing up from the Atlantic he could see, from where he stood under the great beeches, the shining cluster of roofs and the zig-zag line of walls and the forts at the harbour mouth. To-day men will point to where he stood, and one may see it all much as he saw it that October 17th of 1601.

2

It is a commentary on Irish history as it is written that almost every modern historian has taunted Tyrone with either cowardice or incompetence, or both, because he did not at once drive southward after Mountjoy. It is plain from every document of the time that no English official of any authority expected that he would dare to leave Ulster; at most it was thought that he might send his brother Cormac and remain behind himself. Moreover, all these comments on the part of his observers are significantly restrained. The old insulting phrases are now gone—though he is, of course, still the Arch Traitor—and every opinion as to what he will do is tempered by an evident concern as to what he may do. Besides, if it were taken for granted by the generals of 1601 as easily as it has been taken for granted by later historians that he would chase down at once on the heels of Mountjoy, then the whole of Mountjoy's labours to imprison and starve him in the North must likewise be considered a complete failure. Mountjoy had a better opinion of his own work though he leaned towards the belief that Tyrone would have to come south ultimately. Those men knew what was involved in a forced march of three hundred miles, from end to end of the country, from remote Dungannon to remote Kinsale, in midwinter, across flooded rivers, with foreign enemies waiting to trap his army in every county and native rivals ready to pirate him behind his back. Thus, Secretary Fenton wrote to Cecil that he could not imagine what motive would drive Tyrone to make that terrific march 'unless in the humour of a desperate, savage man he will prefer a wilful mind to venture to succour the Spaniards, for a high promise, before all considerations of his own safety and the preservation of his country.'

The military strategy of the thing apart, it was not in O'Neill's character either as a man or as a soldier to chase after Mountjoy. He was a man who had always been unwilling to fight a battle if he could avoid it, a general who relied on Time and Famine and Penury, a prudent man, slow to act and careful in preparation when he did, and the success of that policy over five years of warfare had by now consolidated him in the strategy of temporisation. Whether this occasion was or was not different to all others, whether it was or was not the one crisis in his life that demanded swift action and the greatest risks, he believed otherwise, and both in the opinion of his friends and his enemies it was a defensible judgement. He must have made his decision in the greatest torment. Had the invasion only come one year and a half before he could have followed Mountjoy quickly. If he were able to move swiftly now the English would have been strained to breaking point. Carew, Mountjoy's second, declared—though we must allow that he said so while trying to frighten London into sending them fresh supplies—'If he comes before the supplies come to us from England we shall have to make a retreat and can, we think, make it.' Against that the Munster Irish had been battered by Carew so effectively that the arrival of the Spaniards produced no obvious effect; the best-disposed men refused to rise until they saw some Spanish success and the weaker men came in to protest their loyalty to Mountjoy. All this was in Tyrone's mind as he argued the position with O'Donnell, who was eager for an immediate march southward.

Tyrone saw his army, three hundred miles from its base, in strange country, among a flaccid people, facing the English who had good bases in Cork and Waterford and must, sooner or later, get every possible reinforcement by sea. He saw his men marching—as they finally did march—with their food in bags on their backs, and it would be only meal and butter, and a spare pair of brogues, and every horse carrying a spare set of shoes, no carriages, no wagons, a vast guerilla army, untrained for sieges, and altogether unfit for pitched battles. He refused to face that march until there was no possible way of avoiding it. The enraging fact was that the Spaniards should never have picked on Kinsale, and that their landing there put him into an impossible position on every count. He held his fury, and he held back O'Donnell, who must have been indeed 'desperate,' as was said of him at the time, since he must have known well that if he went south Niall Garv would rip his land to pieces behind him, and that if that southern adventure failed he would have no land to come back to. Tyrone made up his mind to gamble on Time once again, to leave Kinsale to Del Aquila for as long as Del Aquila would tolerate, try to win back Ulster; and so to harrass Dublin that he would at least prevent reinforcements from going to Mountjoy, and might instead force Mountjoy to send assistance to the Pale, or even return North himself.

Accordingly he broke through the ring of forts, thrust to the coast, raided the Pale, pierced Leinster with four thousand men, sacked twenty-two villages, plundered and terrorized all before him, burnt the corn of the settlers, and took great preys of cattle. The Anglo-Irish watched him in a daze, and at once—as he had expected—began to call on Mountjoy and London for protection. But we know Mountjoy's opinion of the Anglo-Irish and the Pale. 'To prevent this clamour of the Pale,' he wrote contemptuously to Elizabeth, 'is unpossible, though it would please Her Majesty to keepe there 10,000 men in her pay. They would not stir, nor raise the crie, but suffer themselves to be so used, out of the malice of their owne hearts, that they might have some colour of complaint, being the worst sort of people in all the Kingdome.' He left them to their fate, and refused to be stirred from the Spaniards even though Tyrone should burn Dublin. He would not even assist his own forts in Ulster. He was content, for the time being at any rate, that Tyrone should now imprison his jailors, win back the allegiance of his allies who had deserted him, such as Ever McCooley and Turlough McHenry, do his best to undo all that had been done against him. Mountjoy, also, was now gambling on Time. He would see to it that the Spaniards would not hold out long enough.

This is a ticklish point which Tyrone, obviously, must have weighed carefully. When he decided that he would allow the Spaniards to be besieged he must have been satisfied that there was no immediate hurry about succouring them. He came in the end to their assistance three months after they landed, and two months after the siege proper began, and it is evident that they could have held out much longer than that. As this is the only prolonged siege of a walled town in the whole of these wars it is interesting to examine the basis of Tyrone's judgement as to how long he could safely leave the Spaniards to their own resources.

The idea of a siege may suggest that the besieged are caught like rats in a trap, their position desperate. In point of military fact for a winter campaign the attackers are in every respect but food much the worse off. They are exposed to the calamities of foul weather—and the siege of Kinsale was carried on in weather of the worst kind—so that their trenches fill with water, they are miserable all the time, their morale is sapped, they die of cold and exposure and malnutrition and disease. There is no effective way of sheltering so enormous an army of men as Mountjoy finally held before Kinsale—over 12,000 men at the end—and the task of feeding them is heart-breaking for the quarter-masters. Furthermore, the greater part of the action lies with the besiegers. The besieged live in comfortable houses—in Kinsale they were supplied with 'vaulted cellars where they lodged securely'—and are chiefly called on to build up breaches made by cannon and to keep the attackers perpetually keyed-up by sorties. If a besieged town has a sufficient supply of food, therefore, and can keep up its own morale it can hold out for a great length of time and cost the enemy dearly in the end. Not long before, Sir John Norreys lost very nearly 1,500 men in besieging a fort in Brittany held by about 200 Spaniards. Neither Tyrone nor del Aquila need, as a result, have been perturbed at the size of Mountjoy's forces. On October 27th his List* was 6,900 men; on November 20th his List was 11,800 foot and 857 horse. The Spaniards were 3,814 men. For such a siege it was not an unequal fight. The Spaniards were all trained fighters. They had a fair supply of provisions. They had a solidly protected and tactically effective position; they had written to Tyrone telling him so, and Mountjoy's despatches and the course of the siege fully confirm that first opinion. In the event they lost far less men than the besiegers. They fought the whole siege bravely and they fought it well, isolated as they were in a strange country—their fleet had gone back to Spain after disembarking the army—and no doubt at a loss to understand the failure of the Irish to come immediately to their assistance.

That danger of bitter misunderstanding was another problem on which neither Tyrone nor the English failed to reckon, and it was probably a much more important problem in the end than any purely military consideration. Tyrone did communicate with del Aquila and del Aquila with him. The first optimistic messages from the Spaniards apparently reached Tyrone by October 20th, three days after Mountjoy appeared on the hills outside the town. Before the end of the month a message from Tyrone, possibly a reply, reached del Aquila. A priest and the servant of a Kinsale landowner, whose name is given as 'McChaire,' had got through the lines by a ruse and reached the walls by creeping on all fours. There the priest called out in Latin to the watch who held his bullet and took them inside. The same two men made the journey back, this time with a clamant appeal from del Aquila to O'Neill to come at once or be for ever

* The 'List' is the paper total. The 'Toll' is the check or practical total.

disgraced before his king. The Spaniards were evidently beginning to take the measure of Mountjoy's attack. It was on receiving this appeal, about November 6th, that Tyrone first seriously considered moving south. Even then he merely fixed November 12th for a conference with all his adherents, and in sum kept del Aquila waiting seven weeks longer. During that period the main contest lay between the Spaniards and the English.

3

To visualize that contest we must imagine a rocky coast broken by the wide estuary of the Bandon River, broad as a harbour-mouth, and sweeping back inland like a sickle. In the hollow of this sickle is the headland and fort of Castle Park. (Park probably implies the park or field of artillery in the fort.) Opposite this fort, eastward across the river, is the fort of Rincorran: the Gaelic word *corran* actually means a sickle. Between these two heavy positions the river flows northward, curves back around to the south in a wide sweep and there, on the opposite side of the headland of Castle Park, to the west and northwest, are the quays of the town. So that the eye, in moving from east to west, hits Rincorran fort, the wide river, Castle Park fort, the river again, and then brushes the quays of Kinsale. The river goes on westward towards Bandon, cutting off a great bleak headland which stretches out to the Old Head of Kinsale. Backing the town is a great, wide, circular sweep of high hills. Only to the immediate east of the town is the land a little more smooth. Mountjoy observed this and noted that another small river flows inland here, roughly parallel to the big Bandon River. This is the entry from Oyster Haven, about a mile east of Kinsale. That little river was invaluable to Mountjoy, because it was navigable at high tide for about two miles, as far as an old mill which still stands and is now called Brown's mills. It meant that English supplies, especially the artillery which could not easily be brought overland, could be sailed right up behind the town on the north-east. From the old mill a hilly road climbs southward towards Kinsale, over that surrounding sweep of hills. In the opposite direction the same road climbs away from the mill and the river past a hill called Knockrobin. It was there that Mountjoy pitched his first camp on October 17th and had his first light skirmish with the Spanish scouts. It was there that he made his plan of campaign.

The terrain decided it. Looking southward he could see how the two forts protected the town and inner harbour. He dismissed for the present the great headland beyond the wide impassable river to the south-west. He also observed that the town climbed the hill to the west and that an attack from that angle was possible but not attractive. His road for supplies was behind him, to the east and north-east. The general direction of assault must be from that point of the compass. But first of all the harbour must be opened to his own ships and closed to Spanish reinforcements, and if he did open it it might also be possible to bombard the town from the water. He might win the two forts.

He first tried to bombard Rincorran with two ships sent around from Oyster Haven. Their guns were too small. Meanwhile the Spanish sortied or the English raided, and the rain fell torrentially by day and night. On the 26th he dislodged his army from Knockrobin and climbed nearer the town, indeed overlooking it, to the opposite hill called the Spittle; but no artillery was landed or mounted until October 29th. In the hope of taking the guns the Spaniards made a sortie by water from the town in the dark, but the ships in the harbour beat them back and the bombardment of Rincorran duly began next day from two culverins trained from the east. One received a flaw at 2 p.m. and fell silent; the other broke its carriage after a few shots. The Spaniards, to draw off the fire, had meantime dragged a demi-cannon out of the town and begun to ply the English camp, and they again sortied that night in an effort to relieve Rincorran. The next morning the mended culverins, augmented by a cannon and a third culverin battered the fort unceasingly, and again the Spaniards sortied in a long and bloody melee that swayed to and fro from the fort in under the very walls of the town so that the English were raked by the fire of the besieged over their heads on the house tops. Still the bombardment went on until dark when town and camp suddenly heard a drum beating over the water for a parley. The men were offering to retire bag and baggage into Kinsale.

The English refused and the batteries kept on vomiting flame all night while the town watched and listened, unable to intervene. At 2 o'clock in the morning the drum again beat for a parley, but it was refused, and in the darkness most of the garrison, both Spanish and Irish escaped down the rocks to the waterside and fought their way free. The battering went on into the morning and at 1 p.m. the Spanish Ensign—the captain had been knocked out—offered to retire, yielding up all their arms, if they might go into the town. That offer was also refused. He then offered that he alone should be permitted to keep his arms and be sent into Kinsale. That third offer likewise was refused. At that he swore that he would be buried in the ruins rather than surrender, but his garrison had not his spirit and threatened to throw him out of the breach unless he yielded. He did so, making now but one condition, that he at least should keep his sword. Mountjoy agreed and the fort fell. Since all those things were managed according to a strict traditional etiquette and the terms graded in proportion to the valour shown in a fight, it does not seem that the defence was strikingly resolute. The prisoners were 65 Spanish soldiers, four women, and a great number of Irish labourers, women and children, but only one Irish swordsman, Dermot MacCarthy, who had come from Spain and was known as Don Dermuchio. The Spanish prisoners were sent to Cork. MacCarthy was hanged.

The fort of Rincorran was evidently a comparatively weak position, and although he took it quickly Mountjoy seems to have been unpleasantly surprised by the vigour of the Spanish sorties during the taking of it, and had formed a much sharper idea of the general strength of the town's defences. At any rate he now decided that there could be no question of taking the town by assault with his present forces, and proposed instead to invest it until reinforcements arrived. In that decision he was confirmed just after the capture (November 3rd) by a warning letter from Elizabeth herself reminding him that he must not 'in venturing too farre make the foe a prey of you.' Better still, other letters on the same day told him that ten ships of war had left Rochester with 2,000 men, thirty more casks of powder, and large provisions of victuals, and in addition 2,000 more men had been levied for Bristol and Barnstable, and another 1,000 had sailed for Lough Foyle to hold down the North. As against that encouragement to take his time, news came that Tyrone was definitely moving south. That meant that the English must now look to their rear, entrench themselves against an attack, and detach a couple of thousand men to cut off the Ulster forces. Here we return to Tyrone and O'Donnell. The Spanish had now been awaiting sight of them for five weeks.

4

In point of fact Tyrone was not yet on the march. He had merely moved into Leinster to that conference with his associates on November 12th which, as already mentioned, had been the result of an earlier appeal from del Aquila to come south at once. To that conference he brought all the forces that he could muster and food for six weeks. It was held on the borders of Cavan and Meath, possibly in the vicinity of Lough Ramor. After a long and fateful discussion he decided to go in person to Kinsale, at the head of a little over 3,700 foot and 670 horse, not counting Red Hugh and the Connaught men. Before he began his hazardous march he made a will appointing his son Hugh as his successor in case anything should happen to himself, sent his brothers and sons to hold Ulster, and then faced the dangers that lay in front of him; 'rivers and waters, and the extremities of winter,' and two armies—that is, those of Mountjoy and Carew. The winter had been terrible, with heavy storms, and the rains had flooded every stream into a river, and every river into a lake, and made all these side-paths which he must travel with his thousands of guerillas impassable for anything but their trudging feet. Slowly he worked his way down towards Trim and there deflected a little to the west. It is a mark of the indecision in men's minds about the whole conflict, and of his considerable power that everywhere the people either threw in their lot with him or sent him fair words and presents. Even the loyalist lords of the Pale, like Delvin, or Dunsany, or Plunkett sent him their gifts of wine or food.

He then sent O'Donnell and O'Rourke and the Connaught men before him into Tipperary where Carew was waiting with the first English army to intercept whom he could. O'Donnell, like any traveller to-day, going southward through Ireland, met the great river Suir, then in full spate, reaching up towards its source through the middle of County Tipperary from the sea; and like any modern traveller, had the choice of proceeding southward either on the east or the west of the river. Carew was waiting for him at Holycross, which lies on the river in the heart of Tipperary, ready to catch him whichever side he went, since the lie of the land, with further rivers to the east and boggy mountains to the west, made any other route normally impossible. Certainly no straggling army of guerillas could have been expected to cross the Slieve Phelim mountain range where, in this foul weather, the lofty moors were little short of a quaking morass. When Carew contacted him, therefore, he felt in no danger of losing his man by falling back to, presumably, a better position. But on that evening of November 21st (1601) O'Donnell suddenly swerved to the west and when darkness fell Carew had, as it turned out, hopelessly lost him. For as dark fell frost also fell, phenomenally severe, and the morasses of Slieve Phelim suddenly became passable. Seizing his luck O'Donnell drove his men, without rest, across the frozen mountain in the darkness.

Four hours before dawn Carew's spies brought him the news. He rose at once and drove after O'Donnell to Cappamore, the only possible entry into Limerick county across the Mulkear, a tributary of the Shannon. He was there by eleven o'clock in the morning. There was no sign of O'Donnell who had not rested after the night's march and was already twenty miles further away at Croom. Carew acknowledged that it was 'the greatest march that had ever been heard of' for a winter campaign, gave up the effort and retired. The way was now wide open for O'Neill. Carew was back in Kinsale, after a rapid march, on November 26th, fearful lest O'Donnell should cut in before him. But O'Donnell did not make for Kinsale at once; he moved southward to Castlehaven. O'Neill joined him later north-west of Kinsale. Captain Tyrrell came after him with a third and final section of the Irish fighting men. The Spaniards were now about two months without sight of their Irish allies.

5

Mountjoy had meanwhile been transforming his camp into a well-entrenched, well-defended position. He had now received all the reinforcements he needed; he was over 12,000 strong, with lavish artillery, seconded by the fleet at sea which had arrived on November 14th. With the arrival of the fleet he decided to attack the remaining fort at the harbour entrance—Castle Park. He bombarded it from sea and land between the 15th and the 20th. The Spanish replied with many sallies and sorties, one of which, across the water from the town, took off most of the garrison at night so that when the fort fell only sixteen fit men were taken out of it. The Spaniards felt the blow of this second surrender, and foreseeing that the town would be bombarded more effectively in the future evacuated all the Irish women and children. These, being loyalists, the English allowed to pass into the surrounding country to their relatives or friends. The town was now invested closely on every side. It was on that same night that O'Donnell dodged Carew across the mountains on his march to the South. Mountjoy closed in. In this evacuation it is to be noted that there was no question of humanity. The English had wished the Anglo-Irish civilian population to stay in Kinsale in order to reduce the supplies available for the Spaniards: they permitted them go without enthusiasm. It would be altogether misleading to talk at any time of humanity in connection with men like Carew, Mountjoy, Dowcra, or Chichester. They were among the most ruthless exponents of total war in history; unscrupulous captains overflowing with a cruel and inventive energy who were, no doubt, regarded by the Spanish of that age with the same bitter scorn as their modern imitators are regarded by their modern descendants.

Four more pieces were now added to the cannon and demi-cannon which had bombarded the fort from the east; three culverins were mounted in the captured Castle Park across the river; the six pieces on the north-eastern hill were augmented and by the 25th of November all were simultaneously beating down on the roofs in a determined barrage. The navy too, ten ships in all, drew in between the lost fort and the town, and its small guns made the foreshore unapproachable. The main effect, however, of the loss of Castle Park was a moral one. The three culverins mounted there were of too short a range to do serious damage and the ships' guns could not reach the higher town and were badly raked by the Spanish when they tried to approach still closer.

On November 28th Mountjoy began to get impatient—for time was getting on and Carew was now returned with news of his failure to cut off O'Donnell and Tyrone. He sent a Trumpet to summon the town to surrender. The messenger was rebuffed at the gate and told that Don Juan del Aquila held the town first for Christ and second for the King of Spain and would therefore defend it *contra tutti*. Spanish soldiers standing by added insulting barrack-room words of their own. In retort the whole artillery of the besiegers spoke all day long and into the night against the eastern gate and finally broke part of it down. Through the darkness the Spaniards worked like devils to repair it. The guns again blazed through the following day and again breached the gate as well as the new works thrown up during the night. It was now the last day of November and O'Donnell was to the west, at Castlehaven, and the English were eager to attack the breach; but their first skirmishes were thrown back and the bombardment had to begin again, still playing against the eastern gate and the wall to the right of it. (This is where, to-day, the traveller enters the town of Kinsale by the road from Cork, a wide peaceful square lapped by the harbour water.) That night again the Spaniards laboured on the gaps, always under fire from the English small-shot, but they worked so well that when 2,000 foot from the English camp made a desperate bravado the next day they had to retire with the report that in spite of all the cannonading the breach could not be ventured. The attack on the east wall was abandoned.

The enemy now turned to the west and under cover of a thick mist began to raise earth-works within less than half a culiver's shot from the walls. When the fog lifted and the Spanish saw these works desperate hand-to-hand fighting followed in the trenches. The east was likewise strongly manned the same night with trenches and gabions (that is, wicker cases full of earth; our sand-bags) and a full complement of artillery still nosed at the east wall and gate. That was the night of the 2nd of December, dark and rainy, and the moon late in rising. Under cover of the blackness and the downpour the Spanish made one of their biggest and bloodiest sorties. They came out with some 2,000 men, first feinting to the west and then wheeling with all their strength on the guns to the east. They fell on them (said an English witness) 'with exceeding fury' and as the musketeers and swordsmen fought for supremacy, the sappers tore at the gabions, and special squads rushed the guns with shovels, mattocks and hammers to 'cloy' them. The main English camp heard the alarum and sallied out and the fight became intensified. But here again the Spanish wheeled back to the west, and in the flitting moonlight they rushed the works that had been thrown up the day before, took them, and slaughtered the garrison. In this, the fiercest and most successful sortie of the siege, it is clear that the Spanish fought *à outrance*, for at dawn on the 3rd their dead littered the gun-emplacements, lay upon the powder, hung across the cannon.

Foiled east and west the English now withdrew, December 4th, to the greater safety of the North, and thought it wise to pull a further regiment out of the main depôt, the Lord Deputy's camp to the N.E. to reinforce them. That made four regiments in all now massed on the North—their fear of the present arrival of Tyrone or O'Donnell was evidently increasing. They furthermore decided that the main camp would have to be more strongly fortified and all the outlying horse was drawn into it for greater protection. From that day on the batteries played only intermittently. In a word, the idea of taking Kinsale by direct assault was given up. In fact, the entire artillery was withdrawn on the 6th into the main northern camp. The reason for these precautions is obvious. Rumour of the approach of Tyrone and O'Donnell became keener and clearer every day. The English realized that they were now in grave danger of being transformed from besiegers into besieged.

Action gave way to talk. Something of the atmosphere of the medieval siege followed in the contention between Don Juan and Mountjoy during the parleys about the burial of the dead. Mountjoy protested against the insulting barrack-room epithets of the Spanish arquebusiers at the time of his first Trumpet, especially those who called the English 'meschini.' Don Juan offered to try the quarrel in personal combat, which Mountjoy declined, adding dryly that he understood the Council of Trent to forbid such combats in the field? He took further umbrage because at his first Drum he had offered to permit certain ladies and women in the town to leave, and had got back the message that Don Juan 'would not be his bawd.' To this Don Juan replied with a shrug. Mountjoy warned him finally that he had offered the courtesies proper between honourable enemies, but that if his courtesy were by any chance being mistaken for timidity, or even for respect for the greatness of Spain, then he would show in future how much he disdained such interpretations.

Nobody would hold it against the English if, at this point, they had begun to feel a little frightened. This was December 5th. The assault had failed. O'Donnell was only fifty miles away. O'Neill's advance cavalry was within three days march. And just before that sortie of the night of the 2nd–3rd news had come that six more Spanish ships under Don Pedro Zubiaur had put in along the coast at Castlehaven with about 700 men and ordnance and ammunition. The English fleet had managed to get around to Castlehaven and the usual 'victory' followed, which, as far as one can make out, means that one Spanish ship was sunk and that the English ships were so severely hammered by the shore batteries that they had to get clear as fast as they could: in brief enough had been accomplished for honour, and no more. Moreover it was commonly believed that more reinforcements were to come after Christmas, and it is most likely that help in plenty would have rewarded any spectacular success.

On December 8th O'Neill's horse was discovered two miles off. He had advanced to a place called Coolcarron Wood, and fortified it with a ditch. From that on the deep woods about Kinsale gradually began to rustle with Irish closing in. O'Neill, the Castlehaven Spanish, and local Irish were soon cutting off Mountjoy's foragers and stopping local supplies. The Spanish, doubly heartened, sallied nightly. The province began to have doubts of an English victory and we have Mountjoy's word for it that most of them were gone 'out.' His own soldiers began to desert freely. Despite the threat of immediate execution if caught, so many stole away that within a few weeks two hundred men were picked up between Cork and Waterford—a good indication of the large number irretrievably gone. Every day O'Neill drew the net closer and closer. By December 13th no food for horse or man was entering the English camp. On the same date Mountjoy wrote to Cecil begging significantly for a diversion in the North to draw off O'Neill. Carew's despatches were even more gloomy. 'There has never been a more miserable siege than this in which many die, many more are too sick to serve, and others run away from faintness of heart. . . . I do not think we have by poll able men in camp to serve the Queen above 1500.' But the most significant sentence of all in these despatches from the English, during those weeks of crisis, refers to the hope of supplies by sea. 'We must further earnestly entreat your Lordships that the fleet may remain upon this coast during the war with the Spaniards and to furnish us with victuals, money, and munitions, for Easterly winds are rare at this time of the year and without every of these this action cannot be maintained but that the army will breake and come to nothing.' It is one of the clichés of history that the weather always favoured England against her would-be invaders. At Kinsale, however, the wind was anti-English: for weeks and weeks it refused obstinately to blow from the east and home, and without its favours—the roads now all in Tyrone's hands—Mountjoy was threatened by starvation. At the end of December he had not six days rations in hand and the wind was still blowing from the west: as it blew for several weeks after.

That week, from about the 17th of December (1601) onward, held Tyrone's fate. It was that point in a duel, a game of chess, a boxing-match when the spectators sit tense, and then suddenly one of the combatants makes a move that decides the game and everybody sinks back with a gasp, knowing that nothing that happens afterwards can retrieve the chance decided at that moment. That week was the decisive moment in the history of Tyrone's life. It was one of the decisive moments in the history of Ireland, incomparably more important than the Battle of the Boyne, or any other battle in the whole course of her history. After it Tyrone was to live out his life in the vain hope of retrieving his position as it was on that 17th December and during the few days after it. Kinsale was to mean to Ireland, for ever, a parting of the ways, a scission with everything that had gone before, an ending as absolute as death. Tyrone had the game in his hands, and he threw it away by deciding to attack. He should have hung on. He should have been faithful to Time who had never been unfaithful to him. He should have turned the screw on Mountjoy as Mountjoy had turned it on him for nearly two years. If he had held out for five years could he not have held out now for five weeks? In deciding to attack he turned his whole attitude, his whole mental outlook, his idea of life, his entire critical opinion of Ireland inside out. For what had been the curse of Ireland for centuries was rashness, and recklessness, and improvidence, and incogitancy, tons of courage and hardly an ounce of brains, all the qualities and faults that naturally depend from the turbulent life of the border. These had created a racial psychosis in which patience and a regard for time and the discipline of restraint played but a small part. His strength had lain in his cultivation of these virtues and his whole life had crowned Time as the goddess of them all.

No doubt O'Donnell was at his elbow, following his own instinct, bursting to give the only virtues he recognized their magnificent opportunity. But what of that? O'Donnell was but a child compared to him. And though Don Juan was, with more reason, also desperately eager for a fight he was in good spirits that could have been encouraged and sustained. That is clear from his letter of December 18th which reads in translation:

'To the Prince O'Neale and Lord O'Donnell.

'I thought your Excellency would have come at Don Ricardo's going, since he had order from you to say, that upon the Spaniards coming to you (from Castlehaven) you would do me that favour. And so I beseech you now you will do it, and come as speedily and well appointed as may be. For I assure you that the enemies are tired, and very few, and they cannot guard the third part of their trenches, which shall not avail them, for, resisting their first fury, all is ended. The manner of your coming your Excellencies know better to take there than I to give it here: for I will give them well to do this way, being always watching to give the blow all that I can, and with some resolution at Your Excellencies fighting as they do always, I hope in God the victory shall be ours without doubt, because the cause is his. And I more desire the victory for the interest of your Excellencies than my owne. And so there is nothing to be done but to bring your squadrons, come well appointed and close with all, and being mingled with the enemies their forts will do as much harm to them as to us. I commend myself to Don Ricardo. The Lord keep your Excellencies. From Kinsale the eight and twentieth of December 1601.' (Old Style.)

Mountjoy intercepted this despatch, but he either permitted it to go through after reading it, since nothing would have pleased him better than a set battle, or a similar one reached Tyrone through another channel. Indeed, to hasten the final gamble, Mountjoy again set about bombarding the town.

The air was now tense with expectation. Any day might bring the clash. On the night of December 21st O'Neill brought his horse and foot within a mile of the English. It was desperate weather, with a great storm raging, the thunder rolling and the lightning flashing so brightly that the whole land was lit up. He must have told the Spanish that he was drawing in for they sallied out in that hellish, fitful light. O'Neill found two English regiments blocking him and after some ineffectual fencing he retired into a fastness of wood and swamp and camped there for the night. He drew out of his fastness in the morning and skirmished again around the northern flank. Mountjoy, furious to come to grips, kept up a stiff bombardment all that day. There must have been more communication between Tyrone and Don Juan because every intelligence warned the English that he would certainly attack that night—the 22nd. Still he held off, possibly because the night was again torn by thunderstorms. That must have been the crucial night when the two Hughs, O'Donnell and O'Neill, quarrelled furiously in Council and Don Juan sent further messages in a strain calculated to sting their pride to the quick. In a heated atmosphere they made their decision: they would attack the next night, the 23rd. The plan was that the Spanish would attack, towards the west, the Quarter or lesser camp—marked on the map as 'The Earl of Thomond's Second Campe'—and that Tyrone, O'Donnell, and Tyrrell would at the same moment attack the major or northern camp. Another possibly more accurate version, from another source, is that Tyrrell was to make a feint on the Quarter while the Spaniards sallied out in force from the West Gate.

All Tyrone's associates agreed later that he faced this battle unwillingly, but that he allowed himself to be overborne by O'Donnell and del Aquila who had, undoubtedly, impressive arguments on their side. For the Spaniards, food was running very low, so low that they were eating rusks steeped in water, and Carew declared on the day after the battle that they had been so reduced as to think it a feast if they could get hold of dogs, cats, or horses. Moreover Don Juan, in his later self-exculpations, declared that his messenger Bustamente had clearly explained his plight to the two Earls, and that all that had been required of them was to dominate the English camp from a hill while he sallied to join them. O'Donnell supported del Aquila, and as for himself pointed out that they could not stay there indefinitely except under conditions of such hardship as would dispirit even the toughest men. That was true enough. Of the three parties to that most wretched of sieges, the Spanish, the English, and the Irish, the Irish were undoubtedly in the worst position of all. They were entirely without shelter. They had brought with them only what they could carry on their backs. Their food must have been bits and scraps. Like all guerillas, who notoriously dislike a country that they do not know well, or on whose friendship they cannot rely implicitly, and who have no talent for any prolonged action—it is simply not their *metier*—their murmurings would reflect their uneasiness, and nothing but decisive action would allay that. Only their own typical recklessness had brought them all that three hundred miles of winter march, and now that they had come there it was terrible for them to find nothing before them but this cold and starvation, the sleeping in sodden clothes in the wet ditches, these incessant storms of the south-west, and no prospect that it would all soon be ended. It was, perhaps, inevitable and inherent in the whole story that these adventurous men should end as desperate men, and that enterprise such as theirs, having constantly wooed Fortune, should tempt it.

The night fell. Midnight came. There was still no sound but the rumbling of that three-day storm. It was now Christmas Eve, and in his house of sods Mountjoy waited with Carew and his Marshal, Sir Richard Wingfield. Kinsale seemed as quiet as sleep, but down there the Spaniards were crouching over their weapons waiting for the zero hour. It was almost dawn, that dismal avantlight about half an hour before the sun makes itself felt, even as a suspicion of dimness under the horizon, when O'Neill walked into the fatal page of his history three quarters of a mile from the English camp. He had no horse. His guerillas were creeping forward in a mass. What followed is as obscure as that half-darkness in which it occurred.

O'Neill's first sight of the English was a Squadron Volant looming up a few hundred yards away as day broke. He saw them being joined by some infantry—that was Wingfield who had gone forward when the first scout reported the presence of the Irish. Then two regiments more, over one thousand men, came up to support these horse and foot. O'Neill retired over a ford. There was not a stir from the town. Wingfield held off for a time —he had sent back a report that the Irish were not in good order and that he would like to attack. Presently Tyrone saw him attacking with a squadron of foot and some horse across the ford. He retired still further behind another stream and a bog to firm ground and waited in the breaking dawn. Still there was not a murmur from the direction of Kinsale. He now saw two more regiments of foot coming up behind those facing him, and presently all four, together with Wingfield and the Squadron Volant began to move up against him. His enemies there must have numbered about 3,000 men, or nearly half the English forces. The remainder were behind in the two camps ready to meet the Spanish assault. It never came. What happened next is inexplicable. It ended everything as suddenly as a thunder-clap.

Wingfield's first attack on the side of the bog was pressed back. He sent out more riflemen and these in turn pressed the Irish van back on its centre. He then found a way around to the firm ground beyond the bog and was able to offer a full attack with horse and foot. The Irish foot took this shock, held it, turned it, and defeated it. Mountjoy, who was watching from a distance, saw the retreat and in haste called up all the remaining horse he had, and with the horse already sent out, managed somehow to take the Irish centre in the rear. This cavalry assault won the hour. The Irish foot in the section that received the brunt of the impact turned and ran. Two other sections however held the assault until the van was now attacked from another angle and broke under pressure. The Castlehaven Spanish held firm, deployed, and were cut to pieces. The Irish centre, or what was left of it, also held its ground and all but a few score were destroyed. The rest were in utter rout. The English horse chased them for two miles until, from sheer exhaustion of man and beast and killing, they desisted. As they came back in the early morning they picked their way among the scattered hundreds upon hundreds of dead.

The traditional explanation for this rout, which was over in an hour, is that the Irish lost their way in the darkness. It is only a tradition. There is also a tradition that an Irish captain gave information about Tyrone's plans to Mountjoy: it is very possible, and even likely, but it contradicts the other explanation since, if Tyrone lost his way, he would not turn up where he was expected, and the evidence in the State Papers, and in Moryson, is definite that the English anticipated an attack without being clear on the details. As to why Don Juan del Aquila did not sally out, there is no explanation. The most reasonable account is in O'Sullivan Beare's chronicle, and as his father took part in the battle he is fairly reliable. It smoothens out most of the contradictions. From him it appears that the battle was not intended at all; that O'Donnell wandered about all night at a loss, owing to the ignorance of his guides; and that when daybreak came he and Tyrone found themselves involved in something they had never anticipated. If this is so, then an earlier hour may have been fixed with del Aquila, and when it passed he may have decided that Tyrone had altered his plans. Yet that leaves us wondering why he did not sally when he heard the sound of the fighting. On that O'Sullivan can only suggest that his scouts reported wrongly that the battle was not a serious affair. Even the English were still, two days after, at a loss to explain what had happened ('No man,' said Carew, 'can yield reasons for this miraculous victory.')

The fleeing Irish did not halt until they reached Innishannon, eight miles to the north-west on the Bandon River, mystified and bewildered and shamed by their collapse. They could already foresee the judgement of history in the scowling looks of the people around them. 'They that did kiss them in their going forward did both strip them and shoot bullets at them on their return; and, for their arms, they did drown them and tread them down in every bog and soft place under their feet.'

Tyrone paused only to confer with his allies. But what outcome could there be to their conference? Six years of hard resistance went like a breath that winter morning. His reputation was ruined. His moral influence was gone. The myth of Spanish aid was finished for ever. His people in the North would be hurrying in to Dowcra immediately they heard the news, even as at that moment the Munster gentlemen were hurrying with dissembled joy to congratulate Mountjoy. A few were, indeed, prepared to go back to Kinsale, collect their forces, blockade Mountjoy—alas, too late!—and retrieve their losses. So hard a realist as Tyrone could not blind himself to the facts as easily as all that. They would have gone back to Kinsale in the bare tackle in which they stood; without a base, without a reputation, without the support of the people, without spirit, without numbers.

That long adventurous march down to Kinsale, through flood and snow and danger, was over. One brief hour had turned everything into a complete debacle. He had become a bush-kerne who had been one of the greatest men in Christendom. It was all like some great structure that patience and intelligence and will-power had built up, and up, until men stood back in astonishment at the size of it—suddenly to hear the ominous rumble and race away for safety as they see the whole thing crash to the ground. It was not his fault. He was the Accuser, not the Defendant at the council-table. He was the modern man who had tried to bear up the rotting edifice of antiquity, and had fallen under its weight. He could not and cannot even be blamed for attempting it, since—by birth, and time, and the urgency of the gifts God gave him, he was fated to 'come forth with callous hands, a chine of steel, and Atlas' shoulders' to a world that Atlas could not have supported indefinitely.

The conference fell silent; broke up, fell apart like its own former power. O'Donnell knew that he was a man without a home, and he refused to face his people as well as the fact. He delegated his title—one cannot say his power—to his brother Rory and took ship for Spain. He would see Philip ! He would force him to collect his fleet again ! He would come back over the western ocean at the head of an army of Victory and Revenge ! Tyrone rose, between a sign and a groan, gathered his followers, and took the road to Ulster.

PART FIVE

1602–1616: EXILE AND EPILOGUE

I

ONE YEAR AFTER Kinsale, at Christmas 1602, one Captain Josias Bodley with some companions paid a very pleasant visit to the house of Sir Richard Moryson in the Magennis country of Lecale, on the east coast of Ulster (and subsequently wrote a very pleasant account of it.) On the way they called at the Magennis home where their hostess was 'that truly beautiful woman' Sara Magennis, a daughter of the Earl of Tyrone. They had the pleasure of drinking her ale and whiskey and, on leaving, they kissed her. Bodley had intended to take his little trip somewhat earlier but, as he explained, Chichester had mobilised all their men to fight Tyrone, who was then at bay in the deep fastnesses of Glankankyne with a herd of cattle and some few fighting men. As a result they had been detained for some sixteen or seventeen days in the field, though 'without doing much harm to Tyrone; for that Tyrone is the worst rascal and very wary and subtil, and will not be beaten except on terms.' However the captain and his colleagues had a couple of brushes with the Arch Traitor and had made him run for his strongholds. This brief respite, of being entertained by Tyrone's sister and brother-in-law, and amusing themselves otherwise and elsewhere, was a welcome break in the winter fighting. The sociable interlude gives us a close-up glimpse of Tyrone's stand during the year then drawing to an end—the once-powerful earl reduced to a wandering guerilla chief, his closest relatives forced to be pleasant with his hunters, his comfortless life contrasted with that of his enemies.

As the winter after Kinsale had waned and spring came on he had felt this pressure increasing gradually, Mountjoy, Dowcra, and Chichester were closing in and in on him, tightening with new forts the ring they had built around him earlier. From that net he could only escape into those rocky depths of Glankankyne over which it could not be cast, or north to O'Kane's country up along the Bann, or south to Maguire's country down across the Blackwater; and from one to the other of these retreats he had dodged when hard pressed. His need all through the year was that same need which had once pressed so hard on the English —Food. For if he could not sow and reap a harvest in some safe fastness, where would he be when the next winter came? It was his aim, therefore, to stay in Glankankyne until he did reap the harvest; it was Mountjoy's aim to keep him on the run so that he should starve when the leaves began to fall again. Bodley's brief reference to one typical sixteen days in the field gives us a picture of the many persistent efforts made to dislodge him, and of his harried, flying defence of his last stronghold.

A glance at the map shows how they had turned the screw on him. Up at the top right-hand, or eastern, corner of Lough Neagh we see a door opened into his recesses by the building of the Fort of Toome. Across Glankankyne we see the garrison at Dungiven coming to meet the garrison from Toome. All along the Blackwater, due south, are half a dozen forts to cut him off from Fermanagh. And he was threatened by more than forts and garrisons; fresh defections by the clans stripped him month by month—his greatest blow being the defection of O'Cahan directly to his North. The result was that the squeezing pressure finally became unbearable. He hung on only until his men had garnered in an early and unripe crop, and then slipped away south to Fermanagh. Mountjoy took possession. Ruined Dungannon became an English fort, and, final symbol, the crowning-stone of Tullyhoge, where O'Neills had been inaugurated from time immemorial, was smashed to pieces. The old Gaelic world fell there like an idol on the grass. Never again would the white stick be handed to one of his name on that little knoll; never again the golden sandal be thrown over an O'Neill's head and fastened to his foot in a ceremony as ancient as the Book of Ruth; never again would the true Bell of Saint Patrick tinkle at the moment of installation. It was even more significant, if less impressively symbolic that, on his return south, Mountjoy received the two remaining sons of Sean who had at last escaped from Tyrone's island-prisons—one of them was the Henry who had escaped from Dublin Castle with Red Hugh O'Donnell—and set them up in the Armagh country until such time as the Queen declared her pleasure concerning them. That long and bitter feud, which began where this story began in Tyrone's childhood, one of the most savage Gaelic vendettas of the century there turned another corner.

All that summer and autumn of 1602, while he was dodging and twisting among the hills of Coleraine and the lakes of Fermanagh, now resting, now fighting, but when he could rather than when he chose to, Tyrone waited for some word from Red Hugh in Spain. There were many rumours that Spring of another Spanish army of 10,000 men who would land this time on the north-eastern coast, and before he was driven from Dungannon Tyrone had still hopefully kept some Spanish soldiers by him as drill-masters for his men. The English fleet likewise had its care for Spain and all through the fine weather it ceaselessly patrolled the Spanish coast. For everybody knew that Red Hugh would work himself to the bone to revenge Kinsale, and he had been, in fact, tireless in his efforts. Still the months passed and no word came, and Tyrone kept his men together and his spirits alive with a gradually decreasing hope. He did not get word about Red Hugh until October—and then the news came that he was dead : poisoned, most men believed, by an English agent named Blake sent after him to Spain. The point has never been conclusively proved but the balance of suspicion is heavily on the side of assassination.

Dead by the will of God, or dead by the hand of an assassin, the passing of Red Hugh broke Tyrone. The winter returned. The rains had begun to fall, the great banks of low cloud shut in the mountains and continued their lofty walls into the dark sky. His lean cattle wandered in search of food in the waste lands where he hid. His followers sat over the stinking fires of bad peat and despair entered their hearts. The glowering days, the long damp nights, the drip of rain outside their bothies, the miserable mooing of the hungry beasts, were a reflection of their own misery that autumn. He was so hard-pressed that he did not dare sleep two nights in succession in the same place but moved on restlessly like Ishmael from hole to hole in his chosen deserts, his wife beside him, his sons bitter as had ever been the sons of Sean. But he could not keep to this hunted life for ever, and he had so few men on whom he could rely that there was no glimmer of hope that the luck would ever turn again. He came back into his own country. Chichester at once drew the gate tight with garrisons on the Bann and lifted his hand to clutch him. It is to this final stand of Tyrone's that Bodley's narrative refers. Shortly after it Tyrone wrote to Mountjoy that he surrendered without terms to the mercy of the Queen. That was December 22nd 1602, almost the anniversary of Kinsale. Mountjoy rejected the surrender.

Unlike Bodley and his friends, Tyrone passed that Christmas (and the first three months of the New Year), like a hunted fox. Elizabeth was dying but she nursed her bitter memories of all that this man had done to shame her, all that he had cost her in honour and in gold. News of his plight reached the Continent, and the King of France, remembering the man's greatness, and fearful of Spain, begged her to yield. Tyrone, in his lost glens, knew nothing either of her sickness or these approaches from France. Had he known he might have risen yet once again, and once again wooed that goddess Time who had so often helped him—for if he could but last until the cold winds of March killed the Queen he would then be treating with her successor, James VI of Scotland—a sympathetic monarch, if not an old friend. In February, 1603, the failing Queen weakened in her resolve. Somebody in London must have passed the hint by devious routes to the Earl, for in March he again offered his submission to Mountjoy, and this time Mountjoy—whose subsequent behaviour shews that he had a genuine admiration for Tyrone—accepted it. The submission was received by Mountjoy on March 23rd. The next day Elizabeth was dead.

Mountjoy tactfully sent Tyrone's old friend Sir Garret Moore with Sir William Godolphin to bring his defeated enemy down to Mellifont. Moore had the tact to leave Godolphin at Charlemont while he rode on into the hills to contact Tyrone. He found him at Tullyhoge, beside his broken coronation-stone. From there he went with Moore back to Charlemont, and on down to Mellifont to meet Mountjoy. The account of the formal surrender by Moryson, who was present, has it that on arriving at the door of the Deputy's chamber Tyrone went upon his knee and remained in that posture for an hour after being permitted to enter and hear the wishes of Her Majesty. For, so far, nobody but Mountjoy and his secretary Moryson knew of the Queen's death and Mountjoy spoke as if she still lived. On his knees he received his rebukes and instructions. He begged for the Queen's gracious pardon. He surrendered to her everything he possessed, lands and rents and titles and all power and influence over his people. He abandoned the name of O'Neill. He renounced all connection with Spain. And if he was pardoned and permitted to return to the North he would loyally, for the future, assist the Queen's officers to civilize the people into English ways, clear the passes, build good houses, abolish all 'barbarous customs,' and do any other work they might allot to him. To the end he maintained, as he had at the beginning, that his motives had been 'neither malice nor ambition but that I was induced by fear of my life to stand upon my guard.' Mountjoy received this humble submission and promised that he would be restored to his title of Earl, and to all the lands that he had held before he went out in rebellion.

The submission concluded Mountjoy embraced Tyrone and they became as two friendly gentlemen. It is a nice situation and one would like to see some Irish Landor recreate the days that followed in another 'Imaginary Conversation.' For all the parties to it were suave and cultivated men and the host, who had been a friend of both his guests, was a perfect interpreter. They remained at Mellifont until April 4th and then the retinue set out for Dublin. As yet no word had been spoken of the death of Elizabeth and Tyrone did not hear it until they arrived at Dublin Castle where Sir Harry Davers met them with the full account. As he gave out his story men looked sideways at Tyrone. He was weeping openly. When somebody said something to him about those tears, he declared that they were for his dear Queen, and continued so, with the tears dripping down into his red beard, shaking with silent rage.

He returned in April to Ulster—a starving, exhausted land. Mountjoy's policy of destruction had been all too successful. No crops had been sown or gathered in some parts of the country for several years. There were stories of children who ate the dead body of their mother in their ravening hunger; of old women who enticed children into their hovels to kill and devour them—possibly untrue, possibly true, at any rate revelatory of the intensity of the famine which could make such stories current. His pardon and return caused a general migration Southward to the Pale where his beaten people could beg or work for food. In that beaten country he met everywhere indifference, contempt, unpopularity, hatred. O'Cahan refused to pay him rents. Niall Garv claimed the lands of the O'Donnells. He was obliged to call on the help of Mountjoy, who knew well that only Tyrone could tidy up the anarchy of this aftermath of war, and at once proclaimed Niall Garv a traitor and called O'Cahan to heel. The wretched men, who had betrayed their own people to assist Dowcra, were thus traitors to every side and went the way of all wretches like them. They repeated the established pattern, dodging and compromising until the English lost patience. In the end they died in the Tower of London, after eating their hearts out in that foreign dungeon for sixteen or seventeen years. Some of their pathetic letters remain begging the Privy Council to get a few pounds out of their tenants to feed their wives and children on whom, at home, every man slammed the door in hatred of the misery brought on the land by these their fathers. (Late in the Cromwellian wars the Duchess of Buckingham came on one of these relicts in the castle of Limavady, an old woman, grimed and wretched, wrapped in a blanket, and the room reeking with the stink of the poor peat over which she crouched. She drew herself up to her full height when asked her name, and said haughtily—'I am O'Cahan's wife.')

Tyrone met that same hatred when he was called to London in May with Rory O'Donnell. All along the route the women whose sons and husbands had been killed in the Irish wars came out and reviled him; he was even battered by volleys of stones and dirt, and had to choose another road for his return and travel under the protection of the sheriffs. His task in trying to reduce his country to order was proportionately bitter. He met his people's savagery with such ruthlessness that those who had gone to the Pale to scratch for food swore that they would rather be strangled than return to him. Yet he held himself before them unbending, as their traditional king, refusing to abandon an inch of his ancient rights. Though defeated he was as uncowed as the first day he went to war.

That mutual hatred, at home and in England, could have

only one end. The words of Sir John Harington who saw him well received in London by James I expressed the general lust to tear him down utterly. 'I have lived to see the damnable rebel Tyrone, brought to England, honoured, and well liked. Oh, what is there that does not prove the inconstancy of worldly matters! How I did labour after that knave's destruction! I adventured perils by sea and land, was near starving, ate horse-flesh in Munster, and all to quell that man who now smileth in peace at those who did hazard their lives to destroy him. And now doth Tyrone dare, us, old commanders, with his presence and protection!' The engines of that spleen became Sir Arthur Chichester, made Lord Deputy in February 1605, and Sir John Davies, the Solicitor General. These two set out to make life impossible for Ulster. They had many willing helpers; greedy churchmen, angry clansmen, every private and public enemy that Tyrone had created during his career. They encouraged every adventurer they could lay hands on to claim lands which he considered to be his own. They searched his titles over and over for legal flaws. They quoted English law against him when it suited, and switched to Celtic law when it suited better. They beset him with spies who invaded his closest privacy. They even set Sir Toby Caulfield to worm himself into the confidence of the Countess and trap her into damaging admissions. They raided his house for priests. They appointed sheriffs and other officials over his country who, they knew, would be distasteful to him. All their practice was in effect to deprive him and his late associates, such as Maguire, of their estates and to push in English officials in their place. That baiting went on all through 1604 and 1605 and into 1606, with Tyrone protesting in vain, corrupt officials pretending to hear his case, no remedy ever made, his rage and his fears feeding one another constantly, every day bringing some new warning that Chichester and Davies would stop at nothing to oust them. The climax came in the autumn of 1605, during one of Chichester's periodic visitations, when one of those spies who gathered about the conquerors like bees about honey informed Chichester that Maguire and Rory O'Donnell were plotting with Henry O'Neill, Tyrone's son, now in the army of the archduke of Austria; that they intended to flee to the Netherlands; and that a plot was on foot to invade Ulster from abroad. After that the clans had no peace. Maguire was arrested. Felon-setters, agents provocateurs, spies, petty officials of every kind dogged them like shadows. Failing to get any evidence to support the story of a plot Chichester egged on his men to badger his victims into some indiscretion that would justify him in proclaiming them traitors. He encouraged O'Cahan, who had not yet exhausted his usefulness, to resist Tyrone's claims to overlordship, and thereby tormented him with a prolonged, humiliating, and indecisive law-suit that dragged on into the summer of 1607. From all this Tyrone's only hope of release was to be made Lord President of Ulster, and he was still awaiting a favourable answer to his petition for the office when he heard that it was to be given to Chichester.

It was now August, 1607. Maguire had been released. Tyrone was due to go to London to hear James arbitrate between himself and O'Cahan. His remaining friends warned him that for him London meant the Tower. He looked about him. Great tracts of land had been taken from him and given to his Irish rivals. Churchmen like Bishop Montgomery of Derry, and the Archbishop of Armagh had filched more. He had lost his fishing rights on the Bann and Lough Foyle. He had been forbidden to practice his religion even in private. Priests in his territory had been deprived of their livings wholesale. The English garrisons mocked him to his beard. His people had been arrested time and again to force them to testify against him. If Chichester, who was the driving-force behind all these torments, were now made Lord President of Ulster he might give up the ghost. In that mood of despair a sea-captain named Bath suddenly appeared by his side to tell him that his son Henry O'Neill had sent a ship from the Low Countries to carry him to Europe; it was at that moment at anchor in Lough Swilly. Tyrone seized the opportunity and it was well for him that he did, for Chichester, on his own admission, was just about to pounce. He made one last gesture either of sentiment or of prudence to his old life—feeling for a friend's goodness, or a shift to throw off Chichester's suspicions—by going down to Mellifont to Sir Garret Moore, the foster-father of his son, a man who had been near to him in his days of greatest power and who had seen him in his abasement on his knees before Mountjoy. Moore was struck by Tyrone's strange display of emotion, so unusual in so undemonstrative a man, but he did not guess the cause and Tyrone would not reveal it lest he should compromise his friend. He remained there for a day and a night, while his wife and his friends were getting ready as quietly as they could for the flight. Then on Sunday afternoon he said good-bye to his 'good Sir Garret,' blessed every member of the household in the Irish fashion, and rode away. By Tuesday he was in one of his *crannoges* or island forts at Creeve, near Dungannon, with his wife and her attendants. On Wednesday they started the long ride through the fern to Rathmullan on Lough Swilly where they saw, on Thursday evening, the French colours on the topmast of the ship and Maguire on the beach loading the boats with provisions.

They went aboard at noon on the next day, Friday, September 14th, 1607, with Rory O'Donnell, Red Hugh's brother, who had become Earl of Tyrconnell when Tyrone surrendered. With them were their nearest relatives—sons, nephews, sisters, including Nuala the wife of the treacherous Niall Garv O'Donnell, and close friends and followers to the number (including the small crew) of ninety-nine. They waited all day until the September dusk and the late darkness came for Tyrone's son, Con, who was away in the hills with his fosterers. He never came. They waited, also, for water and wood-fuel. Those old allies of both O'Donnell and O'Neill, the MacSweeneys of Fanad, would not give them these poor necessities and attacked the crews who ventured to draw the cold water and gather the wood. Until it was midnight and the stars were out Tyrone stood at the gunwale watching for Con. Then the captain refused to wait longer. The sails were spread. The anchor rattled in the dark silence. The ship moved away.

On October 4th they drew into the Seine, worn and battered by storms. Slowly they crossed Europe, honoured as they went by every Court, incommoded occasionally by the English ambassadors, along the road to Rome. They arrived there in May, 1608. One by one they died there during the next ten years of sickness, of age, of repining at the monotony of life.

2

As a boy O'Neill had lived for eight years in the foggy capital of the North, after a childhood spent in the atmosphere of raids and bloodshed and savage vendettas among the Ulster woods. There he met the wide world, and laying its lessons beside the lessons of his fathers made his character, and ordained his life. As an ageing man on, and beyond, the brink of sixty he lived for the last eight years of his life in the warm capital of the South, after a prime spent in the service of his desires, and in the attempt to transmute the courage of his futile local rulers into the courage of a national war. For a year or two of those last eight he dreamed of returning; but as time passed, and his friends died around him, and every post from Ireland told him that (in the poet's words) there is 'no drop of her breast but is sucked by the litter of every foreign sow,' he was driven to accept the rigour of the fact that the game was over and that he would die in exile. Then, settled into his house in Rome, secure in the modest comfort of a Papal and Spanish pension, he gradually became just like any other distinguished emigré habituated to melancholy and homelessness and the routine of idle days. In the mornings there was Mass, in his house, the Salviati palace; for the exiled Archbishop of Armagh, Peter Lombard, lived under the same roof. In the afternoons he must, surely, at intervals toil up the steep path to the Janiculum hill and the Spanish-endowed church of San Pietro from whose terrace the whisper of the fountains mingle with the faint hum of Rome spread beneath. It is one of the most magnificent views in the world; a web of chimneys, domes, truncated columns and broken arches, and on clear days even his fading sight might trace the smoked blur of the Tiber receding to its enveloping haze of sea. In the cool dimness of the church he would sit and pray for his son Hugh and his kin who had died of the fever and were buried there—Rory, Earl of Tyrconnell, and his brother Caffar O'Donnell, O'Multully his secretary and his physician O'Carroll. Over the high altar hung Raphael's Transfiguration. Under the pavement with those Gaelic captains, so tradition said, were the relics of Dante's Beatrice. A place to sit and think, quietly remote from the eyes of the people who hung around him during the day, faces among whom he knew not whom to trust. For Lombard's nephew was now running every week to the English ambassador. Bath, who had brought him out of Lough Swilly, was relaying to Burghley every imaginary or madcap scheme for an invasion of Ireland that his friends, in the way of all refugees, propounded nightly over their wine. And it was only to be expected that the English secret-service agents would dog him ceaselessly. No wonder the old man slept with a naked sword by his side in his great bedroom in that Roman palace, and that everyone who met him found him heavy and gloomy and reserved — except, possibly, as Lombard's ne'er-do-well nephew had it, when he was in his cups at night: then 'both he and his company do usually in that mood dispose of governments and provinces and make new commonwealths'; and the tipsy old man would swear aloud that he would die in Ireland.

In the evening, too, with Lombard—who was writing the whole story down in a book—the years would burn again in the glow of the wine under the two great wax candles, arabesqued with silver and gold, that Paul V had given him the day he canonised Francesca Romana. He would barely hear the flutter of the turtle doves in their corner, muttering in their exquisite cages—another Papal gift. The cool evening air would rest him after the strain of the too-golden sun and the too-incandescent heat. At some query from the Archbishop the wine-glass would turn restlessly in the wrinkled fingers, or he would touch the beard in which now the scarlet hairs were choking their last little flambeaux in the smoke of age. But the Archbishop was not a probing man, and his questions would be answered easily; one feels a little indifferently, for his book was on the surface of things. A query about this man or that battle would leave Tyrone silent after it, turning the glass round and round, weighing less these chances of event than the characters of men and the sources of their achievement or failure, while the Archbishop's squeaking quill races on, designing ideal pictures with men who never existed, and motives so pure that only angels could have been stirred by them, beginning, in fact, the creation of the patriotic myth about Tyrone.

Tyrone knew that he had designed with what he found. He had recognised the inevitability of what limited him—the frailty of the men and the strength of the forces that he could not control; so that even while he had caressed his ambitions he had recoiled from them, and thereby presents a great tragic type—the man who is driven to what his nature inexorably demands and his reason denies. That element of self-perception, powerful in all men both as a coagulant and a dissolvent, to the victor a crown, to the defeated a crucifixion, in both a great human expansion, was central to his nature. That was the element which Dowden perceived in Henry V—the successful nation-builder: his 'noble realization of fact.'

Tyrone had led a host of brave men, but they had been creatures of unconsidered tradition and habit, all impulse and emotion. To those virtues the Archbishop's pen could pay full tribute though he would never see that much of the emotion was ungenerous and the impulse often suicidal, never see that they had been the merest helpless specks in the sludge of an evolution that was leaving them behind among the unfit. The churchman saw life rather more softly (though at the same time more terrifyingly) as a moted sunbeam dancing heavenwards, and those specks were the richer for being attracted by the Sun, helplessly. That conception softens and smudges away the acuity of human tragedy, covers the agony of the man with the veil of the martyr, assuages his misery by referring to his cause; and when it does advert to the mortal man who labours and hopes and struggles and is crushed asks us to find solace in the ideals which supported him in his fight and may be supposed to comfort him in his defeat. It may be true of some men. It is not true of this man. Tyrone was a man of terrific arrogance and terrific ambition and those who found him dour and heavy in his last years were looking at a man who was suffering every hour of his humiliation, who was realizing in himself all the tragedy of his country's defeat.

It is one of the most dismaying falsifications of history that this man, who was a European figure in his intelligent awareness of the large nature of the conflict in which he took part—as intelligent as any man at the time could be expected to be—has been lost to European history, and made part of a merely local piety. The traditional memory of his people has always acknowledged his greatness, but it has never understood and could not therefore acknowledge the true reasons of his greatness. One respects local tradition wherever one finds it, because one knows that unless local, or national feeling is accepted it becomes impossible to understand, let alone appreciate, the national Hero. But any nation that tries to shelter its history and its heroes from comparisons is merely trying to shelter them in a vacuum, the result of which can only be that blank and vacant Requiescat which, as far as the life of this world is concerned, has for centuries obliterated O'Neill. Those who, after the fashion of Archbishop Lombard, made a pious patriot of him have denied him the intellectual judgement to which his stature entitled him. For within his limits, and those of his times, his interest and his virtue is that he applied to his country those tests of comparison, and saw—in the natural confusion and ambiguity of the melee and the natural fallibility that goes with mingled motives—what challenges, what demands the modern world with all its problems thick upon it was making to his people; he saw—at any rate felt intuitively, and certainly acted with the practical effect of a man who understood—that he and they were not merely local pashas fighting for local power but part of a world-conflict whose intensity made these challenges and demands insistent and inescapable. In applying these tests to his country's mind, and in acting on his conclusions as to the pathetic inadequacy of that racial mind, he was the first step that his people made towards some sort of intellectual self-criticism as to their place and their responsibilities in the European system. After him almost until the nineteenth century little else but geography and conquest, and its effects, linked them into world-thought.

In his time the world began that narrowing-in process which has, in our day, finished with the virtual obliteration of all seclusion, removed the word aloofness from the vocabulary of politics, left no corner to the hermit, and condemned to death all the traditions that fail the great modern test of Ubiquity—won by adaptability. The rise of established monarchies which seemed likely to exterminate all local life had, indeed, intensified national life, and the need for more coherent communal endeavour. But international commerce, mercantile competition, the beginnings of industrialisation, which seemed at first to threaten a greater international rivalry than ever before and nothing else, were also beginning to postulate a greater interdependence among nations. All, for a time, that O'Neill or any man in his position in any small country in Europe could be expected to realize was the absolute necessity of conforming swiftly to this trend of world affairs—or of going under. Men like old Archbishop Lombard saw only the passing-away of the old, precious dear-loved ways, having no glimmer of an idea that in civilization—in every aspect of it, even those aspects most closely concerning his own vocation, such as theology and philosophy—the dominating, germinating, fecundate and even preserving factor is Development. It was self-evident to O'Neill, in his own place, in his own problems, in the affairs of his country.

Unfortunately for his country, and it is no doubt part of the whole eddying process by which Development is arrested generally, the fructifying worth of the man's intelligence was ignored by his people; his practical, prudent sense as a man of the world; the intellectual, creative quality in him which entitles him to be called a European figure. It was inevitable since he lived in a society lacking totally (it had always been lacking totally) in speculative energy; a society without the liberating power of the general idea, the concept which reveals and releases, a society without either logic or that intuition which can sometimes take the place of logic. He had worked with a society of blood and soil, founded on a genealogical principle rather than an intellectual principle, with all the limitations and stagnations implicit therein. In his life Tyrone was broken not by England but by Ireland; by its deep atavism and inbreeding, so characteristic of abortive and arrested cultures in all ages of the world's history; after his death he was misrepresented because his people resolutely refused to learn his lesson. Even while he lived they began (in the person of old Archbishop Lombard) to make him the champion of everything to which they clung pathetically and of much that, in fact, he attempted to transform—and of more that he actually rejected. They made him an island patriot, as isolated from the world as themselves. As with pupils whose incapacity frustrates even the best teacher they thereby frustrated him, and diminished him, by denying him the long series of results that could otherwise be traced back to his inspiration. Fortunately for his country, however, he associated his struggle for independence with the whole movement of the Counter-Reformation, and that was a European idea and a European link, and it gave his people access to a great heritage of culture and tradition from which the principle of Development has never been absent. And whether or not they have exploited that European heritage to the full, so enlarging and fructifying, so colourful, so rich in urbanity and tolerance and discipline, and even in the hoary wisdom of the world, he did at any rate spin them that thread, and he did colour all future nationalism with its purple and gold. Had he not done so that old Gaelic world would have died like the Incas and left behind gifts only to the antiquary and the philologist. As it is, by that transfusion, something has persisted, or more accurately may persist, out of the old Gaelic world—purified, chastened, re-enlightened—to form an attractive element in life wherever the Irish nature has the courage to live, like Tyrone, through Ireland into Europe, out of this remote island into the ubiquitous and contemporaneous world of civilized mind.

Clearly, his generation so little understood all this that he may well have wondered, there in Rome, over the wine, with the night sinking on the city, and the doves with their heads on their breasts, and the Archbishop's quill moving a little more slowly as sleep began to call him, whether his people ever would survive. In his despair he may even have wondered whether, if they did, the cost of all wars is not too great for the greatest prize. From his window he could see in the starlight some of the ruins of the greatest empire of the world and he had seen Munster and Ulster all crazed with the thorns and the long grasses, and he knew that the epilogue of all wars is the same, whether won or lost—a great pride, and a little shame, and then, tears and work. . . . . His brief laugh rouses the Archbishop. Men are fated to do what their talents demand of them. There was, after all, little of cold reason in anything he had done who had merely fulfilled himself and God's will in him. He could never have lived like old obese tipsy Turlough, or blustered like Sean the Proud. If his plans had not succeeded that was merely another of those heavenly errors which so profoundly puzzle all men.

The Archbishop looks at the solemn face which has erased its sardonic laugh. The Earl has been melancholy these last weeks. He lays aside the manuscript and speaks of their going to the Farnese palace at Caprarola, for a change and a rest. Tyrone speaks sharply of the costs of such a journey, and the Archbishop sighs to think that so great and good a man should now be mainly concerned with accumulating money. But he says nothing. The 'young and fair' Countess, he knows, has been a great worry—wasting their little money on follies; and 'follies' is a kind word for it. Still . . . they must go somewhere. They will talk of it to-morrow. He gathers up his papers and bids good-night. The Earl sits alone with his glass—he drinks far too much nowadays—in no haste to go to bed since there is so little reason why he should rise betimes.

Through the open window his eyes lift to the great stars in their places. Before their majesty and their indifference he sighs heavily. The nights are endless.

Idly his fingers touch the Archbishop's manuscript and, snuffing the candle, he draws it to him. This is his life, his mind, his soul. Here are thirty crowded years of ambition and of bloodshed, of intrigue and manoeuvre, of victory and utter defeat. The figures rise, a bloody procession. Turlough and Gaveloch and 'that idiot' Florence MacCarthy, Maguire who was a brave man, and Niall Garv who was a braver but a traitor, Harry Hoveden who never lied to him, that wild fellow Tom Lee, young Red Hugh who had more dash than any ten of them—the men he made, the men he tortured, the men he broke, the men he murdered, the men he sold, the men he bought . . . his dead wives . . . his children. . . . And every word that he reads is untrue. Lombard has translated him into a star like those stars over the city roofs. He has seen it all as a glorious story that was in every thread a heartbreak. He has made Life into a Myth. The massive, squat frame shudders into a series of jerking chuckles. The fading eyes peer sardonically through their red eyelashes. Then the chuckle breaks into a sob and the broad body falls on the table, crying as helplessly as a child. Must we Irish always be weaving fancy, living always in the fantastic world of a dream? As the old, drunken man sobs in his rage and misery the glass tumbles, the wine slowly spills across the historian's page a long red streak of blood.

After eight years of that Roman life he began to break. He seemed an old man. The surgeons bled him constantly from the legs. His sight faded. He became blind. On July 20th, 1616, he died. He was buried with the greatest pomp in San Pietro beside his son where a great double slab to-day marks the place beneath the floor. His own stone said:

D . O . M.

HIC. QUIESCUNT.

UGONIS . PRINCIPIS . O'NEILL.

OSSA.

NOTES

1. Urraghs. (Irish : aur-ríg.) Literally means vice-kings or sub-kings, i.e. the heads of the most important non-ruling septs within the Gaelic principality. It is difficult to find any English word for them. They were not 'vassals,' 'tenants,' or 'clients,' since the whole point of Gaelic law is that the king was not in any sense the ultimate owner of any land except his own family land (i.e. the mensal lands of his office).

2. The date of Hugh O'Neill's birth has been now established as around 1550 by Mr. J. K. Graham. *Irish Historical Studies*, I, March, 1938.

3. The usual date given for Hugh's journey to England is 1562. But the usual references for that date do not point to 1562, but to a later crossing in 1567. It is most unlikely that Sidney could possibly have brought Hugh over in 1562 as he was in France about the Guise proposal to marry Mary Queen of Scots to Anthony of Navarre. That was in April. Later in the same year he was on a mission in Scotland. There is no evidence that he was in Ireland that year, whereas he was there in 1559, resigned in August and crossed to England. If my emendation is correct it extends the period Hugh spent in England as a boy—an important point.

4. The fullest account of Mac Aingil is in *Aodh Mac Aingil*, by Thomas O'Cleirigh, (Government Publication, Dublin, n.d.).

5. This is the visit usually confused with his first crossing to England. See Sir Henry Sidney's *Letters and Memorials of State* which is based, here, on Cox's *History of Ireland* and Holinshed.

6. *Church and State in Tudor Ireland.* Robert Dudley Edwards. London, 1935. p. 240.

7. This account of Sanders is based almost exclusively on Dr. Mathew, *The Celtic Peoples and Renaissance Europe*, London, 1933, far and away the most intelligent book written about the period.

8. Those interested in the Bagenals might see further *Vicissitudes of an Anglo-Irish Family*, by Philip Bagenal. London, 1925. Standish O'Grady gives a lively narration of the murder in his *Bog of Stars and Other Stories.*

Tyrone's connivance in the murder of Phelim M'Turlough, is, of course, not proven: it is, however, quite certain that he countenanced it. He was at enmity with Phelim. Three days after the murder he raided Phelim's people for rent. Two weeks after it he was asked if he intended to punish the O'Hagans and he replied: 'If I do them no good I will do them no harm.' To which O'Cahan, standing by, said: 'Seeing you had that within you, you might have kept it well enough within you.' The only evidence for Tyrone's married life with Mabel Bagenal is the Trevelyan Papers.

9. For Red Hugh see *The Life of Hugh Roe O'Donnell* by Lughaidh O'Clery, Ed. Rev. Denis Murphy, Dublin, 1895. Standish O'Grady: *Red Hugh's Captivity*, London, 1889. For the escape, an article by Dr. Paul Walsh, *Irish Ecclesiastical Record*, January, 1930; by Aodh de Blacam, in *The Standard*, February 1, 1930; December 20, 1930; and December 27th, 1930.

10. Tom Lee came over to Ireland with Walter Devereux, the elder Earl of Essex, and became intimate with Tyrone. He was frequently in hot water with the government and was finally executed at Tyburn on a charge of attempting to procure the release of the younger Essex and Southampton by force. Mr. M. A. Cafferkey has written a thesis on Lee.

11. There was no rack in Dublin Castle but there were other engines. Archbishop Hurley, for example, was tortured after the Desmond Revolt by having his legs roasted in the fire in red-hot boots.

12. I cannot claim that these figures are exact. Each report took the old baronies, one by one, for Horse, and for Foot—the Fews, Orier, Kilwarlyn, the Route, etc. But Bagenal omitted Kinalertie and the Glens, and I have filled in by taking the figures for those places from the later report. As these are, presumably, much larger than the actual numbers in these places in 1586, the effect is to minimise the contrast. Neither do I count the 90 men of Captain Piers which only appear in one report from Little Ards. In round figures Tyrone thus appears to command about 6,000 men in 1586, and about 17,000 men in 1592; and by 'command' I mean that that was the strength of the whole district over which he had influential control.

13. O'Sullivan Beare's account of Tyrone's behaviour during the Summer of 1594—it can only be called double-faced and temporising—is as follows: 'Tyrone was perplexed with conflicting anxieties, thinking in his own mind that O'Donnell had started the war in an uncertain hope of aid from Spain, and before seeing the Spanish colours in Ireland, and this put the fate of the Catholics in great peril, even should O'Neill himself come to the rescue. On the other hand, if he did not assist the Catholics, although he was already suspected by the Protestants, he would be regarded as an enemy by both parties.' From the account of Tyrone's behaviour later, in the winter of 1594–5, it will be seen that his public indecision was prolonged long after his practical decision had been made. For that prolonged hesitancy, when it could impress nobody in its later stages, there is, I suggest, no sensible reason.

14. The whole of this period into '97 and '98 was tragic for Bingham. He had indeed been a brutal and ruthless governor and had maddened the people, as the government realised too late. Not until April '96 do we find Burghley commanding Norreys to show more humanity to the people of Connaught, to 'yield somewhat in his own stomach.' Bingham may have collected money and property for his own use but nothing beyond the ordinary manner of the time and he had endured a sufficiently miserable life in the west. That the old man should, exactly for all this, be flung into the Fleet prison is as sharp a commentary on the thanklessness of these Irish wars as there is in all their history.

BIBLIOGRAPHY

As this book makes no pretensions to being an academic study I do not burthen the reader with a list of all the sources used. If he wishes to study the period himself he might best proceed as follows: the article in the D.N.B., a general history such as that by Curtis, a more elaborate history such as Bagwell's *Ireland Under the Tudors*, or O'Clery's *Life of Red Hugh O'Donnell*. He might then start from the beginning again, and move step by step with the *Calendar of State Papers* on his right and the *Annals of the Four Masters* on his left. The problems will then crowd thickly and in trying to solve them the student will soon compile an elaborate bibliography of his own. A knowledge of Gaelic literature is essential. It supplies next to no information but without it one cannot understand the Irish background and point-of-view. For that see Douglas Hyde, or Aodh de Blacam, or individual editions of the poets from whom further lists will accrue.

The main source of this narrative is the State Papers. This biographer has here used only the published Calendars. The secondary source is the Gaelic chronicle, *The Annals of the Four Masters*, and other such chronicles; e.g. Lughaidh O'Clery's *Life of Red Hugh O'Donnell*, or Tadhg O'Cianáin's Gaelic description of *The Flight of the Earls*, or such Gaelic-Latin narratives as Archbishop Lombard's or Don Philip O'Sullivan Beare's. After that come the personal records of English travellers and generals like Fynes Moryson's *Itinerary*, or Sir Henry Dowcra's *Narration*, or Perrot's *Chronicle*. Then come the many books from which one picks up bits and scraps, such as Spenser's *View*, and the pamphlets of other contemporaries like Cuellar, Bodley, Derrick, Dymmok, Rych, Gainsford, etc. A fair idea of these is accessible easily in a little book of extracts, *Ireland through Tudor Eyes*, by E. M. Hinton, Pennsylvania, 1935. The learned journals may then be combed for things like Bagenal's 'Description of Ireland,' in the *Ulster Journal of Archaeology*, or the record of Bingham's services in Connaught, in the Celtic Society's Miscellany. A very useful source-book is Constantia Maxwell's *Irish History from Contemporary Sources*, 1509–1610.

Modern critical studies are few enough. For general information one goes to Bagwell, Maxwell, Curtis, Haverty, Green, and others. For more minute criticism to learned journals like *Irish Historical Studies*, *Studies*, *The Irish Ecclesiastical Record*, the *Transactions* of various learned societies. Of O'Neill himself there is only one published biography, *The Life and Times of Hugh O'Neill* by John Mitchel, a slight and rather unreliable book which, however, was the first attempt to give a straight record of his life from the sources available at the time: 1845. There is a useful record in Bagwell, in Lord Hamilton's *Elizabethan Ulster*, in *The Indestructible Nation* by P. S. O'Hegarty, and the *Fate and Fortunes of the Earls of Tyrone and Tyrconnell*, by C. P. Meehan.

On various aspects of the life and problems of the period there are many useful books, from Ada Longfield's *Anglo-Irish Trade in the Sixteenth Century* to Dr. Dudley Edwards' *Church and State in Tudor Ireland*, from Eoin MacNeill's *Celtic Ireland* to G. A. Hayes-McCoy's *Scots Mercenary Forces in Ireland, 1565–1603*.

I have, throughout, been guided and assisted more than I can say by a thesis presented for the M.A. degree at Queen's University, Belfast, by Mr. J. K. Graham, entitled *An Historical Study of the Career of Hugh O'Neill, Second Earl of Tyrone*, and for that I again wish to return special thanks.

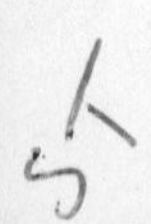